A New Canon
of English Poetry

A New Canon
of English Poetry

CHOSEN AND EDITED BY

JAMES REEVES

&

MARTIN SEYMOUR-SMITH

BARNES & NOBLE, INC.

PUBLISHERS : BOOKSELLERS : SINCE 1873

TO

TERENCE HARDS

First published in the United States by Barnes & Noble,
New York 10003
Printed in Great Britain by Morrison and Gibb Ltd
London and Edinburgh

Contents

Introduction

Non-specialist readers are likely to rely for their knowledge of standard, classic (as distinct from modern) English poetry on a comparatively few general anthologies. *Palgrave* and the *Oxford Book*—or for convenience, 'Oxgrave'—often represents the limits of the poetry they know really well. To these may be added a few volumes which have come into comparatively wide circulation in the last thirty or forty years, such as the poems of Donne and Blake. To say this is not to disparage the taste of the general reader or his love of poetry. The standard anthologies perform an indispensable function and are rightly valued by those who, at an impressionable age, learnt their poetry from them.

Nevertheless Oxgrave, as well as the many other general anthologies which are more or less based on them, have their limitations—limitations due to either the taste or the knowledge of their editors, to current poetic fashions, or to the inaccessibility of certain poems. The general excellence of these two collections is in one sense a disadvantage: because of the authority they enjoy, and because of their wide use in education, there is a tendency to regard them as representing 'the best' in English poetry; their contents are by implication stamped as canonical. Many tend to forget or to ignore what is not in Oxgrave; it passes out of currency. So also do those poems in the standard anthologies which, with the passing of time, turn out to be inferior. Little that is new is added to replace the casualties, with the result that the reader tends to enjoy a contracting canon of classic poetry. True, most readers now know poems not in Oxgrave, but because not all these are easily accessible, they are lost to general view.

It is the purpose of this book to offer a substantial body of poems, mostly short, both English and American, which in our opinion deserve to rank in the canon. In our title, following the precedent of the *Oxford Book of English Verse*, we use 'English' comprehensively. We believe that everything here reprinted can stand alongside the Oxgrave canon. These poems deserve to be known, not only by literary specialists, but by all who care for poetry. They have that quality, in some degree, which can best be called 'classic'. The proof

xv

of this claim can of course only be found in the poems themselves; but some further account of our terms of reference and our principles of inclusion and exclusion is called for.

We have limited ourselves to the same period of time as is covered by Oxgrave. To go beyond this would be to claim obvious advantages denied to the earlier editors. Moreover, however good, however generally accepted any favourite modern poem may be, its very modernity is proof that it has not yet been overlooked. Modern poetry is, as it were by definition, that which has not had time to suffer neglect or to become classic.

While we have included nothing which is in Oxgrave, we have not felt justified in selecting from all the poems outside them. We have denied ourselves much of the best of such poets as Donne and Blake and Hopkins as being too well known: these poets have been read almost as if they were modern. We regard most very long poems as outside our scope, as they were outside the scope of the earlier editors. Otherwise we might have included Sir John Davies's *Orchestra*. But we have included Ralegh's *Cynthia*, not only because of its poetic beauty but also because no other anthology gives a reliable text. Among other poems not easily available elsewhere in authentic texts are many of the lyrics from Elizabethan song-collections, William Baldwin's poem from *A Mirror for Magistrates*, Skelton's poems, and two lyrics probably by Suckling never printed in book form.

To some readers our non-inclusion of traditional ballads and songs will be a matter for regret. It cannot be denied, however, that Q gives a good and generous representation to traditional ballads as understood by Child. We might have included these on the ground that Q's texts are bad. After long consideration, however, we reluctantly concluded that poems of the oral tradition were of a special order, and could not be grouped in the same volume. Only those ballads can be regarded as truly classic which are known by everyone in one form or another.

We have included a few, but not many, poems to be found in the other Oxford books of verse. We have modernized or regularized text and punctuation, and expanded contractions, only very sparingly. Certain medieval poems, for instance, have been taken out of the realm of the specialist without, however, our indulging in more adaptation than the general reader absolutely requires.

American poetry presents something of a problem. There is a sense in which all American poetry is neglected in Britain, and we might therefore have doubled the size of this volume by including a hundred or so of the best poems in the *Oxford Book of American Verse*. We have in fact, for the sake of our American readers, given almost nothing in that admirable collection; we have preferred to give mainly what can fairly be regarded as overlooked, even in America. Certain poems of Emily Dickinson, we feel, demand a place here, as do many by the most conspicuously neglected of all American poets, Trumbull Stickney. On the other hand, we have reluctantly passed over Whitman because—like that of Donne and Hopkins—none of his work can truthfully be called neglected.

To return to English poetry, the last thing we wished to do was to go into the hedges and ditches in search of poems which Oxgrave quite rightly left out. Certain poets, it is true, such as Fulke Greville and Hartley Coleridge, have been consistently under-represented by anthologists; but it is not for this reason alone that we have chosen a number of their poems. These poems—and not simply *any* poems by these poets—are here on their own merits. It might be objected that Clare is now too well known to require inclusion, despite the neglect of earlier anthologists; but there is still a tendency, which we wish to combat, to regard him as in some way a special case rather than a classic English poet. He has always suffered from being something of a cult-figure. On the other hand we feel that Wordsworth has been so thoroughly assimilated that nothing in his work is requisite to our present purpose. Even the surprisingly late *Extempore Effusion on the Death of James Hogg* has at last achieved fame.

In conclusion we repeat that no poem or poet is here solely on account of former neglect. We have read a good many poets in whom we believed we might find something worthy of inclusion, only to be disappointed. We think that it would be eccentric to include James Montgomery, Barry Cornwall, Erasmus Darwin or Henry James Pye, simply because others have excluded them. We have tried rather to concentrate on the *unaccountably* neglected—the poems which Oxgrave ought to have known about and admired. Admittedly our selections from well-known poets, such as Coleridge and Rossetti, have the appearance of being marginal in comparison with more fully representative selections. But there seems to us to be no excuse for omitting *The Pains of Sleep* or the original version of *Dejection*. The poems we give by Rossetti seem to us to be better in every way than the more popular *Blessed Damozel*; while there is really no reason why every anthologist should always reprint the same sonnets by Keats and not the largely unknown but superior two we quote. We do not deny that there are certain poets, notably Scott and Byron, whom we consider earlier editors to have over-valued; at the same time, we must insist that it is no part of our purpose to supplant the canon they laid down.

We wish simply to modify, supplement and extend it.

1966.   J. R.
                                                                           M. S-S.

Acknowledgment

The editors wish to thank Charles Graves, Vivian de Sola Pinto and David Wright for helpful advice.

Now Goeth Sun under Wood

Nou goth sonne under wod,—
me reweth, marie, thi faire Rode.[1]
Nou goth sonne under tre,—
me reweth, marie, thi sone and the.

ANONYMOUS

[1] rood

Fowls in the Frith

Foweles in the frith,[1]
The fisses in the flod,
And i mon waxe wod.[2]
Mulch sorw I walke with
for beste of bon and blod.

ANONYMOUS

[1] wood   [2] shall go mad

Benedicite, What Dreamed I this Night?

Benedicite, what dreamed I this night?
  Methought the world was turned up so down;
The sun, the moon, had lost their force and light;
  The sea also drowned both tower and town.
  Yet more marvel how that I heard the sound
    Of ones voice saying 'Bear in thy mind,
    Thy lady hath forgotten to be kind.'

To complain me, alas, why should I so,
  For my complaint it did me never good?
But by constraint now must I shew my woe
  To her only which is mine eyes food,
  Trusting sometime that she will change her mood.
    And let me not always be guerdonless,
    Sith for my truth she needeth no witness.

ANONYMOUS

Suddenly afraid

Sodenly afraid,
   Halfe wakinge halfe sleping,
And gretly dismayd,
   A woman sate weping,
With favour in her face far passing my reson,
And of her sore weping this was the encheson.[1]
Her sone in her lappe laid, sche seid, slein by treson,
If weping might ripe be, hit semed then in seson.
   Jhesus, so sche sobbed,
   So her sone was bobbed[2]
   And of his live robbed;
Seinge this wordes as I sey thee,
'Who can not wepe, com lerne of me.'

I seid I coude not wepe, I was so hard herted.
Sche answerd me schortly with wordes that smarted,
'Lo, nature schall meve thee, thau must be converted,
Thine owne fader this night is dede?' This sche thwerted.[3]
   'Jhesus, so my sone is bobbed,
   And of his live robbed,
   For soth then I sobbed
Verifying this wordes, seing to thee,
Who can not wepe com lerne at me.

'Now breke hert, I thee praye! this cors lieth so rewlie,[4]
So beten, so wounded, entreted so foully.
What wight may behold, and wepe not? None truly,
To see my ded dere sone bledinge, lo, this newly.'
   Ever stille sche sobbed,
   So her sone was bobbed
   And of his live robbed.
Newing these wordes, as I sey thee,
'Who can not wepe, com lerne at me.'

On me sche cast her ye, and seid 'See, man, thy brother!'
Sche kiste him and seid 'Swete, am I not thy moder?'

And swoninge sche felle; ther hit wold be no nother.
I not which more dedlie, the tone or the toder.
>   Yett sche revived and sobbed
>   How her sone was bobbed
>   And of his live robbed.
'Who can not wepe,' this is the lay,
And with that wordes sche vanisched away

ANONYMOUS

¹ cause   ² mocked   ³ replied   ⁴ pitiable

Knowledge, Acquaintance . . .

Knolege, aquayntance, resort, favour with grace;
>   Delyte, desyre, respyte wyth lyberte;
Corage¹ wyth lust,² convenient tyme and space;
>   Dysdayns, dystres, exylyd cruelte;
>   Wordys well set with good habylyte;
Demure demenaunce, womanly of porte;
Transendyng plesure, surmountyng all dysporte;

Allectuary³ arrectyd⁴ to redres⁵
>   These feverous axys,⁶ the dedely wo and payne
Of thoughtfull⁷ hertys plungyd in dystres;
>   Refresshyng myndys the Aprell shoure of rayne;
>   Condute of comforte, and well most soverayne;
Herber⁸ enverduryd, contynuall fressh and grene;
Of lusty somer the passyng goodly quene;

The topas rych and precyouse in vertew;
>   Your ruddys⁹ wyth ruddy rubys may compare;
Saphyre of sadnes,¹⁰ envayned wyth indy blew;
>   The pullyshed perle youre whytenes doth declare;
>   Dyamand poyntyd to rase oute hartly care;
Geyne¹¹ surfetous suspecte the emeraud comendable;
Relucent smaragd,¹² objecte imcomperable;

Encleryd myrroure and perspectyve[13] most bryght,
   Illumynyd wyth feturys far passyng my reporte;
Radyent Esperus, star of the clowdy nyght,
   Lode star to lyght these lovers to theyr porte,
   Gayne dangerous stormys theyr anker of supporte,
Theyr sayll of solace most comfortably clad,
Whych to behold makyth hevy hartys glad:

Remorse[14] have I of youre most goodlyhod,
   Of youre behavoure curtes and benynge,
Of your bownte and of youre womanhod,
   Which makyth my hart oft to lepe and sprynge,
   And to remember many a praty thynge;
But absens, alas, wyth tremelyng fere and drede
Abashyth me, albeit I have no nede.

You I assure, absens is my fo,
   My dedely wo, my paynfull hevynes;
And if ye lyst to know the cause why so,
   Open myne hart, beholde my mynde expres:
   I wold ye coud! then shuld ye se, mastres,
How there nys thynge that I covet so fayne
As to enbrace you in myne armys twayne.

Nothynge yerthly to me more desyrous
   Than to beholde youre bewteouse countenaunce:
But, hatefull absens, to me so envyous,
   Though thou withdraw me from her by long dystaunce,
   Yet shall she never oute of remembraunce;
For I have gravyd her wythin the secret wall
Of my trew hart, to love her best of all!
                Qd Skelton, laureat.

                        JOHN SKELTON

[1] heart   [2] pleasure   [3] Electuary   [4] considered sovereign
[5] remedy   [6] paroxysms   [7] anxious   [8] herb-garden
[9] ruddy complexion   [10] constancy   [11] against
[12] another name for emerald   [13] mirror   [14] recollection

Womanhood, Wanton, ye Want

Womanhood, wanton, ye want;
  Youre medelyng, mastres, is manerles;
Plente of yll, of goodnes skant,
  Ye rayll at ryot, recheles:[1]
  To prayse youre porte it is nedeles;
For all your draffe[2] yet and youre dreggys,
As well borne as ye full oft tyme beggys.

Why so koy and full of skorne?
  Myne horse is sold, I wene, you say;
My new furryd gowne, when it is worne,
  Put up youre purs, ye shall non pay.
  By crede, I trust to se the day,
As proud a pohen as ye sprede,
Of me and other ye may have nede.

Though angelyk be youre smylyng,
  Yet is youre tong an adders tayle,
Full lyke a scorpyon styngyng
  All those by whom ye haue avayle:[3]
  Good mastres Anne, there ye do shayle:[4]
What prate ye, praty pyggysny?
I truste to quyte you or I dy.

Youre key is mete for euery lok,
  Youre key is commen and hangyth owte;
Youre key is redy, we nede not knok,
  Nor stand long wrestyng there aboute;
  Of youre doregate ye have no doute:
But one thyng is, that ye be lewde:
Holde youre tong now, all beshrewde!

To mastres Anne, that farly[5] swete,
That wonnes[6] at the Key in Temmys strete.

JOHN SKELTON

---

[1] reckless   [2] refuse   [3] profit   [4] shamble
[5] strange   [6] dwells

With Lullay, Lullay . . .

With, Lullay, lullay, lyke a chylde,
Thou slepyst to long, thou art begylde.

My darlyng dere, my daysy floure,
  Let me, quod he, ly in your lap.
Ly styll, quod she, my paramoure,
  Ly styll hardely,[1] and take a nap.
  Hys hed was hevy, such was his hap,
All drowsy dremyng, dround in slepe,
That of hys love he toke no kepe,
          With, Hey, lullay, &c.

With ba, ba, ba, and bas, bas, bas,
  She cheryshed hym both cheke and chyn,
That he wyst never where he was;
  He had forgoten all dedely syn.
  He wantyd wyt her loue to wyn:
He trusted her payment, and lost all hys pray:
She left hym slepyng, and stale away,
          Wyth, Hey, lullay, &c.

The ryvcrs rowth,[2] the waters wan;
  She sparyd not to wete her fete;
She wadyd over, she found a man
  That halsyd her hartely and kyst her swete:
  Thus after her cold she cought a hete.
My lefe, she sayd, rowtyth[4] in hys bed;
I wys he hath an hevy hed,
          Wyth, Hey, lullay, &c.

What dremyst thou, drunchard, drousy pate!
  Thy lust and lykyng is from the gone;
Thou blynkerd blowboll,[5] thou wakyst to late,
  Behold, thou lyeste, luggard, alone!
  Well may thou sygh, well may thou grone,
To dele wyth her so cowardly:
I wys, powle hachet, she bleryd thyne I.[6]
          Qd Skelton, laureate.

                    JOHN SKELTON

[1] boldly   [2] rough   [3] clasped round the neck: embraced
[4] snoreth   [5] a term of abuse   [6] eye; *bleryd thyne I*: cheated you

Go, Piteous Heart . . .

Go, pytyous hart, rasyd[1] with dedly wo,
  Persyd with payn, bleding with wondes smart,
Bewayle thy fortune, with vaynys wan and blo.[2]
  O Fortune unfrendly, Fortune unkynde thow art,
  To be so cruell and so overthwart,[3]
To suffer me so carefull to endure,
That wher I love best I dare not dyscure![4]

One ther is, and ever one shalbe,
  For whose sake my hart is sore dyseasyd;
For whose love, welcom dysease to me!
  I am content so all partys be pleasyd:
  Yet, and God wold, I wold my payne were easyd!
But Fortune enforsyth me so carefully to endure,
That where I love best I dare not dyscure.
                              Skelton, laureat,
                    At the instance of a nobyll lady.

                                   JOHN SKELTON

[1] torn [2] livid [3] perverse [4] discover: i.e., cannot declare my love

By a Forest . . .

Bi a forrest as I gan fare,
  Walkyng al myselven a-lone,
I hard a mornyng of an haare,
  Rouffully schew mad here mone.

Dere-worth god, how schal I leve
  And leyd my lyve in lond?
ffrom dale to doune I am I-drevfe;
  I not where I may syte or stond!

I may nother rest nor slepe
   By no wallay[1] that is so derne,[2]
Nor no covert may me kepe,
   But ever I rene fro herne to herne.[3]

hontteris wyll not heyre ther mase
   In hope of hunttyng for to wend;
They cowpyllyt[4] ther howndes more and lase
   And bryngyth theme to the feldys ende.

Rochis[5] rennyn on euery syde
   In forrovs that hoppe me to fynd;
honteris takythe ther horse and ryde,
   And cast the conttray to the wynd.

Anone as they commyth me be-hynde,
   I loke and syt ful style and love;
The furst mane that me doth fynde
   Anon he cryit: 'so howe! so hoowe!'

'lo,' he sayth, 'where syttyt an haare—
   Aryse vpe, Watte, & go forth blyue!'[6]
With sorroe and with mych care
   I schape a-way with my lyve.

Att wyntter in the depe snove
   Men wyl me seche for to trace,
And by my steyppes I ame I-knowe;
   And followyt me fro place to place.

And yf I to the toune come or torne,
   Be hit in worttes[7] or in leyke,[8]
Then wyl the wyffys al-so eorne[9]
   flece me with here dogis heyke.[10]

And yf I syt and crope the kovle,[11]
   And the wyfe be in the waye,
A-none schowe wyll swere, 'by cokkes soule!
   There is an haare in my haye!'

Anone sche wyle clepe, 'forth, cure,[12] knave!'
   And loke ryt weel wer I syte;
By-hynd sche wyl with a stave
   fful wel porpos me to hette.

'Go forthe, Wate, Wit crystus curse,
   And yf I leve, thou schalt be take;
I have an hare-pype[13] in my purce,[14]
   hit schal be set al for thi sauke!'

Ten hath this wyffys two dogges grete,
   On me sche byddyt heme goe;
And as a scrowe[15] sche wyll me thret,
   And ever sche cryit, 'go, dooge, gooe!'

But all way this most I goo,
   By no banke I may a-byde;
lord god, that me is woo!
   Many a hape hath me bytyde.

There is no best in the word, I wene,
   hert, hynd, buke ne dowe,
That suffuris halfe so myche tene
   As doth the sylly wat—go where he go.

eyfe a genttylmane wyl have any game,
   And fynd me in forme where I syte,
ffor dred of lossynge of his name
   I wot wele he wyle not me hyte.

ffor an acuris[16] bred[17] he wyll me leve,
   Or he wyll let his hondes rene;
Of all the men that beth a-lyve
   I am most be-hold to genttyl-men!

As sone as I can ren to the laye,
   A-non the grey-hondys wyl me have;
My bowels beth I-throwe a-waye,
   And I ame bore home on a stavfe.

Als son as I am come home,
I ame I-honge hye vp-on a pyne,
With leke-worttes I am eette a-none,
And whelpes play with my skyne!

ANONYMOUS

[1] valley   [2] out-of-the-way   [3] hiding-place
[4] couple   [5] dogs   [6] quickly   [7] herbs
[8] leek   [9] eagerly   [10] also   [11] kale
[12] cur   [13] hare-trap   [14] bag
[15] scolding woman   [16] acres   [17] breadth

January by this Fire . . .

Januar	By thys fyre I warme my handys;
Februar	And with my spade I delfe my landys.
Marche	Here I sette my thynge[1] to sprynge;
Aprille	And here I here the fowlis synge.
Maij	I am as lyght as byrde in bowe;
Junij	And I wede my corne well I-now.
Julij	With my sythe my mede I mawe;[2]
Auguste	And here I shere my corne full lowe.
September	With my flayll I erne my brede;
October	And here I sawe my whete so rede.
November	At Martynesmasse I kylle my swyne;
December	And at Christesmasse I drynke redde wyne.

ANONYMOUS

[1] seeds   [2] mow

Maiden in the Moor lay

Maiden in the mor lay—
in the mor lay—
sevenyst[1] fulle,
sevenyst fulle.

Maiden in the mor lay—
   in the mor lay—
  sevenistes fulle ant a day.

Welle was hire mete.
wat was hire mete?
  the primerole² ant the—
   the primerole ant the—
Welle was hire mete.
Wat was hire mete?
  the primerole ant the violet.

Welle was hire dryng.³
  wat was hire dryng?
  the chelde water of the—
   the chelde water of the—
Welle was hire dryng.
Wat was hire dryng?
  the chelde water of the welle-spring.

Welle was hire bour.⁴
wat was hire bour?
  the rede rose an te—
   the reed rose an te—
Welle was hire bour.
Wat was hire bour?
  the reed rose an te lilie flour.

ANONYMOUS

¹ seven nights   ² primrose   ³ drink   ⁴ bed

I have a Gentle Cock

I have a gentil cook,
  crowyt me day;
he doth me rysyn erly,
  my matyins for to say.

I have a gentil cook,
   comyn he is of gret;[1]
his comb is of reed corel,
   his tayil is of get.[2]

I have a gentyl cook,
   comyn he is of kynde;
his comb is of red corel,
   his tayl is of Inde.

his legges ben of asor,[3]
   so geintil and so smale;
his spores arn of sylver qwyt,[4]
   in-to the worte-wale.[5]

His eynyn arn of cristal,
   lokyn al in aumbyr;
and every nygt he perchit hym
   in myn ladyis chaumbyr.

ANONYMOUS

[1] of noble descent   [2] jet   [3] azure
[4] white   [5] root of cock's spur

I must go Walk the Wood so wild

I must go walke the woed so wyld
   And wander here and there
   in dred and dedly fere,
for where I trusted I am begyld,
   and all for on.[1]

Thus am I banysshyd from my blys
   by craft and false pretens,
   fautles with-out offens,
as off return no certen ys,
   and all for fer off on.

my bed schall be under the grenwod tre,
   a tufft off brakes under my hed,
   as on from Joye were fled;
thus from my lyff day by day I flee,
   and all for on.

The Ronnyng stremes shall be my drynke,
   acrons schalbe my fode;
   nothyng may do me good,
but when of your bewty I do thunk,
   and all for lowe off on.

ANONYMOUS

[1] one

The last time I the Well woke

The last tyme I the wel woke
Ser John caght me with a croke,
he made me to swere be bel and boke
   I shuld not tell-ey.

yet he did me a wel wors turne,
he leyde my hed agayn the burne,[1]
he gafe my mayden-hed a spurne
   and rofe[2] my kell-ey.[3]

Ser John came to oure hows to play
fro evensong tyme til light of the day;
we made as mery as flowres in may—
   I was begyled-ay

Sir John he came to our hows,
he made hit wondur copious
he seyd that I was gracious
   to beyre a childe-ey.

I go with childe, wel I wot;
I schrew⁴ the fadur that hit gate,
with-outen he fynde hit mylke and pap
    a long while-ey.

    Byuan hys my name iet.

ANONYMOUS

¹ well   ² tore   ³ maidenhead   ⁴ curse

May no Man sleep . . .

May no man slepe in youre halle
for dogges, madam—for dogges, madam,
But yf¹ he have a tent² of fifteen ynche
    with twey clogges³
to dryve awey the dogges, madame.
    I-blessyd be such Clogges,
    that yeveth such bogges,⁴
    by-twyne my lady legges,
to dryve awey the dogges, madame.

May no man slepe in youre halle
for rattys, madam—for rattys, madame,
but yf he have a tent of fifteen enche
    wyt letheryn knappes,⁵
to dryve awey the rattys, madame.
    I-blessyd be suche knappes
    that gyveth such swappes
    under my lady lappes
to dryve awey the rattys, madame.

May no man slepe in youre halle
for flyes, madam—for flyes, madame,
but yf he have a tent of fifteen enche
    wyt a peir of byes⁶
to dryve awey the flyes, madame,

I-blessyd be such byes,
that maketh such suyes[7]
by-tuynne my lady thyes,
to dryve awey the flyes, madame.

ANONYMOUS

[1] But yf: unless   [2] surgical probe
[3] wooden blocks   [4] movements   [5] knobs
[6] rings (testicles)   [7] movements

We bear about no Cats' Skins

We bern[1] abowtyn non cattes skynnys,
pursis, perlis, sylver pynnis,
smale wympeles for ladyis chynnys.
    Damsele, bey sum ware of me.

I have a poket for the nonys,
therine ben tweyne precyous stonys.
Damsele, hadde the asayid next hem onys,
    the xuld the rathere gon with me.

i have a Jelyf[2] of godes sonde,[3]
Withoutyn fyt[4] it can stonde.
It can smytyn and hath non honde.
    Ryd[5] yourself quat it may be.

I have a powder for to selle,
Quat it is can I not telle—
It makit maydenys wombys to swelle,
    Thereof I have a quantyte.

ANONYMOUS

[1] carry   [2] jelly   [3] sent from God
[4] feet   [5] guess

O Lord, so sweet . . .

O Lord, so swett ser John dothe kys
  at every tyme when he wolde pley,
off hym-selfe so plesant he ys,
  I have no powre to say hym nay.

ser John loves me and I love hym,
  the more I love hym the more I maye.
he says, swett hert, cum kys me trym—
  I have no powre to say hym nay.

ser John to me Is proferynge
  for hys plesure ryght well to pay,
and In my box he puttes hys offrynge—
  I have no powre to say hym nay.

ser John ys taken In my mouse-trappe.
  Fayne wold I have hem bothe nyght and day.
He gropith so nyslye a-bought my lape,
  I have no pore to say hym nay.

ser John gevyth me reluys[1] rynges,
  With praty plesure for to assay—
furres of the fynest with other thynges.
  I have no powre to say hym nay.

ANONYMOUS

[1] glittering

The Cutty Wren

O where are you going? says Milder to Malder,
O I cannot tell, says Festel to Fose,
We're going to the woods, says John the Red Nose,
We're going to the woods, says John the Red Nose.

O what will you do there? says Milder to Malder,
O I cannot tell, says Festel to Fose,
We'll shoot the Cutty Wren, says John the Red Nose,
We'll shoot the Cutty Wren, says John the Red Nose.

O how will you shoot her? says Milder to Malder,
O I cannot tell, says Festel to Fose,
With arrows and bows, says John the Red Nose,
With arrows and bows, says John the Red Nose.

O that will not do, says Milder to Malder,
O, what will do then? says Festel to Fose,
Big cannons and guns, says John the Red Nose,
Big cannons and guns, says John the Red Nose.

O how will you bring her home? says Milder to Malder,
O, I cannot tell, says Festel to Fose,
On four strong men's shoulders, says John the Red Nose,
On four strong men's shoulders, says John the Red Nose.

O that will not do, says Milder to Malder,
O what will do then? says Festel to Fose,
In carts and wagons, says John the Red Nose,
In carts and wagons, says John the Red Nose.

O what will you cut her up with? says Milder to Malder,
O I cannot tell, says Festel to Fose,
With knives and with forks, says John the Red Nose,
With knives and with forks, says John the Red Nose.

O that will not do, says Milder to Malder,
O what will do then? says Festel to Fose,
With hatchets and cleavers, says John the Red Nose,
With hatchets and cleavers, says John the Red Nose.

O how will you boil her? says Milder to Malder,
O I cannot tell, says Festel to Fose,
In kettles and pots, says John the Red Nose,
In kettles and pots, says John the Red Nose.

O that will not do, says Milder to Malder,
O what will do then? says Festel to Fose,
Brass pans and cauldrons, says John the Red Nose,
Brass pans and cauldrons, says John the Red Nose.

O who'll have the spare ribs? says Milder to Malder,
O I cannot tell, says Festel to Fose,
We'll give them to the poor, says John the Red Nose,
We'll give them to the poor, says John the Red Nose.

ANONYMOUS

Riddle of Snow and Sun

White bird featherless
Flew from Paradise,
Pitched on the castle wall;
Along came Lord Landless,
Took it up handless,
And rode away horseless to the King's white hall.

ANONYMOUS

Nottamun Town

In Nottamun Town not a soul would look up,
Not a soul would look up, not a soul would look down,
Not a soul would look up, not a soul would look down
To tell me the way to Nottamun Town.

I rode a big horse that was called a grey mare,
Grey mane and tail, grey stripes down his back,
Grey mane and tail, grey stripes down his back,
There weren't a hair on him but what was called black.

She stood so still, she threw me to the dirt,
She tore my hide and bruised my shirt;
From stirrup to stirrup I mounted again
And on my ten toes I rode over the plain.

Met the King and the Queen and a company of men
A-walking behind and a-riding before.
A stark naked drummer came walking along
With his hands in his bosom a-beating his drum.

Sat down on a hot and cold frozen stone,
Ten thousand stood round me yet I was alone.
Took my heart in my hand to keep my head warm.
Ten thousand got drowned that never were born.

ANONYMOUS

Meditation in Winter

I

In to thir dirk and drublie dayis,
Quhone sabill all the hewin arrayis,
    With mystie vapouris, cluddis and skyis,
    Nature all curage me denyis
Off sangis, ballattis, and of playis.

II

Quhone that the nycht dois lenthin houris,
With wind, with haill, and havy schouris,
    My dule spreit dois lurk for schoir;
    My hairt for languor dois forloir,
For laik of symmer with his flouris.

III

I walk, I turne, sleip may I nocht,
I vexit am with havy thocht;
    This warld all ouir I cast about,
    And ay the mair I am in dout,
The mair that I remeid have socht.

IV

I am assayit on everie syde,
Dispair sayis ay, 'In tyme prowyde,
　　And get sum thing quhairon to leif;
　　Or with grit trouble and mischeif,
Thow sall in to this court abyde.'

V

Than Patience sayis, 'Be not agast:
Hald Hoip and Treuthe within the fast;
　　And lat Fortoun wirk furthe hir rage,
　　Quhone that no rasoun may assuage,
Quhill that hir glas be run and past.'

VI

And Prudence in my eir sayis ay,
'Quhy wald thow hald that will away?
　　Or craif that thow may have no space,
　　Thow tending to ane uther place,
A journay going everie day?'

VII

And than sayis Age, 'My freind, cum neir,
And be not strange, I the requeir:
　　Cum, brodir, by the hand me tak,
　　Remember thow hes compt to mak
Off all thi tyme thow spendit heir.'

VIII

Syne Deid castis upe his ettis wyd,
Saying, 'Thir oppin sall the byd;
　　Albeid that thow were never sa stout,
　　Vndir this lyntall sall thow lowt:
Thair is nane uther way besyd.'

IX

For feir of this all day I drowp;
No gold in kist, nor wyne in cowp;
　　No ladeis bewtie, nor luiffis blys
　　May lat me to remember this:
How glaid that ever I dyne or sowp.

X

Yit, quhone the nycht begynnis to schort,
It dois my spreit sum pairt confort,
    Off thocht oppressit with the schouris.
    Cum, lustie symmer: with thy flouris,
That I may leif in sum disport.
                    Quod Dunbar.

WILLIAM DUNBAR

I am called Childhood . . .

I am called Chyldhod, in play is all my mynde,
To cast a coyte, a cokstele, and a ball.
A toppe can I set, and dryve it in his kynde.
But would to god these hateful bookes all,
Were in a fyre brent to pouder small.
Than myght I lede my lyfe alwayes in play:
Whiche lyfe god sende me to myne endyng day.

SIR THOMAS MORE

Art thou Heywood . . .

Art thou Heywood with the mad mery wit?
Ye forsooth maister, that same is even hit.
Art thou Heywood that applieth mirth more then thrift?
Ye sir, I take mery mirth a golden gift.
Art thou Heywood that hath made many mad plaies?
Ye many plaies, fewe good woorkes in all my daies.
Art thou Heywood that hath made men mery long?
Ye: and will, if I be made mery among.
Art thou Heywood that woulde be made mery now?
Ye sir: helpe me to it now I beseche yow.

JOHN HEYWOOD

Norfolk Sprang Thee . . .

Norfolk sprang thee, Lambeth holds thee dead,
Clere, of the County of Cleremont, though hight.
Within the womb of Ormonds race thou bred,
And sawest thy cousin crowned in thy sight.
Shelton for love, Surrey for lord, thou chase;—[1]
Aye, me! while life did last that league was tender.
Tracing whose steps thou sawest Kelsall blaze,
Laundersey burnt, and battered Bullen render.
At Muttrel gates, hopeless of all recure,
Thine Earl, half dead, gave in thy hand his will;
Which cause did thee this pining death procure.
Ere summers four times seven thou couldst fulfill.
Ah, Clere! if love had booted, care, or cost,
Heaven had not wonne, nor earth so timely lost.

HENRY HOWARD, EARL OF SURREY

[1] chosest

In the Rude Age . . .

In the rude age when scyence was not so rife,
If Jove in Crete, and other where they taught
Artes to reverte to profyte of our lyfe,
Wan[1] after deathe to have their temples sought;
If vertue yet, in no unthankfull tyme,
Fayled of some to blast her endles fame—
A goodlie meane bothe to deter from cryme
And to her steppes our sequell to enflame;
In deyes of treuthe, if Wyattes frendes then waile—
The onelye debte that ded of quycke may clayme—
That rare wit spent, employde to our avayle,
Where Christe is tought, deserve they monnis blame?
His livelie face thy brest how did it freate,[2]
Whose cynders yet with envye doo the eate.

HENRY HOWARD, EARL OF SURREY

[1] won   [2] filled with envy

Divers thy Death . . .

Dyvers thy death doo dyverslye bemone.
Some, that in presence of that livelye hedd
Lurked, whose brestes envye with hate had sowne,
Yeld Cesars teres uppon Pompeius hedd.
Some, that watched with the murdrers knyfe,
With egre thurst to drynke thy guyltles blood,
Whose practyse brake by happye end of lyfe,
Weape envyous teares to here thy fame so good.
But I that knewe what harbourd in that hedd,
What vertues rare were temperd in that brest,
Honour the place that such a jewell bredd,
And kysse the ground, where as thy coorse doth rest,
With vaporde eyes; from whence suche streames avayle
As Pyramus did on Thisbes brest bewayle.

HENRY HOWARD, EARL OF SURREY

Wyatt resteth here . . .

Wyatt resteth here, that quick could never rest;
Whose heavenly giftes encreased by disdain,
And vertue sank the deper in his brest:
Such profit he by envy could obtain.

A hed, where wisdom misteries did frame;
Whose hammers bet styll in that lively brayn
As on a stithe, where that some work of fame
Was dayly wrought, to turne to Britaines gayn.

A visage, stern and myld; where bothe did grow,
Vice to contemne, in vertue to rejoyce;
Amid great stormes, whom grace assured so,
To lyve upright, and smile at fortunes choyce.

A hand, that taught what might be sayd in ryme;
That reft Chaucer the glory of his wit;
A mark, the which—unparfited, for time—
Some may approche, but never none shall hit.

A toung, that served in forein realmes his king;
Whose courteous talke to vertue did enflame
Eche noble hart; a worthy guide to bring
Our English youth, by travail, unto fame.

An eye, whose judgement none affect could blinde,
Frendes to allure, and foes to reconcile;
Whose persing loke did represent a mynde
With vertue fraught, reposed, voyd of gyle.

A hart, where drede was never so imprest
To hyde the thought that might the trouth avance;
In neyther fortune lost, nor yet represt,
To swell in wealth, or yeld unto mischance.

A valiant corps, where force and beawty met,
Happy, alas! to happy, but for foes,
Lievd, and ran the race that nature set;
Of manhodes shape, where she the molde did lose.

But to the heavens that simple soule is fled;
Which left with such, as covet Christ to know,
Witnesse of faith that never shall be ded;
Sent for our helth, but not received so.

Thus, for our gilte, this jewel have we lost;
The earth his bones, the heavens possesse his gost.

HENRY HOWARD, EARL OF SURREY

How Collingbourne was Cruelly Executed for Making a Foolish Rhyme

How like you this my maisters (quoth I?) very wel said one: The tragedy excelleth: the invencion also of the induction, and the discriptions are notable. But where as he faineth to talke with the princes in hel, that I am sure will be mislyked, because it is moste certayne, that some of their soules be in heaven. And although he herein do follow allowed Poetes, in theyr discription of Hel, yet it savoreth so much of Purgatory, whiche the papistes have digged thereout, that the ignorant maye therby be deceyved. Not a whit I warrant you (quoth I) For he meaneth not by his Hell the place eyther of damned soules, or of such as lye for their fees, but rather the Grave, wherin the dead bodies of al sortes of people do rest till tyme of the resurrection. And in this sence is Hel taken often in the scriptures, & in the writynges of learned christians. And so (as he himselfe hath tolde me) he meaneth, and so would have it taken. Tush (quoth an other) what stande we here upon? it is a Poesie and no divinitye, and it is lawfull for poetes to fayne what they lyst, so it be appertinent to the matter: And therefore let it passe even in such sort as you have read it. With a good will (quoth I) But where as you say a poet may faine what he list: In deede my thynke it should bee so, and ought to be well taken of the hearers: but it hath not at al times been so allowed. Ye saye troth quoth the reader: For here followeth in the story, that after the death of this duke, one called Collingborne was cruelly put to death for makyng of a ryme. I have his Tragedie here (quoth I) For the better perceyving whereof, you must ymagin that you se him a mervaylous wel favoured man, holdinge in his hand, his owne hart, newely ripped out of his brest, and smoking forth the lively spirit: and with his other hand, beckening to and fro, as it were to warne us to avoyde: and with his faynte tounge and voyce, sayeng as coragiously as he may, these wordes that folowe.

Beware, take heede, take heede, beware, beware
You Poetes you, that purpose to rehearce
By any arte what Tyrantes doynges are,
Erinnis rage is growen so fell and fearce
That vicious actes may not be toucht in verse:
The Muses freedoome, graunted them of elde,
Is barde, slye reasons treasons hye are held.

Be rough in ryme, and then they say you rayle,
Though Juvenal so be, that makes no matter:
With Jeremye you shal be had to jayle,
Or forst with Marciall, Ceasars faultes to flatter,
Clarkes must be taught to clawe and not to clatter:
Free Hellicon, & franke Pernassus hylles,
Are Helly hauntes, & ranke pernicious ylles.

Touche covertly in termes, and then you taunt,
Though praysed Poetes, alway dyd the lyke,
Controll us not, else traytour vyle avaunt,
What passe we what the learned do mislyke?
Our sinnes we see, wherin to swarme we seeke.
We passe not what the people saye or thynke.
Theyr shyttle hate maketh none but cowardes shrinke.

We knowe say they the course of Fortunes wheele,
Howe constantly it whyrleth styll about,
Arrearing nowe, whyle elder headlong reele.
Howe al the riders alwaye hange in doubt.
But what for that? we count him but a lowte
That stickes to mount, and basely like a beast
Lyves temperately for feare of blockam feast.

In dede we would of all be deemed gods
What ever we doe: and therfore partely hate
Rude preachers that dare threaten us plages & rods,
And blase the blots whereby we stayne our state:
But nought we passe what any such do prate.
Of course and office they must say theyr pleasure,
And we of course must heare and mend at leasure.

But when these pelting[1] poetes in theyr rymes
Shall taunt, and jest, or paynt our wicked wurkes,
And cause the people knowe, and curse our crymes,
This ougly fault, no Tyrant lyves but urkes.
And therefore lothe we taunters worse than Turkes.
They minde thereby to make us knowe our mis,[2]
And so to amend, but they but doate in this.

We knowe our faultes as wel as any other,
We also doubt[3] the daungers for them due:
Yet styll we trust so ryght to guyde the rother,[4]
That skape we shal the sourges that ensue.
We thinke we knowe moe shiftes than other knewe.
In vayne therfore for us are counsayles wryt:
We knowe our faultes, and wil not mend a whit.

These are the affections of the wycked sorte,
That preace[5] for honours, welth, and pleasure vayne.
Ceas therfore Baldwyn, ceas I thée exhort,
Withdrawe thy pen, for nothing shalt thou gayne
Save hate, with losse of paper, ynke and payne.
Fewe hate theyr sinnes, all hate to heare them touched,
Howe covertly so ever they be couched.

Thy entent I knowe is godly, playne, and good,
To warne the wyse, to fraye[6] the fond fro yll:
But wycked worldelinges are so wytles wood,
That to the wurst they all thinges construe styl.
Wyth rygour oft they recompence good wyll:
They racke the wurdes tyl tyme theyr synowes burst,
In doubtfull sences, strayning styll the wurst.

A paynefull proofe taught me the truth of this,
Through Tyrauntes rage, and Fortunes cruel tourne:
They murdred me, for metryng thinges amys.
For wotst thou what? I am that Colingbourne
Whych rymed that whych made full many mourne:
The Cat, the Rat, and Lovel our Dog,
Do rule al England, under a Hog.

Whereof the meanyng was so playne and true,
That every foole perceyved it at furst:
Most liked it, for most that most thinges knewe,
In hugger mugger, muttred what they durst.
The kyng him selfe of most was held accurst,
Both for his owne and for his faultours[7] faultes,
Of whom were three, the naughtiest of all naughtes.

The chyefe was Catisby whom I called a Cat,
A crafty lawyer catching all he could.
The second Ratclife, whom I named a Rat,
A cruel beast to gnawe on whom he should.
Lord Lovell barkt & byt whom Rychard would.
Whom therfore ryghtly I dyd terme our Dog,
Wherewyth to ryme I cleped the Kyng a Hog.

Tyll he usurped the crowne, he gave the Bore,
In whych estate would God he had deceased,
Than had the realme not ruyned so sore.
His Nephewes reygne should not so soone have ceassd,
The noble blud had not bene so decreased.
His Rat, his Cat, and Bloudhound had not noyed
So many thousandes as they have destroyed.

Theyr laweles dealynges al men dyd lament,
And do dyd I, and therfore made the rymes
To shewe my wyt, howe wel I could invent,
To warne withal the careles of theyr crymes,
I thought the freedome of the auncient tymes
Stoode styll in force. *Ridentem dicere verum
Quis vetat?* None, save clymers stil in *ferum.*

Belyke no Tyrantes were in Horace dayes,
And therefore Poetes freely blamed vyce.
Witnes theyr Satyr sharpe, and tragicke playes,
With chyefest Prynces chyefly had in pryce.
They name no man, they myxe theyr gall with spyce,
No more do I, I name no man outryght,
But ryddle wise, I meane them as I myght.

When bruyt had brought this to theyr gylty eares,
Who rudely named were noted in the ryme,
They all conspyred like most greedy Beares,
To charge me wyth most haynous traytrous cryme:
And damned me the gallow tree to clyme,
And strangled fyrst in quarters to be cut,
Whych should on hye over London gates be put.

This wicked judgement vexed me so sore,
That I exclamed agaynst theyr tyranny:
Wherewyth encenst, to make my payne the more,
They practised a shamefull villanye:
They cut me downe alyve, and cruelly
Rypt up my paunche and bulke to make me smart,
And lingred long eare they tooke out my hart.

Here Tyraunt Rychard played the eager Hog,
His grashyng tuskes my tender grystels shore:
His bloudhound Lovell playd the ravenyng Dog,
His wulvishe teeth, my gylteles carkas toar:
His Rat, and Cat, did what they myght, and more,
Cat Catesby clawed my guts to make me smart,
The Rat Lord Ratclyve gnawed me to the hart.

If Jewes had kylde the justest kyng alyve,
If Turkes had burnt up churches, Gods, and all,
What greater payne could cruel hartes contryve,
Than that I suffred, for this trespas smal?
I am not Prince nor Piere, but yet my fall
Is wurthy to be thought upon for this,
To see how cankard Tyrantes malyce is.

To teach also all subjectes to take heade
They meddle not with Magistrates affayres.
But praye to God to mende them if it nede:
To warne also all Poetes that be strayers,
To kepe them close in compas of their chayers,
And whan they touch thinges which they wish amended.
To sause them so, that fewe nede be offended.

And so to myxe theyr sharpe rebukes with myrth,
That they maye pearce, not causyng any payne,
Save such as followeth every kyndly byrth,
Requyted strayte, with gladnes of the gayne.
A poet must be pleasaunt, not to playne,
No flatterer, no bolsterer of vyce,
But sound and swete, in all thinges ware and wyse.

The Greekes do paynt a Poetes office whole
In Pegasus, theyr fayned horse wyth wynges,
Whom shaped so Medusaes blud did foale,
Who with his feete strake out the Muses sprynges
Fro flintie rockes to Hellicon that clynges.
And then flewe up unto the starrye skye,
And there abides among the heavens hye.

For he that shal a perfect Poete be,
Must fyrst be bred out of Medusaes blud:
He must be chaste and vertuous as was she,
Who to her power the Ocean god wythstoode.
To thende also his doome be just and good,
He must (as she had) have one onlye iye,
Regarde of truth, that nought maye leade awrye.

In courage eke he must be like a horse,
He maye not feare to register the ryght.
And that no power or fansie do him force,
No byt nor reyne his tender Jawes may twight.
He must be armed wyth strength of wyt and spryght
To dashe the rockes, darke causes and obscure,
Tyll he attayne the sprynges of truth most pure.

His hooves must also plyant be and strong,
To ryve the rockes of lust and errors blynde,
In brayneles heades, that alway wander wrong:
These must he bryse wyth reasons playne and kinde,
Tyll sprynges of grace do gushe out of the minde.
For tyl affections from the fond be dryven,
In vayne is truth tolde, or good counsayle geven.

Like Pegasus a Poet must have wynges,
To flye to heaven, thereto to feede and rest:
He must have knoweledge of eternal thynges,
Almighty Jove must harber in his brest.
With worldly cares he may not be opprest,
The wynges of skyll and hope must heave him hyer,
That al the joyes which worldly wyts desyre.

He must be also nymble, free, and swyft
To travayle farre to viewe the trades of men,
Great knowledge oft is gotten by the shyft:
Thynges notable he must be quicke to pen,
Reprovyng vyces sharpely now and then.
He must be swyft when touched tyrants chafe,
To gallop thence to kepe his carkas safe.

These propertyes yf I had well consydered,
Especially that whych I touched last,
With speedy flyght my feete should have delyvered
My feble body from the stormy blast:
They should have caught me, ere I had be cast.
But trusting vaynely to the Tyrauntes grace,
I never shronke, nor chaunged porte or place.

I thought the Poetes auncient liberties
Had bene allowed plea at any barre.
I had forgot howe newefound tyrannies
Wyth ryght and freedome were at open warre,
That lust was lawe, that myght dyd make and mar,
That with the lewde save this no order was,
Sic volo, sic iubeo, stet pro ratione voluntas.

Where this is lawe, it booteth not to pleade,
No pryvilege or libertyes avayle.
But wyth the learnde whom lawe and wisedome lead
Although through rashenes Poetes hap to rayle,
A plea of dotage may all quarels quayle:
Their libertyes theyr wrytinges to expounde,
Doth quyt them clere from faultes by Momus founde.

This auncient freedome ought not be debarred
From any wyght that speaketh ought, or wryteth.
The authours meanyng should of ryght be heard,
He knoweth best to what ende he endyteth:
Wordes sometyme beare more than the hart behiteth.
Admyt therefore the authours exposicion,
Yf playne, for truth: if forst, for his submission.

C.E.P.—4

Of slaunderers just lawes requyre no more
Save to amend that seemed evel sayd:
Or to unsaye the slaunders sayd afore,
And aske forgevenes for the hasty brayd:
To Heretykes no greater payne is layed
Than to recant theyr errours or retract:
And wurse than these can be no wryters acte.

Yes (quoth the Cat) thy rayling wordes be treason
And treason is far worse than heresye.
Then must it folowe by this foolyshe reason,
That kynges be more than God in majestie,
And soules be lesse than bodyes in degree.
For Heretikes both soules and God offend,
Traytours but seeke to bryng mans lyfe to ende.

I speake not this to abase the haynous faulte
Of traytrous actes abhord of God and man,
But to make playne theyr judgement to be naught
That heresye for lesser sinne do ban,
I curse them both as deepe as any can,
And alway dyd: yet through my foolyshe ryme,
They arraynde & staynde me wyth that shameful crime.

I never meant the kyng or counsayle harme,
Unles to wyshe them safetye were offence.
Agaynst theyr power I never lyfted arme,
Neyther pen nor tounge for any yll pretence.
The ryme I made, though rude, was sound in sence,
For they therein whom I so fondly named,
So ruled all that they were fowle defamed.

This was no treason but the very troth,
They ruled all, none could denye the same:
What was the cause then why they were so wroth?
What, is it treason in a riming frame
To clyp, to stretche, to adde, or chaunge a name?
And this reserved, there is no rime or reason,
That any craft can clowt to seeme a treason.

For where I meant the kyng by name of Hog,
I only alluded to his badge the Boare:
To Lovels name I added more our Dog,
Because most Dogs have borne that name of yore.
These metafors I use with other more,
As Cat, and Rat, the halfe names of the rest.
To hide the sense which they so wrongly wrest,

I praye you nowe what treason fynde you here?
Enough: you rubbed the gylty on the gal,
Both sence and names do note them very nere.
I graunt that was the chiefe cause of my fall,
Yet can you finde therein no treason at all:
There is no worde agaynst the prynce or state,
Nor harme to them whom al the realme dyd hate.

But sith the gylty alwayes are suspicious,
And dread the ruyne that must sewe by reason,
They can not chose but count theyr counsayle vicious
That note theyr faultes, and therfore cal it treason:
All grace and goodnes with the lewde is geason.[8]
This is the cause why they good thinges detest,
Whereas the good take yll thynges to the best.

And therfore Baldwyn boldly to the good
Rebuke thou vice, so shalt thou purchase thankes
As for the bad thou shalt but move his mood,
Though plesantly thou touch his sinfull prankes:
Warne poetes therfore not to passe the bankes
Of Hellicon, but kepe them in the streames,
So shall their freedome save them from extreames.

WILLIAM BALDWIN

[1] paltry   [2] faults   [3] fear   [4] rudder   [5] compete
[6] frighten   [7] i.e., his bad advisers   [8] scanty

In the Wracks of Walsingham

In the wrackes of Walsingam
   Whom should I chuse,
But the Queene of Walsingam
   to be guide to my muse
Then thou Prince of Walsingam
   graunt me to frame,
Bitter plaintes to rewe thy wronge,
   bitter wo for thy name,
Bitter was it soe to see,
   The seely sheepe
Murdred by the raveninge wolves
   Whilc the sheephards did sleep
Bitter was it oh to rewe
   the sacred vyne
Whiles the gardiners plaied all close
   rooted up by the swine
Bitter bitter oh to behould
   the grasse to growe
Where the walles of Walsingam
   so statly did shewe,
Such were the workes of Walsingam:
   while shee did stand
Such are the wrackes as now do shewe
   of that holy land,
Levell Levell with ground
   the towres doe lye
Which with their golden glitteringe tops
   Pearsed once to the skye,
Wher weare gates no gates ar nowe,
   the waies unknowen
Wher the press of peares did passe
   While her fame far was blowen.
Oules de scrike wher the sweetest himnes
   lately weer songe
Toades and serpentes hold ther dennes,
   Wher the Palmers did thronge

Weepe weepe o Walsingam
　　whose dayes are nightes
Blessings turned to blasphemies
　　Holy deedes to dispites,
Sinne is wher our: Ladie sate
　　Heaven turned is to Hell.
Sathan sittes wher our Lord did swaye
　　Walsingam oh farewell

ANONYMOUS

Nature in Her Working . . .

Nature in her woorcking soometyme dooth pinche lyke a niggard,
Disfiguring creatures, lyms with deformitye dusking.
This man is unjoyncted, that swad[1] lyke a monster abydeth:
Shee limps in the going, this slut with a cammoysed[2] haucks nose,
And as a Cow wasted plods on, with an head lyke a lutecase.
Theese faultes fond Hodipecks[3] impute too Nature, as yf she
Too frame were not habil gems with rare dignitye lustring.
Wherfor in advis'ment laboring too cancel al old blots,
And toe make a patterne of price, thee maystrye toe publish:
For toe shape a peerlesse paragon shee mynded, asembling
Her force and cunning for a spirt lands sundrye refusing,
And with al her woorckmat's travayling shee lighteth in *Holland*,
Round too the *Hage* posting, to the world *Marye* matchles avauncing.
In bodye fine fewterd,[4] a brave Brownnetta; wel handed;
Her stature is coomly; not an ynch toe superfluus holding;
Gratius in visadge; with a quick eye prittelye glauncing;
Her lips lyke corral rudye, with teeth lillye whit eevened.
Yoong in age, in manners and nurture sage she remayneth;
Bashful in her speaking; not rash, but watchful in aunswer;
Her look's, her simpring, her woords with curtesye sweetning;
Kynd and also modest; lyking with chastitye lyncking;
And in al her gesturs observing coomlye *Decorum*.
But toe what eend labor I, me toe presse with burden of Aetna:

Thee stars too number, poincts playnely uncounctabil opning.
Whust: not a woord: a silence such a task impossibil asketh.
Her *vertu* meriteth more prayse, than parlye can utter.

RICHARD STANYHURST

[1] fat, squat fellow
[2] pug-nosed, concave-nosed: either this contradicts 'haucks' or, more probably, it means
'slut with a nose like a pug-nosed hawk'   [3] blockhead   [4] like a greyhound

Sometime lively Gerald . . .

Soomtyme liv'lye *Girald* in grave now liv'les is harbourd.
A matchlesse gallant, in byrth and auncestrye nobil.
His nobil linnadge *Kyldaer* with *Mountegue* warrants.
Proper in his person, with gyfts so hym nature adorned.
In valor and in honor wel knowne too no man unequal.
And a true sound subject, to his Prince most faythful abyding.
Theese not with standing his liefe too to hastelye vannisht.
Nipt were thee blossooms, care fruictful season approched.
Wherefor his acquayntaunce his death so untymelye bewayleth.
Maynoth lamenteth, *Kilka* and *Rathangan* ar howling.
Nay rather is mated bye this hard hap desolat *Ireland*.
Such claps of batter that seally unfortunat *Island*.
O that I thy prayses could wel decipher in order,
Lyke *Homer* or *Virgil*, lyke *Geffray Chauncer* in English:
Then would thy *Stanyhurst* in pen bee liberal holden.
Thee poet is barrayn; for prayse rich matter is offred.
Heere percase *carpers* wyl twight his jollitye youthful.
Strong reason unstrayned that weake objection aunswers.
Hee must bee peerlesse who in yong yeers faultles abydeth.
Such byrds flee seldoom, such black swans scantlye be floating.
In world of mischiefe who finds such glorius angels?
Soom stars passe oothers; al perls doe not equalye luster.
Thee soundest wheatcorne with chaffy filthod is husked.
What shal I say further, this loare divinitye telleth;
Vertuus hee lived, through grace that vertuus eended.
What may be then better, than a godly and gratius upshot?

Too *God* in al pietee, too *Prince* in dutye remayning.
Whearefor (woorthye *Girald*) syth thy eend was hertye repentaunce,
Thy sould *God* gladdeth with saincts in blessed *Olympus*,
Thogh tumbd bee carcasse in towne of martyred *Alban*.

RICHARD STANYHURST

And if I did What then?

And if I did what then?
Are you agreev'd therfore?
The Sea hath fishe for every man,
And what would you have more?

Thus did my Mistresse once,
Amaze my mind with doubt:
And popt a question for the nonce,
To beat my braynes about.

Whereto I thus replied,
Eche fisherman can wishe,
That all the Sea at every tyde,
Were his alone to fishe.

And so did I (in vaine),
But since it may not be:
Let such fishe[1] there as finde the gaine,
And leave the losse for me.

And with such lucke and losse,
I will content my selfe:
Till tydes of turning time may tosse,
Such fishers on the shelfe.

And when they sticke on sandes,
That every man may see:
Then will I laugh and clappe my handes,
As they doe now at mee.

GEORGE GASCOIGNE

[1]used here as a verb

Gascoigne's Passion

I smile sometimes although my griefe be great,
To heare and see these lovers paint their paine,
And how they can in pleasaunt rimes repeate,
The passing pangs, which they in fancies faine.
But if I had such skill to frame a verse
I could more paine than all their panges reherse.

   Some say they find nor peace, nor power to fight.
Which seemeth strange: but stranger is my state:
I dwell in dole, yet sojorne with delight,
Reposed in rest, yet weried with debate.
For flatte repulse, might well apease my will
But fancie fights, to trie my fortune still.

   Some other say they hope, yet live in dread,
They friese, they flame, they flie alofte, they fall,
But I nor hope with happe to raise my hed,
Nor feare to stoupe, for why my gate is small.
Nor can I friese, with colde to kill my harte,
Nor yet so flame, as might consume my smarte.

   How live I then, which thus drawe foorth my daies?
Or tell me how, I found this fever first?
What fits I feele? what distance? what delayes?
What griefe? what ease? what like I best? what worst?
These things they tell, which seeke redresse of paine,
And so will I, although I coumpt it vaine.

I live in love, even so I love to live,
(Oh happie state, twice happie he that finds it)
But love to life this cognisance doth give,
This badge this marke, to every man that minds it,
Love lendeth life, which (dying) cannot die,
Nor living live: and such a life lead I.

   The sunny dayes which gladde the saddest wights,
Yet never shine to cleare my misty Moone,
No quiet sleepe, amidde the mooneshine nights
Can close mine eies, when I am wo by gone.
Into such shades my peevish sorow shrowdes,
That Sunne and Moone, are still to me in clowdes.

And feverlike I feede my fancie still,
With such repast, as most empaires my helth,
Which fever first I caught by wanton will,
When coles of kind did stirre my bloud by stelth:
And gazing eies, in bewtie put such trust
That love enflamd my liver all with lust.

My fits are like the fever Ectyck fits,
Which one day quakes within and burnes without,
The next day heate within the boosoms sits,
And shivring cold the body goes about.
So is my harte most hote when hope is cold,
And quaketh most when I most heate behold.

Tormented thus without delaies I stand,
Alwaies in one and evermore shal be,
In greatest griefe when helpe is nearest hand,
And best at ease if death might make me free:
Delighting most in that which hurts my hart,
And hating change which might renue my smart.

Lenvoie. Yet you dere dame: to whome this cure perteines,
    Devise betimes some drammes for my disease,
    A noble name shall be your greatest gaines,
    Whereof be sure, if you will worke mine ease.
    And though fond fooles set forth their fitts as fast,
    Yet grant with me that *Gascoignes* passions past.
                    Ever or Never.

                    GEORGE GASCOIGNE

Caelica, while you swear . . .

Caelica, while you doe sweare you love me best,
And ever loved onely me,
I feele that all powers are opprest
By Love, and Love by Destinie.

For as the child in swadling-bands,
When it doth see the Nurse come nigh,
With smiles and crowes doth lift the hands,
Yet still must in the cradle lie:
   So in the boate of Fate I rowe,
   And looking to you, from you goe.

When I see in thy once-beloved browes,
The heavy marks of constant love,
I call to minde my broken vowes,
And child-like to the Nurse would move;

   But *Love* is of the *Phoenix-kind*,
And burnes it selfe, in selfe-made fire,
To breed still new birds in the minde,
From ashes of the old desire:
   And hath his wings from constancy,
   As mountaines call'd of *moving* be.

Then *Caelica* lose not heart-eloquence,
Love understands not, come againe:
Who changes in her owne defence,
Needs not cry to the deafe in vaine.

Love is no true made *Looking-glasse*,
Which perfect yeelds the shape we bring,
It ugly showes us all that was,
And flatters every future thing.
   When *Phoebus* beames no more appeare
   Tis darker that the day was here.

Change I confesse it is a hatefull power,
To them that all at once must thinke,
Yet *Nature made both sweet and sower,*
She gave the eye a lid to winke:

And though the Youth that are estrang'd
From Mothers lap to other skyes,
Doe thinke that Nature there is chang'd
Because at home their knowledge lyes;

Yet shall they see who farre have gone,
That *Pleasure speaks more tongues than one.*

The Leaves fall off, when Sap goes to the root,
The warmth doth clothe the bough againe;
But to the dead tree what doth boot,
The silly mans manuring paine?

Unkindnesse may peece up againe,
But kindnesse either chang'd or dead,
Selfe-pittie may in fooles complaine;
Put thou thy Hornes on others head:
   For *constant faith is made a drudge,*
   But when requiting love is judge.

       FULKE GREVILLE, LORD BROOKE

Satan, no Woman . . .

Sathan, no Woman, yet a wandring spirit,
When he saw ships saile two wayes with one wind,
Of Saylers trade he hell did disinherit:
The Divell himselfe loves not a halfe-fast mind.

The *Satyre* when he saw the Shepheard blow
To warme his hands, and make his pottage coole,
Manhood forsweares, and halfe a beast did know,
Nature with double breath is put to schoole.

Cupid doth head his shafts in Womens faces,
Where smiles and teares dwell ever neere together,
Where all the Arts of Change give Passion graces;
While these clouds threaten, who feares not the weather?
   Saylers and *Satyres*, *Cupids* Knights, and I,
   Feare Women that Sweare, *Nay*; and know they lye.

       FULKE GREVILLE, LORD BROOKE

Juno, that on Her Head . . .

Juno, that on her head *Loves* liverie[1] carried,
Scorning to weare the markes of *Io's* pleasure,
Knew while the Boy in *Aequinoctiall* tarried,
His heats would rob the heaven of heavënly treasure,
Beyond the *Tropicks* she the Boy doth banish,
Where smokes must warme, before his fire do blaze,
And Childrens thoughts not instantly grow Mannish,
Feare keeping lust there very long at gaze:
But see how that poore Goddesse was deceived,
For Womens hearts farre colder there than ice,
When once the fire of lust they have received,
With two extremes so multiply the vice,
    As neither partie satisfying other,
    Repentance[2] *still becomes desires mother.*

FULKE GREVILLE, LORD BROOKE
[1] cuckold's horns   [2] shame

The Nurse-life Wheat . . .

The *nurse-life*[1] Wheat within his greene huske growing,
Flatters our hope and tickles our desire,
Natures true riches in sweet beauties shewing,
Which set all hearts, with labours love, on fire.

No lesse faire is the Wheat when golden eare
Showes unto hope the joyes of neare enjoying:
Faire and sweet is the bud, more sweet and faire
The Rose, which proves that time is not destroying.

Caelica, your youth, the morning of delight,
Enamel'd o're with beauties white and red,
All sense and thoughts did to beleefe invite,
That Love and Glorie there are brought to bed;
    And your ripe yeeres love-noone (he goes no higher),
    Turnes all the spirits of Man into desire.

FULKE GREVILLE, LORD BROOKE
[1] life-fostering

Merlin, they say . . .

Merlin, they say, an English Prophet borne,
When he was yong and govern'd by his Mother,
Took great delight to laugh such fooles to scorne,
As thought, by Nature we might know a Brother.

His Mother chid him oft, till on a day,
They stood, and saw a Coarse to buriall carried,
The Father teares his beard, doth weepe and pray;
The Mother was the woman he had married.

Merlin laughs out aloud in stead of crying;
His Mother chides him for that childish fashion;
Sayes, Men must mourne the dead, themselves are dying,
Good manners doth make answer unto passion.

The Child (for children see what should be hidden)
Replies unto his Mother by and by,
'Mother, if you did know, and were forbidden,
'Yet you would laugh as heartily, as I.'

FULKE GREVILLE, LORD BROOKE

Cupid, *Thou Naughty Boy* . . .

Cupid, thou naughtie Boy, when thou wert loathed,
Naked and blind, for vagabunding noted,
Thy nakednesse I in my reason clothed,
Mine eyes I gave thee, so was I devoted.

Fye Wanton, fie; who would shew children kindnesse?
No sooner he into mine eyes was gotten,
But straight he clouds them with a seeing blindnesse,
Makes reason wish that reason were forgotten.

From thence to *Myra's* eyes the Wanton strayeth,
Where while I charge him with ungratefull measure,
So with faire wonders he mine eyes betrayeth,
That my wounds, and his wrongs, become my pleasure;
   Till for more spite to *Myra's* heart he flyeth,
   Where living to the world, to me he dieth.

FULKE GREVILLE, LORD BROOKE

Who ever Sails . . .

Who ever sailes neere to *Bermuda* coast,
Goes hard aboord the Monarchy of Feare,
Where all desires (but Lifes desire) are lost,
For wealth and fame put off their glories there.

Yet this Ile poyson-like, by mischiefe knowne,
Weanes not desire from her sweet nurse, the Sea;
But unseene showes us where our hopes be sowne,
With woefull signes declaring joyfull way.
   For who will seeke the wealth of Westerne Sunne,
   Oft by Bermuda's *miseries must runne.*

Who seeks the God of *Love*, in Beauties skye,
Must passe the Empire of confused Passion,
Where our desires to all but Horrors die,
Before that joy and peace can take their fashion.

Yet this faire Heaven that yeelds this Soule-despaire,
Weanes not the heart from his sweet God, *Affection*;
But rather shewes us what sweet joyes are there,
Where constancy is servant to perfection.
   Who *Caelica's* chast heart then seeks to move,
   Must joy to suffer all the woes of *Love*.

FULKE GREVILLE, LORD BROOKE

Absence, *the Noble Truce* . . .

Absence, the noble truce
Of *Cupids* warre:
Where though desires want use,
They honoured are.
Thou art the just protection,
Of prodigall affection,
Have thou the praise;
When bankrupt *Cupid* braveth,
Thy mines his credit saveth,
With sweet delayes.

Of wounds which presence makes
With Beauties shot,
Absence the anguish slakes,
But healeth not:
Absence records the Stories,
Wherein Desire glories,
Although she burne;
She cherisheth the spirits
Where Constancy inherits
And passions mourne.

Absence, like dainty Clouds,
On glorious-bright,
Natures weake senses shrowds,
From harming light.
Absence maintaines the treasure
Of pleasure unto pleasure,
Sparing with praise;
Absence doth nurse the fire,
Which starves and feeds desire
With sweet delayes.

Presence to every part
Of Beauty tyes,
Where Wonder rules the Heart
There Pleasure dyes:

Presence plagues minde and senses
With modesties defences,
Absence is free:
Thoughts doe in absence venter
On *Cupids* shadowed center,
They winke and see.

But Thoughts be not so brave,
With absent joy;
For you with that you have
Your selfe destroy:
The absence which you glory,
Is that which makes you sory,
And burne in vaine:
For Thought is not the weapon,
Wherewith *thoughts-ease* men cheapen,
Absence is paine.

FULKE GREVILLE, LORD BROOKE

I offer Wrong to My Beloved Saint

I offer wrong to my beloved Saint,
I scorne, I change, I falsify my love,
Absence and time have made my homage faint,
With *Cupid* I doe every where remove.

I sigh, I sorrow, I doe play the foole,
Mine eyes like Weather-cocks, on her attend:
Zeale thus on either side she puts to schoole,
That will needs have inconstancy to friend.

I grudge, she saith, that many should adore her,
Where love doth suffer, and thinke all things meet,
She saith, All selfe-nesse must fall downe before her:
I say, Where is the sauce should make that sweet?
   Change and contempt (you know) *ill speakers be:*
   Caelica: and such are all your thoughts of me.

FULKE GREVILLE, LORD BROOKE

Satire septimus contra sollistam[1]

There where the sottish ignoraunt adore,
The vaine transparant, splendor of the Sun,
Accounting no felicity before,
The rising of his glory be begun,
Yet darke drownde vices will not seeke to shun:
I was: but now the shade of men I tooke,
Those that the substance of their soule forsooke.

Croesus said wealth was chiefe felicity,
Onely authority deserv'd a throne,
That war for kingdomes was tranquility,
And to be honor'd was true heaven alone,
But when by thraldome all this pompe was gone:
Solon (quoth he) my soule must needes confesse,
In dying well is onely happines.

The sun shines when the Scepter's in the hand,
The sun shines where the golden Fleece doth rest,
Where Ladyes wanton with a carpet band,[2]
(Though it be shut) within the Misers chest,
And where fat Epicures delight to feast:
O golden glory, shall this ever vanish,
Where such a God with swaying power doth vanquish.

Behold, the morning cheeres the springing flower,
The heate of heaven glads the twining vine,
The glasse full brimmed with the sandy hower,
These are more glorious than that pride of thine,
Yet see how sodainely they shall decline:
When like the flower, thy beawty, vine, thy wit,
Thy glasse-dust run, and thou in dust shalt sit.

How like a King the Marygould doth spred,
The golden circuit of her impald brow,
A whiffing winde that coronet hath shed,
And made her prowde unknobbed stalke to bow
No longer will the plants her pompe alow,

So have I seene ere now a goulden Crowne,
In a darke vault his pretious head lay downe.

Let him then thinke, that happines will thinke,
It lyes not in the glosse of humaine eyes,
How sodainely that vading[3] joy would shrinke,
When every minute, living pleasure dyes,
Like the bright clowded mistnes of the skyes.
If wild-bred Satyres so their lesson can,
Tis better be a Satyre than a man.

Spes Imperfecta

Thou Treasurer of heaven where hast thou clos'd
This hidden wealth of mens true happines?
In nothing humane fancy hath compos'd,
Yet on the earth once dwelt this blessednes,
To bring the earth from cursed wretchednes:
Open that secret coffer we may see,
(If not possesse) that heavenly treasury.

WILLIAM RANKINS

[1] Those born under the Sun are the natural possessors of
high place
[2] In his edition Davenport interprets this line 'where ladies
flirt with a base fellow who lives in society only because he
has mortgaged his property to a usurer for ready money, and
so, can shine as a gentleman for a time'
[3] fading

The 11th: and last book of the Ocean to Cynthia

Sufficeth it to yow my joyes interred,
In simpell wordes that I my woes cumplayne,
Yow that then died when first my fancy erred,
Joyes under dust that never live agayne.

If to the livinge weare my muse adressed,
Or did my minde her own spirrit still inhold,
Weare not my livinge passion so repressed,
As to the dead, the dead did thes unfold,

Sume sweeter wordes, sume more becumming vers,
Should wittness my myshapp in hygher kynd,
But my loves wounds, my fancy in the hearse,
The Idea but restinge, of a wasted minde,

The blossumes fallen, the sapp gon from the tree,
The broken monuments of my great desires,
From thes so lost what may th' affections bee,
What heat in Cynders of extinguisht fiers?

Lost in the mudd of thos hygh flowinge streames,
Which through more fayrer feilds ther courses bend,
Slayne with sealf thoughts, amasde in fearfull dreams,
Woes without date, discumforts without end,

From frutfull trees I gather withred leves
And glean the broken eares with misers hands,
Who sumetyme did injoy the waighty sheves
I seeke faire floures amidd the brinish sand.

All in the shade yeven in the faire soon dayes
Under thos healthless trees I sytt alone,
Wher joyfull byrdds singe neather lovely layes
Nor Phillomen recounts her direfull mone.

No feedinge flockes, no sheapherds cumpunye
That might renew my dollorus consayte,
While happy then, while love and fantasye
Confinde my thoughts onn that faire flock to waite;

No pleasinge streames fast to the ocean wendinge
The messengers sumetymes of my great woe,
But all onn yearth as from the colde stormes bendinge
Shrinck from my thoughts in hygh heavens and below.

Oh, hopefull lowe my object, and invention,
Oh, trew desire the spurr of my consayte,
Oh, worthiest spirrit, my minds impulsion,
Oh, eyes transpersant, my affections bayte,

Oh, princely forme, my fancies adamande,
Devine consayte, my paynes acceptance,
Oh, all in onn, oh heaven on yearth transparant,
The seat of joyes, and loves abundance!

Out of that mass of mirakells, my Muse,
Gathered thos floures, to her pure sences pleasinge,
Out of her eyes (the store of joyes) did chuse
Equall delights, my sorrowes counterpoysinge.

Her regall lookes, my rigarus sythes suppressed,
Small dropes of ioies, sweetned great worlds of woes,
One gladsume day a thowsand cares redressed.
Whom Love defends, what fortune overthrowes?

When shee did well, what did ther elce amiss?
When shee did ill what empires could have pleased?
No other poure effectinge wo, or bliss,
Shee gave, shee tooke, shee wounded, shee apeased.

The honor of her love, Love still devisinge,
Woundinge my mind with contrary consayte,
Transferde it sealf sumetyme to her aspiringe
Sumetyme the trumpett of her thoughts retrayt;

To seeke new worlds, for golde, for prayse, for glory,
To try desire, to try love severed farr,
When I was gonn shee sent her memory
More stronge then weare ten thowsand shipps of warr,

To call mee back, to leve great honors thought,
To leve my frinds, my fortune, my attempte,
To leve the purpose I so longe had sought
And holde both cares, and cumforts in contempt.

Such heat in Ize, such fier in frost remaynde,
Such trust in doubt, such cumfort in dispaire,
Mich like the gentell Lamm, though lately waynde,
Playes with the dug though finds no cumfort ther.

But as a boddy violently slayne
Retayneath warmth although the spirrit be gonn,
And by a poure in nature moves agayne
Till it be layd below the fatall stone;

Or as the yearth yeven in cold winter dayes
Left for a tyme by her life gevinge soonn,
Douth by the poure remayninge of his rayes
Produce sume green, though not as it hath dunn;

Or as a wheele forst by the fallinge streame,
Although the course be turnde sume other way
Douth for a tyme go rounde uppon the beame
Till wantinge strenght to move, it stands att stay;

So my forsaken hart, my withered mind,
Widdow of all the joyes it once possest,
My hopes cleane out of sight, with forced wind
To kyngdomes strange, to lands farr off addrest,

Alone, forsaken, frindless onn the shore
With many wounds, with deaths cold pangs inebrased,
Writes in the dust as onn that could no more
Whom love, and tyme, and fortune had defaced,

Of things so great, so longe, so manefolde
With meanes so weake, the sowle yeven then departing
The weale, the wo, the passages of olde
And worlds of thoughts discribde by onn last sythinge:

As if when after Phebus is dessended
And leves a light mich like the last dayes dawninge,
And every toyle and labor wholy ended
Each livinge creature draweth to his restinge

Wee should beginn by such a partinge light
To write the story of all ages past
And end the same before th' aprochinge night.

Such is agayne the labor of my minde
Whose shroude by sorrow woven now to end
Hath seene that ever shininge soonn declynde
So many yeares that so could not dissende

But that the eyes of my minde helde her beames
In every part transferd by loves swift thought;
Farr off or nire, in wakinge or in dreames,
Imagination stronge their luster brought.

Such force her angellike aparance had
To master distance, tyme, or crueltye,
Such art to greve, and after to make gladd,
Such feare in love, such love in majestye.

My weery lymes, her memory imbalmed,
My darkest wayes her eyes make cleare as day.
What stormes so great but Cinthias beames apeased?
What rage so feirce that love could not allay?

Twelve yeares intire I wasted in this warr,
Twelve yeares of my most happy younger dayes,
Butt I in them, and they now wasted ar,
Of all which past the sorrow only stayes.

So wrate I once, and my mishapp fortolde,
My minde still feelinge sorrowfull success
Yeven as before a storme the marbell colde
Douth by moyste teares tempestious tymes express.

So fealt my hevy minde my harmes att hande
Which my vayne thought in vayne sought to recure;
Att middell day my soonn seemde under land
When any littell cloude did it obscure.

And as the Isakells in a winters day
When as the soonn shines with unwounted warme,

So did my joyes mealt into secreat teares
So did my hart desolve in wastinge dropps;
And as the season of the year outweares
And heapes of snow from off the mountayn topps

With suddayne streames the vallies overflow,
So did the tyme draw on my more dispaire.
Then fludds of sorrow and whole seas of wo
The bancks of all my hope did overbeare

And drovnd my minde in deapts of missery.
Sumetyme I died, sumetyme I was distract,
My sowle the stage of fancies tragedye.
Then furious madness wher trew reason lackt

Wrate what it would, and scurgde myne own consayte.
Oh, hevy hart who cann thee wittnes beare,
What tounge, what penn could thy tormentinge treat
But thyne owne mourning thoughts which present weare,

What stranger minde beleve the meanest part
What altered sence conceve the weakest wo
That tare, that rent, that peirsed thy sadd hart?

And as a man distract, with trebell might
Bound in stronge chaynes douth strive, and rage in vayne,
Till tyrde and breathless, he is forst to rest,
Fyndes by contention but increas of payne,
And fiery heat inflamde in swollen breast,

So did my minde in change of passion
From wo to wrath, from wrath returne to wo,
Struglinge in vayne from loves subiection.

Therfore all liveless, and all healpless bounde
My fayntinge spirritts sunck, and hart apalde,
My joyes and hopes lay bleedinge on the ground
That not longe since the highest heaven scalde.

I hated life and cursed destiney
The thoughts of passed tymes like flames of hell,

Kyndled a fresh within my memorye
The many deere achiuements that befell

In thos pryme yeares and infancy of love
Which to discribe weare butt to dy in writinge.
Ah those I sought, but vaynly, to remove
And vaynly shall, by which I perrish livinge.

And though strong reason holde before myne eyes
The Images, and formes of worlds past
Teachinge the cause why all thos flames that rize
From formes externall, cann no longer last,

Then that thos seeminge bewties hold in pryme
Loves ground, his essence, and his emperye,
All slaves to age, and vassalls vnto tyme
Of which repentance writes the tragedye.

But this, my harts desire could not conceve
Whose Loue outflew the fastest fliinge tyme;
A bewty that cann easely deseave
Th' arrest of yeares, and creepinge age outclyme.

A springe of bewties which tyme ripeth not
Tyme that butt workes onn frayle mortallety,
A sweetness which woes wronges outwipeth not,
Whom love hath chose for his devinnitye,

A vestall fier that burnes, but never wasteth,
That looseth nought by gevinge light to all
That endless shines eachwher and endless lasteth
Blossumes of pride that cann nor vade nor fall.

Thes weare thos marvelous perfections,
The parents of my sorrow and my envy
Most deathfull and most violent infections,
Thes be the Tirants that in fetters tye

Their wounded vassalls, yet nor kill nor cure,
But glory in their lastinge missery

That as her bewties would our woes should dure
Thes be th' effects of pourfull emperye . . .

Yet have thes wounders want which want cumpassion,
Yet hath her minde some markes of humayne race
Yet will shee bee a wooman for a fashion
So douth shee pleas her vertues to deface.

And like as that immortall pour douth seat
An element of waters to allay
The fiery soonn beames that on yearth do beate
And temper by cold night the heat of day.

So hath perfection, which begatt her minde,
Added therto a change of fantasye
And left her the affections of her kynde
Yet free from evry yevill but crueltye.

But leve her prayse, speak thow of nought but wo,
Write on the tale that Sorrow bydds ther tell,
Strive to forgett, and care no more to know
Thy cares are known, by knowinge thos too well,

Discribe her now as shee appeeres to thee,
Not as shee did apeere in dayes fordunn.
In love thos things that weare no more may bee,
For fancy seildume ends wher it begunn.

And as streame by stronge hand bounded in
From natures course, wher it did sumetyme runn,
By some small rent or loose part douth beginn
To finde escape, till it a way hath woone,

Douth then all unawares in sunder teare
The forsed bounds and raginge, runn att large,
In th'auncient channells as they wounted weare,
Such is of weemens love the carefull charge,

Helde, and mayntaynde with multetude of woes,
Of longe arections such the suddayne fall,

Onn houre deverts, onn instant overthrowes
For which our lives, for which our fortunes thrale,

So many yeares thos joyes have deerely bought,
Of which when our fonde hopes do most assure
All is desolvde, our labors cume to nought,
Nor any marke therof ther douth indure;

No more then when small dropps of rayne do fall
Uppon the parched grounde by heat up dried,
No coolinge moysture is percevde att all
Nor any shew or signe of weet douth byde.

But as the feildes clothed with leves and floures
The bancks of roses smellinge pretious sweet
Have but ther bewties date, and tymely houres,
And then defast by winters cold, and sleet,

So farr as neather frute nor forme of floure
Stayes for a wittnes what such branches bare,
Butt as tyme gave, tyme did agayne devoure
And chandge our risinge joy to fallinge care;

So of affection which our youth presented,
When shee that from the soonn reves[1] poure and light
Did but decline her beames as discontented
Convertinge sweetest dayes to saddest night;

All droopes, all dyes, all troden under dust
The person, place, and passages forgotten
The hardest steele eaten with softest ruste,
The firme and sollide tree both rent and rotten;

Thos thoughts so full of pleasure and content
That in our absence weare affections foode
Ar rased out and from the fancy rent
In highest grace and harts deere care that stood,

Ar cast for pray to hatred, and to scorne,
Our deerest treasors and our harts trew joyes,

The tokens hunge onn brest, and kyndly worne
Ar now elcewhere disposde, or helde for toyes;

And thos which then our Jelosye removed,
And others for our sakes then valued deere,
The one forgot, the rest are deere beloved,
When all of ours douth strange or vilde² apeere.

Thos streames seeme standinge puddells which, before,
Wee saw our bewties in, so weare they cleere.
Bellphebes course is now observde no more,

That faire resemblance weareth out of date.
Our Ocean seas are but tempestius waves
And all things base that blessed wear of late . . .

And as a feilde wherin the stubbell stands
Of harvest past, the plowmans eye offends,
Hee tills agayne or teares them up with hands,
And throwes to fire as foylde and frutless ends,

And takes delight another seed to sow. . . .
So douth the minde root up all wounted thought
And scornes the care of our remayninge woes;
The sorrowes, which themsealvs for us have wrought,

Ar burnt to Cinders by new kyndled fiers,
The ashes ar dispeirst into the ayre,
The sythes, the grones of all our past desires
Ar cleane outworne, as things that never weare . . .

With youth, is deade the hope of loves returne,
Who lookes not back to heare our after cryes.
Wher hee is not, hee laughts att thos that murne,
Whence hee is gonn, hee scornes the minde that dyes,

When hee is absent hee beleves no words,
When reason speakes hee careless stopps his ears,
Whom he hath left hee never grace affords
But bathes his wings in our lamentinge teares.

Unlastinge passion, soune outworne consayte
Whereon I built, and onn so dureless trust!
My minde had wounds, I dare not say desaite,
Weare I resolvde her promis was not Just.

Sorrow was my revendge, and wo my hate;
I pourless was to alter my desire.
My love is not of tyme, or bound to date
My harts internall heat, and livinge fier

Would not, or could be quencht, with suddayn shoures.
My bound respect was not confinde to dayes
My vowed fayth not sett to ended houres.
I love the bearinge and not bearinge sprayes

Which now to others do ther sweetnes send,
Th'incarnat, snow driven white, and purest asure,
Who from high heaven douth on their feilds dissend
Fillinge their barns with grayne, and towres with treasure.

Erringe or never erringe, such is Love,
As while it lasteth scornes th'accompt of thos
Seekinge but sealf contentment to improve,
And hydes if any bee, his inward woes,

And will not know while hee knowes his own passion
The often and unjust perseverance
In deeds of love, and state, and every action
From that first day and yeare of their joyes entrance;

But I unblessed, and ill borne creature,
That did inebrace the dust, her boddy bearinge,
That loved her both, by fancy, and by nature,
That drew yeven with the milke in my first suckinge

Affection from the parents brest that bare mee,
Have found her as a stranger so severe
Improvinge my mishapp in each degree.
But love was gonn. So would I, my life weare!

A Queen shee was to mee, no more Belphebe,
A Lion then, no more a milke white Dove;
A prissoner in her brest I could not bee,
Shee did untye the gentell chaynes of love.

Love was no more the love of hydinge
All trespase, and mischance, for her own glorye.
It had bynn such, it was still for th'ellect,
But I must bee th'exampell in loves storye,
This was of all forpast the sadd effect . . .

But thow my weery sowle and hevy thought
Made by her love a burden to my beinge,
Dust know my error never was forthought
Or ever could proceed from sence of Lovinge.

Of other cause if then it had proceedinge
I leve th'excuse syth Judgment hath bynn geven;
The lymes devided, sundred and a bleedinge
Cannot cumplayne the sentence was unyevunn.

This did that natures wonder, Vertues choyse,
The only parragonn of tymes begettinge
Devin in wordes, angellicall in voyse;
That springe of joyes, that floure of loves own settinge,

Th'Idea remayninge of thos golden ages,
That bewtye bravinge heavens, and yearth imbalminge,
Which after worthless worlds but play onn stages,
Such didsst thow her longe since discribe, yet sythinge,

That thy unabell spirrit could not fynde ought
In heavens bewties, or in yearths delighte
For likeness, fitt to satisfy thy thought.
Butt what hath it avaylde thee so to write?

Shee cares not for thy prayse, who knowes not thers;
Its now an Idell labor, and a tale
Tolde out of tyme that dulls the heerers eares;
A marchandise wherof ther is no sale.

Leve them, or lay them vp with thy dispaires;
She hath resolvde, and Judged thee longe ago;
Thy lines ar now a murmeringe to her eares
Like to a fallinge streame which passinge sloe

Is wovnt to nurrishe sleap, and quietnes.
So shall thy paynfull labors bee pervsde
And draw on rest, which sumetyme had regard.
But thos her cares, thy errors have excusde,

Thy dayes foredun have had ther dayes reward.
So her harde hart, so her estranged minde,
In which above the heavens, I once reposed,
So to thy error have her eares inclined,

And have forgotten all thy past deservinge,
Holdinge in minde butt only thyne offence
And only now affecteth thy depravinge
And thincks all vayne that pleadeth thy defence.

Yet greater fancye bewtye never bredd,
A more desire the hart bludd never nourished,
Her sweetness an affection never fedd
Which more in any age hath ever floryshedd.

The minde and vertue never have begotten
A firmer love, since love on yearth had poure,
A love obscurde, but cannot be forgotten,
Too great and stronge for tymes Jawes to devour;

Contayninge sych a fayth as ages wound not,
Care, wackfull ever of her good estate,
Feare, dreadinge loss, which sythes, and ioyes not
A memory, of the joyes her grace begate,

A lastinge gratfullness, for thos cumforts past
Of which the cordiall sweetness cannot dye.
Thes thoughts, knitt up by fayth, shall ever last,
Thes, tyme assayes, butt never can untye;

Whose life once lived in her perrellike brest,
Whose joyes weare drawne but from her happines,
Whose harts hygh pleasure, and whose minds trew rest
Proceeded from her fortunes blessedness,

Who was intentive, wakefull, and dismayde,
In feares, in dreames, in feeverus Jelosye,
Who longe in sylence served, and obayed
With secret hart, and hydden loyaltye;

Which never change to sadd adversetye,
Which never age, or natures overthrow,
Which never sickness, or deformetye,
Which never wastinge care, or weeringe wo,
If subject unto thes she could have bynn. . . .

Which never words, or witts mallicious,
Which never honors bayte, or worlds fame
Atchyved by attemptes adventerus,
Or ought beneath the soonn, or heavens frame,

Can so desolve, dissever, or distroye
The essentiall love, of no frayle parts cumpounded,
Though of the same now buried bee the joy,
The hope, the cumfort, and the sweetness ended,

But that the thoughts, and memories of thees
Worke a relapps of passion, and remayne
Of my sadd harte the sorrow suckinge bees.
The wrongs recevde, the scornes perswade in vayne. . . .

And though thes medcines worke desire to end
And ar in others the trew cure of likinge,
The salves that heale loves wounds and do amend
Consuminge woe, and slake our harty sythinge,

They worke not so, in thy minds long deseas:
Externall fancy tyme alone recurethe
All whose effects do weare away with ease.
Love of delight while such delight indureth
Stayes by the pleasure, but no longer stayes. . . .

But in my minde so is her love inclosde
And is therof not only the best parte
But into it the essence is disposde . . .
Oh love (the more my wo) to it thow art

Yeven as the moysture in each plant that growes,
Yeven as the soonn unto the frosen ground,
Yeven as the sweetness, to th' incarnate rose,
Yeven as the Center in each perfait rounde,

As water to the fyshe, to men as ayre,
As heat to fier, as light unto the soonn.
Oh love it is but vayne, to say thow weare,
Ages, and tymes, cannot thy poure outrun. . . .

Thow are the sowle of that unhappy minde
Which beinge by nature made an Idell thought
Begon yeven then to take immortall kynde
When first her vertues in thy spirrights wrought. . . .

From thee therfore that mover cannot move
Because it is becume thy cause of beinge;
What ever error may obscure that love
What ever frayle effect of mortall livinge,

What ever passion from distempered hart
What absence, tyme, or iniuries effect,
What faythless frinds, or deipe dissembled art
Present, to feede her most unkynde suspect.

Yet as the eayre in deip caves vnder grovnd
Is strongly drawne when violent heat hath rent
Great clefts therin, till moysture do abound,
And then the same imprisoned, and uppent,

Breakes out in yearthquakes teringe all asunder,
So in the Center of my cloven hart,
My hart, to whom her bewties wear such wounder,
Lyes the sharpe poysoned heade of that loves dart,

Which till all breake and all desolve to dust
Thence drawne it cannot bee, or therin knowne.
Ther, mixt with my hart bludd, the fretting rust
The better part hath eaten, and outgrown. . . .

Butt what of thos, or thes, or what of ought
Of that which was, or that which is, to treat?
What I possess is butt the same I sought;
My love was falce, my labors weare desayte.

Nor less then such they ar esteemde to bee,
A fraude bought att the prize of many woes,
A guile, whereof the profitts unto mee—
Coulde it be thought premeditate for thos?

Wittnes thos withered leves left on the tree,
The sorrow worren face, the pensive minde,
The externall shews what may th' internall bee;
Cold care hath bitten both the root, and vinde. . . .

Butt stay my thoughts, make end, geve fortune way,
Harshe is the voice of woe and sorrows sounde,
Cumplaynts cure not, and teares do but allay
Greifs for a tyme, which after more abounde.

To seeke for moysture in th'Arabien sande
Is butt a losse of labor, and of rest.
The lincks which tyme did break of harty bands

Words cannot knytt, or waylings make a new.
Seeke not the soonn in cloudes, when it is sett . . .
On highest mountaynes wher thos Sedars grew,
Agaynst whose bancks, the trobled ocean bett,

And weare the markes to finde thy hoped port,
Into a soyle farr off them sealves remove,
On Sestus shore, Leanders late resorte,
Hero hath left no lampe to Guyde her love;

Thow lookest for light in vayne, and stormes arise;
Shee sleaps thy death that erst thy danger syth-ed
C.E.P.—6

Strive then no more, bow down thy weery eyes,
Eyes, which to all thes woes thy hart have guided.

Shee is gonn, Shee is lost! Shee is found, shee is ever faire!
Sorrow drawes weakly, wher love drawes not too.
Woes cries, sound nothinge, butt only in loves eare.
Do then by Diinge, what life cannot doo . . .

Unfolde thy flockes, and leve them to the feilds
To feed on hylls, or dales, wher likes them best,
Of what the summer, or the springe tyme yeildes,
For love, and tyme, hath geven thee leve to rest.

Thy hart, which was their folde, now in decay
By often stormes, and winters many blasts
All torne and rent, becumes misfortunes pray,
Falce hope, my shepherds staff, now age hath brast.

My pipe, which loves own hand, gave my desire
To singe her prayses, and my wo uppon,
Dispaire hath often threatned to the fier,
As vayne to keipe now all the rest ar gonn.

Thus home I draw, as deaths longe night drawes onn
Yet every foot, olde thoughts turne back myne eyes,
Constraynt mee guides as old age drawes a stonn
Agaynst the hill, which over wayghty lyes

For feebell armes, or wasted strenght to move.
My steapps are backwarde, gasinge on my loss,
My minds affection, and my sowles sole love,
Not mixte with fancies chafe, or fortunes dross

To God I leve it, who first gave it me,
And I her gave, and she returnd agayne,
As it was herrs. So lett his mercies bee,
Of my last cumforts, the essentiall meane.
But be it so, or not, th'effects, ar past.
Her love hath end; my woe must ever last.

SIR WALTER RALEGH.

¹ steals   ² vile

The Advice

Many desire, but few or none deserve
To win the Fort of thy most constant will:
Therefore take heed, let fancy never swerve
But unto him that will defend thee still.
  For this be sure, the fort of fame once won,
  Farewell the rest, thy happy dayes are done.

Many desire, but few or none deserve
To pluck the flowers and let the leaves to fall;
Therefore take heed, let fancy never swerve,
But unto him that will take leaves and all.
  For this be sure, the flower once pluckt away,
  Farewell the rest, thy happy days decay.

Many desire, but few or none deserve
To cut the corn, not subject to the sickle.
Therefore take heed, let fancy never swerve,
But constant stand, for Mowers mindes are fickle.
  For this be sure, the crop being once obtain'd
  Farewell the rest, the soil will be disdain'd.

SIR WALTER RALEGH

Feed still Thyself

Feede still thy selfe, thou fondling with beliefe,
Go hunt thy hope, that never tooke effect,
Accuse the wrongs that oft hath wrought thy griefe,
And reckon sure where reason would suspect.

Dwell in the dreames of wish and vaine desire,
Pursue the faith that flies and seekes to new,
Run after hopes that mocke thee with retire,
And looke for love where liking never grew.

Devise conceits to ease thy carefull hart,
Trust upon times and daies of grace behinde,
Presume the rights of promise and desart,
And measure love by thy beleeving minde.

Force thy affects that spite doth daily chace,
Winke at the wrongs with wilfull oversight,
See not the soyle and staine of thy disgrace,
Nor recke disdaine, to doate on thy delite.

And when thou seest the end of thy reward,
And these effects ensue of thine assault,
When rashnes rues, that reason should regard,
Yet still accuse thy fortune for the fault.

And crie, O Love, O death, O vaine desire,
When thou complainst the heate, and feeds the fire.

                              SIR WALTER RALEGH

The Shadow of Night

TO MY DEARE AND MOST WORTHY FRIEND
MASTER MATHEW ROYDON

It is an exceeding rapture of delight in the deepe search of knowledge,
(none knoweth better then thy selfe sweet *Mathew*) that maketh men manfully
indure th'extremes incident to that *Herculean* labour: from flints must the
Gorgonean fount be smitten. Men must be shod by *Mercurie*, girt with *Saturnes*
Adamantine sword, take the shield from Pallas, the helme from *Pluto*, and
have the eyes of *Graea* (as *Hesiodus armes Perseus* against *Medusa*) before they
can cut of the viperous head of benumming ignorance, or subdue their
monstrous affections to most beautifull judgement.

How then may a man stay his marvailing to see passion-driven men, reading
but to curtoll a tedious houre, and altogether hidebownd with affection to
great mens fancies, take upon them as killing censures as if they were judge-
ments Butchers, or as if the life of truth lay tottering in their verdits.

Now what a supererogation in wit this is, to thinke skil so mightilie pierst
with their loves, that she should prostitutely shew them her secrets, when she
will scarcely be lookt upon by others but with invocation, fasting, watching;
yea not without having drops of their soules like an heavenly familiar. Why

then should our *Intonsi Catones* with their profit-ravisht gravitie esteeme her
true favours such questionlesse vanities, as with what part soever thereof they
seeme to be something delighted, they queimishlie commende it for a pretie
toy. Good Lord how serious and eternall are their Idolatrous platts for
riches! no marvaile sure they here do so much good with them. And heaven
no doubt will grovill on the earth (as they do) to imbrace them. But I stay
this spleene when I remember my good *Mat.* how joyfully oftentimes you
reported unto me, that most ingenious *Darbie*, deepe searching *Northumberland*,
and skill-imbracing *heire of Hunsdon* had most profitably entertained learning
in themselves, to the vitall warmth of freezing science, & to the admirable
luster of their true Nobilitie, whose high deserving vertues may cause me
hereafter strike that fire out of darknesse, which the brightest Day shall envie
for beautie. I should write more, but my hasting out of towne taketh me from
the paper, so preferring thy allowance in this poore and strange trifle, to the
passport of a whole Cittie of others, I rest as resolute as *Seneca*, satisfying my
selfe if but a few, if one, or if none like it.

By the true admirour of thy vertues and perfectly vowed friend.

G. Chapman.

HYMNUS IN NOCTEM

Great Goddesse to whose throne in Cynthian fires,
This earthlie Alter endlesse fumes exspires,
Therefore, in fumes of sighes and fires of griefe,
To fearefull chances thou sendst bold reliefe,
Happie, thrise happie, Type, and nurse of death,
Who breathlesse, feedes on nothing but our breath,
In whom must vertue and her issue live,
Or dye for ever; now let humor give
Seas to mine eyes, that I may quicklie weepe
The shipwracke of the world: or let soft sleepe
(Binding my sences) lose my working soule,
That in her highest pitch, she may controule
The court of skill, compact of misterie,
Wanting but franchisement and memorie
To reach all secrets: then in blissfull trance,
Raise her (deare Night) to that perseverance,
That in my torture, she all earths may sing,
And force to tremble in her trumpeting
Heauens christall temples: in her powrs implant
Skill of my griefs, and she can nothing want.

Then like fierce bolts, well rammd with heate & cold
In Joves Artillerie; my words unfold,
To breake the labyrinth of everie eare,
And make ech frighted soule come forth and heare,
Let them breake harts, as well as yeelding ayre,
That all mens bosoms (pierst with no affaires,
But gaine of riches) may be lanced wide,
And with the threates of vertue terrified.
　　Sorrowes deare soveraigne, and the queene of rest,
That when unlightsome, vast, and indigest
The formelesse matter of this world did lye,
Fildst euery place with thy Divinitie,
Why did thy absolute and endless sway,
Licence heavens torch, the scepter of the Day,
Distinguisht intercession to thy throne,
That long before, all matchlesse rulde alone?
Why letst thou order, orderlesse disperse,
The fighting parents of this uniuerse?
When earth, the ayre, and sea, in fire remain
When fire, the sea, and earth, the ayre containd
When ayre, the earth, and fire, the sea enclosde
When sea, fire, ayre, in earth were indisposde
Nothing, as now, remainde so out of kinde
All things in grosse, were finer than refinde,
Substance was sound within, and had no being,
Now forme gives being; all our essence seeming,
Chaos had soule without a bodie then,
Now bodies live without the soules of men,
Lumps being digested; monsters, in our pride.
　　And as a wealthie fount, that hils did hide,
Let forth by labor of industrious hands,
Powres out her treasure through the fruitefull strands,
Seemely divided to a hundred streames,
Whose bewties shed such profitable beames,
And make such Orphean Musicke in their courses,
That Citties follow their enchanting forces,
Who running farre, at length ech powres her hart
Into the bosome of the gulfie desart,
As much confounded there, and indigest,
As in the chaos of the hills comprest:

So all things now (extract out of the prime)
Are turnd to chaos, and confound the time.
   A stepdame Night of minde about us clings,
Who broodes beneath her hell obscuring wings,
Worlds of confusion, where the soule defamde,
The bodie had bene better never framde,
Beneath thy soft, and peace-full covert then,
(Most sacred mother both of Gods and men)
Treasures unknowne, and more unprisde did dwell;
But in the blind borne shadow of this hell,
This horrid stepdame, blindnesse of the minde,
Nought worth the sight, no sight, but worse then blind,
A Gorgon that with brasse, and snakie brows,
(Most harlot-like) her naked secrets shows:
For in th'expansure, and distinct attire,
Of light, and darcknesse, of the sea, and fire,
Of ayre, and earth, and all, all these create,
First set and rulde, in most harmonious state,
Disjunction showes, in all things now amisse,
By that first order, what confusion is:
Religious curb, that manadgd men in bounds,
Of publique wellfare; lothing private grounds,
(Now cast away, by selfe-lov's paramores)
All are transformd to Calydonian bores,
That kill our bleeding vines, displow our fields,
Rend groves in peeces; all things nature yeelds
Supplanting: tumbling up in hills of dearth,
The fruitefull disposition of the earth,
Ruine creates men: all to slaughter bent,
Like envie, fed with others famishment.
   And what makes men without the parts of men,
Or in their manhoods, lesse then childeren,
But manlesse natures? all this world was namde
A world of him, for whom it first was framde,
(Who (like a tender Chevrill), shruncke with fire
Of base ambition, and of selfe-desire,
His armes into his shoulders crept for feare
Bountie should use them; and fierce rape forbeare,
His legges into his greedie belly runne,
The charge of hospitalitie to shunne)

In him the world is to a lump reverst,
That shruncke from forme, that was by forme disperst,
And in nought more then thanklesse avarice,
Not rendring vertue her deserved price.
Kinde Amalthaea was transferd by Jove,
Into his sparckling pavement, for her love,
Though but a Goate, and giving him her milke,
Basenesse is flintie; gentrie softe as silke,
In heavens she lives, and rules a living signe
In humane bodies: yet not so divine,
That she can worke her kindnesse in our harts.
    The sencelesse Argive ship, for her deserts,
Bearing to Colchos, and for bringing backe,
The hardie Argonauts, secure of wracke,
The fautor and the God of gratitude,
Would not from number of the starres exclude.
A thousand such examples could I cite,
To damne stone-pesants, that like Typhons fight
Against their Maker, and contend to be
Of kings, the abject slaves of drudgerie:
Proud of that thraldome: love the kindest lest,
And hate, not to be hated of the best.
    If then we frame mans figure by his mind,
And that at first, his fashion was assignd,
Erection in such God-like excellence
For his soules sake, and her intelligence:
She so degenerate, and growne deprest,
Content to share affections with a beast,
The shape wherewith he should be now indude,
Must beare no signe of mans similitude.
Therefore Promethean Poets with the coles
Of their most geniale, more-then-humane soules
In living verse, created men like these,
With shapes of Centaurs, Harpies, Lapithes,
That they in prime of erudition,
When almost savage vulgar men were growne,
Seeing them selves in those Pierean founts,
Might mend their mindes, asham'd of such accounts.
So when ye heare, the sweetest Muses sonne,
With heavenly rapture of his Musicke, wonne

Rockes, forrests, floods, and winds to leave their course
In his attendance: it bewrayes the force
His wisedome had, to draw men growne so rude
To civill love of Art, and Fortitude.
And not for teaching others insolence,
Had he his date-exceeding excellence
With soveraigne Poets, but for use applyed,
And in his proper actes exemplified;
And that in calming the infernall kinde,
To wit, the perturbations of his minde,
And bringing his Eurydice from hell,
(Which Justice signifies) is proved well.
But if in rights observance any man
Looke backe, with boldnesse lesse then Orphean,
Soone falls he to the hell from whence he rose:
The fiction then would temprature dispose,
In all the tender motives of the minde,
To make man worthie his hel-danting kinde.
The golden chaine of Homers high device
Ambition is, or cursed avarice,
Which all Gods haling being tyed to Jove,
Him from his setled height could never move:
Intending this, that though that powrefull chaine
Of most Herculean vigor to constraine
Men from true vertue, or their pristine states
Attempt a man that manlesse changes hates,
And is enobled with a deathlesse love
Of things eternall, dignified above:
Nothing shall stirre him from adorning still
This shape with vertue, and his powre with will.
   But as rude painters that contend to show
Beastes, foules or fish, all artlesse to bestow
On every side his native counterfet,
Above his head, his name had neede to set:
So men that will be men, in more then face,
(As in their foreheads) should in actions place
More perfect characters, to prove they be
No mockers of their first nobilitie:
Else may they easly passe for beasts or foules:
Soules praise our shapes, and not our shapes our soules.

And as when Chloris paints th'ennamild meads,
A flocke of shepherds to the bagpipe treads
Rude rurall dances with their countrey loves:
Some a farre off observing their removes,
Turnes, and returnes, quicke footing, sodaine stands,
Reelings aside, od actions with their hands;
Now backe, now forwards, now lockt arme in arme,
Now hearing musicke, thinke it is a charme,
That like loose froes at Bacchanalean feasts,
Makes them seeme franticke in their barraine jestes;
And being clusterd in a shapelesse croude,
With much lesse admiration are allowd.
So our first excellence, so much abusd,
And we (without the harmonie was usd,
When Saturnes golden scepter stroke the strings
Of Civill governement) make all our doings
Sauour of rudenesse, and obscuritie,
And in our formes shew more deformitie,
Then if we still were wrapt, and smoothered
In that confusion, out of which we fled.
    And as when hosts of starres attend thy flight,
(Day of deepe students, most contentfull night)
The morning (mounted on the Muses stead)
Ushers the sonne from Vulcans golden bed,
And then from forth their sundrie roofes of rest,
All sorts of men, to sorted taskes addrest,
Spreade this inferiour element: and yeeld
Labour his due: the souldier to the field,
States-men to counsell, Judges to their pleas,
Merchants to commerce, mariners to seas:
All beasts, and birds, the groves and forrests range,
To fill all corners of this round Exchange,
Till thou (deare Night, ô goddesse of most worth)
Letst thy sweet seas of golden humor forth
And Eagle-like dost with thy starrie wings,
Beate in the foules, and beasts to Somnus lodgings,
And haughtie Day to the infernall deepe,
Proclaiming scilence, studie, ease, and sleepe.
All things before thy forces put in rout,
Retiring where the morning fir'd them out.

So to the chaos of our first descent,
(All dayes of honor, and of vertue spent)
We basely make retrait, and are no lesse
Then huge impolisht heapes of filthinesse.
Mens faces glitter, and their hearts are blacke,
But thou (great Mistresse of heavens gloomie racke)
Art blacke in face, and glitterst in thy heart.
There is thy glorie, riches, force, and Art;
Opposed earth, beates blacke and blewe thy face,
And often doth thy heart it selfe deface,
For spite that to thy vertue-famed traine,
All the choise worthies that did ever raigne
In eldest age, were still preferd by Jove,
Esteeming that due honor to his love.
There shine they: not to sea-men guides alone,
But sacred presidents to everie one.
There fixt for ever, where the Day is driven,
Almost foure hundred times a yeare from heauen.
In hell then let her sit, and never rise,
Till Morns leave blushing at her cruelties.
    Meane while, accept, as followers of thy traine,
(Our better parts aspiring to thy raigne)
Vertues obscur'd, and banished the day,
With all the glories of this spongie sway,
Prisond in flesh, and that poore flesh in bands
Of stone, and steele, chiefe flowrs of vertues Garlands.
    O then most tender fortresse of our woes,
That bleeding lye in vertues overthroes,
Hating the whoredome of this painted light:
Raise thy chast daughters, ministers of right,
The dreadfull and the just Eumenides,
And let them wreake the wrongs of our disease,
Drowning the world in bloud, and staine the skies
With their spilt soules, made drunke with tyrannies.
    Fall Hercules from heaven in tempestes hurld,
And cleanse this beastly stable of the world:
Or bend thy brasen bow against the Sunne,
As in Tartessus, when thou hadst begunne
Thy taske of oxen: heat in more extreames
Then thou wouldst suffer, with his envious beames:

Now make him leave the world to Night and dreames.
Never were vertues labours so envy'd
As in this light: shoote, shoote, and stoope his pride:
Suffer no more his lustfull rayes to get
The Earth with issue: let him still be set
In Somnus thickets: bound about the browes,
With pitchie vapours, and with Ebone bowes.
    Rich-tapird sanctuarie of the blest,
Pallace of Ruth, made all of teares, and rest,
To thy blacke shades and desolation,
I consecrate my life; and living mone,
Where furies shall for ever fighting be,
And adders hisse the world for hating me,
Foxes shall barke, and Night-ravens belch in grones,
And owles shall hollow my confusions:
There will I furnish up my funerall bed,
Strewd with the bones and relickes of the dead.
Atlas shall let th'Olimpick burthen fall,
To cover my untombed face withall.
And when as well, the matter of our kind,
As the materiall substance of the mind,
Shall cease their revolutions, in abode
Of such impure and ugly period,
As the old essence, and insensive prime:
Then shall the ruines of the fourefold time,
Turnd to that lumpe (as rapting Torrents rise)
For ever murmure forth my miseries.
    Ye living spirits then, if any live,
Whom like extreames, do like affections give,
Shun, shun this cruell light, and end your thrall,
In these soft shades of sable funerall:
From whence with ghosts, whom vengeance holds from rest,
Dog-fiends and monsters hanting the distrest,
As men whose parents tyrannie hath slaine,
Whose sisters rape, and bondage do sustaine.
But you that ne'er had birth, nor ever prov'd,
How deare a blessing tis to be belov'd,
Whose friends idolatrous desire of gold,
To scorne, and ruine have your freedome sold:
Whose vertues feele all this, and shew your eyes,

Men made of Tartar, and of villanies:
Aspire th'extraction, and the quintessence
Of all the joyes in earths circumference:
With ghosts, fiends, monsters: as men robd and rackt,
Murtherd in life: from shades with shadowes blackt:
Thunder your wrongs, your miseries and hells,
And with the dismall accents of your knells,
Reviue the dead, and make the living dye
In ruth, and terror of your torturie:
Still all the powre of Art into your grones,
Scorning your triviall and remissive mones,
Compact of fiction, and hyperboles,
(Like wanton mourners, cloyd with too much ease)
Should leave the glasses of the hearers eyes
Unbroken, counting all but vanities.
But paint, or else create in serious truth,
A bodie figur'd to your vertues ruth,
That to the sence may shew what damned sinne,
For your extreames this Chaos tumbles in.
But wo is wretched me, without a name:
Vertue feeds scorne, and noblest honor, shame:
Pride bathes in teares of poore submission,
And makes his soule, the purple he puts on.
   Kneele then with me, fall worm-like on the ground,
And from th'infectious dunghill of this Round,
From mens brasse wits, and golden foolerie,
Weepe, weepe your soules, into felicitie:
Come to this house of mourning, serve the night,
To whom pale day (with whoredome soked quite)
Is but a drudge, selling her beauties use
To rapes, adultries, and to all abuse.
Her labors feast imperiall Night with sports,
Where Loves are Christmast, with all pleasures sorts:
And whom her fugitive, and far-shot rayes
Disjoyne, and drive into ten thousand wayes,
Nights glorious mantle wraps in safe abodes,
And frees their neckes from servile labors lodes:
Her trustie shadowes, succour men dismayd,
Whom Dayes deceiptfull malice hath betrayd:
From the silke vapors of her Iveryport,

Sweet Protean dreames she sends of every sort:
Some taking formes of Princes, to perswade
Of men deject, we are their equals made,
Some clad in habit of deceased friends,
For whom we mournd, and now have wisht amends,
And some (deare favour) Lady-like attyrd,
With pride of Beauties full Meridian fir'd:
Who pitie our contempts, reviue our harts:
For wisest Ladies love the inward parts.
    If these be dreames, euen so are all things else,
That walke this round by heavenly sentinels:
But from Nights port of horne she greets our eyes
With graver dreames inspir'd with prophesies,
Which oft presage to us succeeding chances,
We prooving that awake, they shew in trances.
If these seeme likewise vaine, or nothing are
Vaine things, or nothing come to vertues share:
For nothing more then dreames, with us shee findes:
Then since all pleasures vanish like the windes,
And that most serious actions not respecting
The second light, are worth but the neglecting,
Since day, or light, in anie qualitie,
For earthly uses do but serve the eye.
And since the eyes most quicke and dangerous use,
Enflames the heart, and learnes the soule abuse,
Since mournings are preferd to banquettings,
And they reach heaven, bred under sorrowes wings.
Since Night brings terror to our frailties still,
And shamelesse Day, doth marble us in ill.
    All you possest with indepressed spirits,
Indu'd with nimble, and aspiring wits,
Come consecrate with me, to sacred Night
Your whole endevours, and detest the light.
Sweete Peaces richest crowne is made of starres,
Most certaine guides of honord Marinars,
No pen can any thing eternall wright,
That is not steept in humor of the Night.
    Hence beasts, and birds to caves and bushes then.
And welcome Night, ye noblest heires of men,
Hence Phebus to thy glassie strumpets bed,

And never more let Themis daughters spred,
Thy golden harnesse on thy rosie horse,
But in close thickets run thy oblique course.
　　See now ascends, the glorious Bride of Brides,
Nuptials and triumphs, glittring by her sides,
Iuno and Hymen do her traine adorne,
Ten thousand torches round about them borne:
Dumbe Silence mounted on the Cyprian starre,
With becks, rebukes the winds before his carre,
Where she advanst; beates downe with cloudie mace,
The feeble light to blacke Saturnius pallace:
Behind her, with a brase of silver Hynds,
In Ivorie chariot, swifter then the winds,
Is great Hyperions horned daughter drawne
Enchantresse-like, deckt in disparent lawne,
Circkled with charmes, and incantations,
That ride huge spirits, and outragious passions:
Musicke, and moode, she loves, but love she hates,
(As curious Ladies do, their publique cates)
This traine, with meteors, comets, lightenings,
The dreadfull presence of our Empresse sings:
Which grant for ever (ô eternal Night)
Till vertue flourish in the light of light.

HYMNUS IN CYNTHIAM

Natures bright eye-sight, and the Nights faire soule,
That with thy triple forehead dost controule
Earth, seas, and hell: and art in dignitie
The greatest, and swiftest Planet in the skie:
　　Peacefull, and warlike, and the powre of fate,
In perfect circle of whose sacred state,
The circles of our hopes are compassed:
All wisedome, beautie, majestie and dread,
Wrought in the speaking pourtrait of thy face:
Great Cynthia, rise out of thy Latmian pallace,
Wash thy bright bodie, in th'Atlanticke streames,
Put on those robes that are most rich in beames:
And in thy All-ill-purging puritie,

(As if the shadie Cytheron did frie
In sightfull furie of a solemne fire)
Ascend thy chariot, and make earth admire
Thy old swift changes, made a yong fixt prime,
O let thy beautie scorch the wings of time.
That fluttering he may fall before thine eyes,
And beate him selfe to death before he rise.
And as heavens' Geniall parts were cut away
By Saturnes hands, with adamantine Harpey,
Onely to shew, that since it was composd
Of uniuersall matter: it enclosd
No powre to procreate another heaven:
So since that adamantine powre is given
To thy chast hands, to cut of all desire
Of fleshly sports, and quench to Cupids fire:
Let it approve: no change shall take thee hence,
Nor thy throne beare another inference.
For if the envious forehead of the earth
Lowre on thy age, and claime thee as her birth:
Tapers, nor torches, nor the forrests burning,
Soule-winging musicke, nor teare-stilling mourning,
(Usd of old Romanes and rude Macedons
In thy most sad, and blacke discessions)
We know can nothing further thy recall,
When Nights darke robes (whose objects blind us all)
Shall celebrate thy changes funerall.
But as in that thrise dreadfull foughten field
Of ruthlesse Cannae, when sweet Rule did yeeld,
Her beauties strongest proofs, and hugest love:
When men as many as the lamps above,
Armd Earth in steele, and made her like the skies,
That two Auroraes did in one day rise;
Then with the terror of the trumpets call,
The battels joynd as if the world did fall:
Continewd long in life-disdaining fight,
Joves thundring Eagles featherd like the night,
Hou'ring above them with indifferent wings,
Till Bloods sterne daughter, cruell Tyche flings
The chiefe of one side, to the blushing ground,
And then his men (whom griefs, and feares confound)

Turnd all their cheerfull hopes to grimme despaire,
Some casting of their soules into the aire,
Some taken prisners, some extreamely maimd,
And all (as men accurst) on fate exclaimd;
So (gracious Cynthia) in that sable day,
When interposed earth takes thee away,
(Our sacred chiefe and soveraigne generall),
As chrimsine a retrait, and steepe a fall
We feare to suffer from this peace, and height,
Whose thancklesse sweet now cloies us with receipt.
    The Romanes set sweet Musicke to her charmes,
To raise thy stoopings, with her ayrie armes:
Usde loud resoundings with auspicious brasse:
Held torches up to heauen, and flaming glasse,
Made a whole forrest but a burning eye,
T'admire thy mournefull partings with the skye.
The Macedonians were so stricken dead,
With skillesse horrour of thy changes dread:
They wanted harts, to lift up sounds, or fires,
Or eyes to heauen; but usd their funerall tyres,
Trembld, and wept; assur'd some mischiefs furie
Would follow that afflicting Augurie.
    Nor shall our wisedomes be more arrogant
(O sacred Cynthia) but beleeve thy want
Hath cause to make us now as much affraid:
Nor shall Democrates who first is said,
To reade in natures browes, thy chaunges cause,
Perswade our sorrowes to a vaine applause.
    Times motion, being like the reeling sunnes,
Or as the sea reciprocallie runnes,
Hath brought us now to their opinions;
As in our garments, ancient fashions
Are newlie worne; and as sweet poesie
Will not be clad in her supremacie
With those straunge garments (Romes Hexameters)
As she is English: but in right prefers
Our native robes, put on with skilfull hands
(English heroicks) to those antick garlands,
Accounting it no meede but mockerie,
When her steepe browes alreadie prop the skie,

To put on startups, and yet let it fall.
No otherwise (O Queene celestiall)
Can we beleeve Ephesias state wilbe
But spoile with forreine grace, and change with thee
The purenesse of thy never-tainted life.
Scorning the subiect title of a wife,
Thy bodie not composed in thy birth,
Of such condensed matter as the earth,
Thy shunning faithlesse mens societie,
Betaking thee to hounds, and Archerie
To deserts, and inaccessible hills,
Abhorring pleasure in earths common ills,
Commit most willing rapes on all our harts:
And make us tremble, lest thy soveraigne parts
(The whole preservers of our happinesse)
Should yeeld to change, Eclips, or heavinesse.
And as thy changes happen by the site,
Neare, or farre distance, of thy fathers light,
Who (set in absolute remotion) reaves
Thy face of light, and thee all darkned leaues:
So for thy absence, to the shade of death
Our soules fly mourning, wingd with our breath.
   Then set thy Christall, and Imperiall throne
(Girt in thy chast, and never-loosing zone
Gainst Europs Sunne directly opposit,
And give him darknesse, that doth threat thy light.
   O how accurst are they thy favour scorne?
Diseases pine their flockes, tares spoile their corne:
Old men are blind of issue, and young wives
Bring forth abortive frute, that never thrives.
   But then how blest are they thy favour graces,
Peace in their hearts, and youth raignes in their faces:
Health strengths their bodies, to subdue the seas,
And dare the Sunne, like Thebane Hercules
To calme the furies, and to quench the fire:
As at thy altars, in thy Persicke Empire,
Thy holy women walkt with naked soles
Harmelesse, and confident, on burning coles:
The vertue-temperd mind, ever preserves,
Oyles, and expulsatorie Balme that serves

To quench lusts fire, in all things it annoints,
And steeles our feet to march on needles points:
And mongst her armes, hath armour to repell
The canon, and the firie darts of hell:
She is the great enchantresse that commands
Spirits of every region, seas, and lands,
Round heaven it selfe, and all his seven-fold heights,
Are bound to serve the strength of her conceipts:
A perfect type of thy Almightie state,
That holdst the thread, and rul'st the sword of fate.
  Then you that exercise the virgine Court
Of peacefull Thespya, my muse consort,
Making her drunken with Gorgonean Dews,
And therewith, all your Extasies infuse,
That she may reach the top-lesse starrie brows
Of steepe Olympus, crownd with freshest bows
Of Daphnean Laurell, and the praises sing
Of mightie Cynthia: truely figuring,
(As she is Heccate) her soveraigne kinde.
And in her force, the forces of the mind:
An argument to ravish and refine
An earthly soule, and make it meere divine.
Sing then withall, her Pallace brightnesse bright,
The dasle-sunne perfections of her light.
Circkling her face with glories, sing the walkes,
Where in her heavenly Magicke mood she stalkes,
Her arbours, thickets, and her wondrous game,
(A huntresse, being never matcht in fame).
Presume not then ye flesh confounded soules,
That cannot beare the full Castalian bowles,
Which sever mounting spirits from the sences,
To looke in this deepe fount for thy pretenses:
The juice more cleare then day, yet shadows night,
Where humor challengeth no drop of right:
But judgement shall displaie, to purest eyes
With ease, the bowells of these misteries.
  See then this Planet of our lives discended
To rich Ortigia, gloriouslie attended,
Not with her fiftie Ocean Nimphs: nor yet
Hir twentie forresters: but doth beget

By powrefull charmes, delightsome servitors
Of flowrs, and shadows, mists, and meteors:
Her rare Elisian Pallace she did build
With studied wishes, which sweet hope did guild
With sunnie foyle, that lasted but a day:
For night must needs, importune her away.
The shapes of everie wholesome flowre and tree
She gave those types of hir felicitie.
And Forme her selfe, she mightilie conjurd
Their priselesse values, might not be obscurd,
With disposition baser then divine,
But make that blissfull court of hers to shine
With all accomplishment of Architect,
That not the eye of Phebus could detect.
Forme then, twixt two superior pillers framd
This tender building, Pax Imperii nam'd,
Which cast a shadow, like a Pyramis
Whose basis, in the plaine or back part is
Of that queint worke: the top so high extended,
That it the region of the Moone transcended:
Without, within it, everie corner fild
By bewtious Forme, as her great mistresse wild.
Here as she sits, the thunder-louing Jove
In honors past all others showes his love,
Proclaiming her in compleat Emperie,
Of what soever the Olympick skie
With tender circumvecture doth embrace,
The chiefest Planet, that doth heaven enchace:
Deare Goddesse, prompt, benigne, and bounteous,
That heares all prayers, from the least of us
Large riches gives, since she is largely given,
And all that spring from seede of earth and heaven
She doth commaund: and rules the fates of all,
Old Hesiod sings her thus celestiall:
And now to take the pleasures of the day,
Because her night starre soone will call away,
She frames of matter intimate before,
(To wit, a bright, and daseling meteor)
A goodlie Nimph, whose bewtie, bewtie staines
Heau'ns with her jewells; gives all the raines

Of wished pleasance; frames her golden wings,
But them she bindes up close with purple strings,
Because she now will have her run alone.
And bid the base, to all affection.
And Euthimya is her sacred name,
Since she the cares and toyles of earth must tame:
Then straight the flowrs, the shadowes and the mists,
(Fit matter for most pliant humorists)
She hunters makes: and of that substance hounds
Whose mouths deafe heaven, & furrow earth with wounds.
And marvaile not a Nimphe so rich in grace
To hounds rude pursutes should be given in chase:
For she could turne her selfe to everie shape
Of swiftest beasts, and at her pleasure scape.
Wealth faunes on fooles: vertues are meate for vices,
Wisdome conformes her selfe to all earths guises,
Good gifts are often given to men past good,
And Noblesse stoops sometimes beneath his blood.
    The hounds that she created, vast, and fleete
Were grimme Melampus, with th'Ethiops feete,
White Leucon; all eating Pamphagus,
Sharp-sighted Dorceus, wild Oribasus
Storme-breathing Lelaps, and the savage Theron,
Wingd-footed Pterelas, and Hinde-like Ladon,
Greedie Harpyia, and the painted Stycté,
Fierce Tigris, and the thicket-searcher Agre,
The blacke Melaneus, and the bristled Lachne,
Leane-lustfull Cyprius, and big chested Alce.
These and such other now the forrest rang'd,
And Euthimya to a Panther changd.
Holds them sweet chase; their mouths they freely spend,
As if the earth is sunder they would rend.
Which change of Musick likt the Goddesse so,
That she before her formost Nimphe would go,
And not a huntsman there was eagrer seene
In that sports love, (yet all were wondrous keene)
Then was their swift, and windie-footed queene.
And now this spotted game did thicket take,
Where not a hound could hungred passage make
Such proofe the covert was, all armd in thorne,

With which in their attempts, the doggs were torne,
And fell to howling in their happinesse:
As when a flocke of schoole-boys, whom their mistresse
(Held closelie to their bookes) gets leave to sport,
And then like toyle-freed deare, in headlong sort
With shouts, and shriekes, they hurrey from the schoole.
Some strow the woods, some swimme the silver poole:
All as they list to severall pastimes fall,
To feede their famisht wantonnesse with all.
When strait, within the woods some wolfe or beare,
The heedlesse lyms of one doth peecemeale teare,
Affrighteth other, sends some bleeding backe,
And some in greedie whirle pitts suffer wracke:
So did the bristled covert check with wounds
The licorous hast of these game greedie hounds.
  In this vast thicket (whose descriptions task
The penns of furies, and of feends would aske:
So more then humane thoughted horrible)
The soules of such as liv'd implausible,
In happie Empire of this Goddesse glories,
And scorned to crowne hir Phanes with sacrifice
And ceaselesse walke; exspiring fearefull grones,
Curses, and threats for their confusions.
Her darts, and arrowes, some of them had slaine,
Others hir doggs eate, painting hir disdaine,
After she had transformd them into beasts:
Others her monsters carried to their nests,
Rent them in peeces, and their spirits sent
To this blind shade, to waile their banishment.
The huntsmen hearing (since they could not heare)
Their hounds at fault; in eager chase drew neare,
Mounted on Lyons, Unicorns, and Bores,
And saw their hounds lye licking of their sores,
Some yerning at the shroud, as if they chid
Her stinging toungs, that did their chase forbid:
By which they knew the game was that way gone.
Then ech man forst the beast he rode upon,
T'assault the thicket; whose repulsive thorns
So gald the Lyons, Bores, and Unicorns,
Dragons, and wolves; that halfe their courages

Were spent in rores, and sounds of heavines:
Yet being the Princeliest and hardiest beasts,
That gave chiefe fame to those Ortygian forests,
And all their riders furious of their sport,
A fresh assault they gave, in desperate sort:
And with their falchions made their wayes in wounds:
The thicket opend, and let in the hounds.
But from her bosome cast prodigious cries,
Wrapt in her Stigian fumes of miseries:
Which yet the breaths of those couragious steads
Did still drinke up, and cleerd their ventrous heads:
As when the fierie coursers of the sunne,
Up to the pallace of the morning runne,
And from their nosthrills blow the spitefull day:
So yet those foggie vapors, made them way.
But preasing further, saw such cursed sights,
Such Aetnas filld with strange tormented sprites,
That now the vaprous obiect of the eye
Out-pierst the intellect in facultie.
Basenesse was Nobler then Nobilitie:
For ruth (first shaken from the braine of Love,
And love the soule of vertue) now did move,
Not in their soules (spheres meane enough for such)
But in their eyes: and thence did conscience touch
Their harts with pitie: where her proper throne,
Is in the minde, and there should first have shone:
Eyes should guide bodies, and our soules our eyes,
But now the world consistes on contraries:
So sence brought terror, where the mindes presight
Had saft that feare, and done but pittie right,
But servile feare, now forgd a wood of darts
Within their eyes, and cast them through their harts.
Then turnd they bridle, then halfe slaine with feare,
Ech did the other backwardes overbeare.
As when th'Italian Duke, a troupe of horse
Sent out in hast against some English force,
From statelie sited sconce-torne Nimigan,
Under whose walles the Wall most Cynthian,
Stretcheth her silver limms loded with wealth,
Hearing our horse were marching downe by stealth.

(Who looking for them) warres quicke Artizan
Fame-thriving Vere, that in those Countries wan
More fame then guerdon; ambuscadoes laide
Of certaine foote, and made full well appaide
The hopefull enemie, in sending those
The long-expected subjects of their blowes
To move their charge; which strait they give amaine,
When we retiring to our strength againe,
The foe pursewes assured of our lives,
And us within our ambuscado drives,
Who straight with thunder of the drums and shot,
Tempest their wraths on them that wist it not.
Then (turning headlong) some escapt us so,
Some left to ransome, some to overthrow,
In such confusion did this troupe retire,
And thought them cursed in that games desire:
Out flew the houndes, that there could nothing finde,
Of the slye Panther, that did beard the winde,
Running into it full, to clog the chase,
And tire her followers with too much solace.
And but the superficies of the shade,
Did onely sprinckle with the sent she made,
As when the sunne beames on high billowes fall,
And make their shadowes dance upon a wall,
That is the subiect of his faire reflectings:
Or else; as when a man in summer evenings,
Something before sunneset, when shadows bee
Rackt with his stooping to the highest degree,
His shadow clymes the trees, and skales a hill,
While he goes on the beaten passage still,
So sleightlie toucht the Panther with her sent,
This irksome covert, and away she went,
Downe to a fruitfull Iland sited by,
Full of all wealth, delight, and Emperie,
Ever with child of curious Architect,
Yet still deliverd: pav'd with Dames select,
On whom rich feete, in fowlest bootes might treade,
And never fowle them: for kinde Cupid spreade,
Such perfect colours, on their pleasing faces,
That their reflects clad fowlest weeds with graces,

Bewtie strikes fancie blind; pyed show deceav's us,
Sweet banquets tempt our healths, when temper leaues us
Inchastitie, is ever prostitute,
Whose trees we loth, when we have pluckt their fruite.
   Hither this Panther fled, now turnd a Bore
More huge then that th'Aetolians plagud so sore,
And led the chase through noblest mansions,
Gardens and groves, exempt from Parragons,
In all things ruinous, and slaughtersome,
As was that scourge to the Aetolian kingdome:
After as if a whirlewind drave them one,
Full crie, and close, as if they all were one
The hounds pursew, and fright the earth with sound,
Making her tremble; as when windes are bound
In her cold bosome, fighting for event:
With whose fierce Ague all the world is rent.
   But dayes arme (tir'd to hold her torch to them)
Now let it fall within the Ocean streame,
The Goddesse blew retraite, and with her blast,
Her morns creation did like vapours wast:
The windes made wing, into the upper light,
And blew abroad the sparckles of the night.
Then (swift as thought) the bright Titanides
Guide and great soveraigne of the marble seas,
With milkwhite Heiffers, mounts into her Sphere,
And leaues us miserable creatures here.
   Thus nights, faire dayes: thus griefs do joyes supplant:
Thus glories graven in steele and Adamant
Never supposd to wast, but grow by wasting,
(Like snow in rivers falne) consume by lasting.
O then thou great Elixer of all treasures,
From whom we multiplie our world of pleasures,
Discend againe, ah never leave the earth,
But as thy plenteous humors gave us birth,
So let them drowne the world in night, and death
Before this ayre, leave breaking with thy breath.
Come Goddesse come, the double fatherd sonne,
Shall dare no more amongst thy traine to runne,
Nor with poluted handes to touch thy vaile:
His death was darted from the Scorpions taile,

For which her forme to endlesse memorie,
With other lamps, doth lend the heavens an eye,
And he that shewd such great presumption,
Is hidden now, beneath a little stone.
   If proude Alpheus offer force againe,
Because he could not once thy love obtaine,
Thou and thy Nimphs shall stop his mouth with mire,
And mocke the fondling, for his mad aspire.
Thy glorious temple (great Lucifera)
That was the studie of all Asia,
Two hundred twentie sommers to erect,
Built by Chersiphrone thy Architect,
In which two hundred, twentie columns stood,
Built by two hundred twentie kings of blood,
Of curious bewtie, and admired height,
Pictures and statues, of as praysefull sleight,
Convenient for so chast a Goddesse phane,
(Burnt by Herostratus) shall now againe,
Be reexstruct, and this Ephesiabe
Thy countries happie name, come here with thee,
As it was there so shall it now be framde,
And thy faire virgine-chamber ever namde:
And as in reconstruction of it there,
There Ladies did no more their jewells weare,
But franckly contribute them all to raise,
A work of such a chast Religious prayse:
So will our Ladies; for in them it lyes,
To spare so much as would that worke suffice:
Our Dames well set their jewels in their myndes,
In-sight illustrates; outward braverie blindes,
The minde hath in her selfe a Deitie,
And in the stretching circle of her eye
All things are compast, all things present still,
Will framd to powre, doth make us what we will,
But keep your jewels, make ye braver yet,
Elisian Ladies; and (in riches set,
Vpon your foreheads), let us see your harts:
Build Cyanthiaes Temple in your vertuous parts,
Let everie jewell be a vertues glasse:
And no Herostratus shall ever race,

Those holy monuments: but pillers stand,
Where every Grace, and Muse shall hang her garland.
   The minde in that we like, rules euery limme,
Gives hands to bodies, makes them make them trimme:
Why then in that the body doth dislike,
Should not his sword as great a vennie strike?
The bit, and spurre that Monarcke ruleth still,
To further good things, and to curb the ill,
He is the Ganemede, the birde of love,
Rapt to his soueraignes bosome for his loue,
His bewtie was it, not the bodies pride,
That made him great Aquarius stellified:
And that minde most is bewtifull and hye,
And nearest comes to a Divinitie,
That furthest is from spot of earths delight,
Pleasures that lose their substance with their sight,
Such one, Saturnius ravisheth to love,
And fills the cup of all content to love.
   If wisedome be the mindes true bewtie then,
And that such bewtie shines in vertuous men,
If those sweet Ganemedes shall onely finde.

      *   *   *   *

Loue of Olimpius, are those wizerds wise,
That nought but gold, and his dyjections prise?
This bewtie hath a fire vpon her brow,
That dimmes the Sunne of base desires in you,
And as the cloudie bosome of the tree,
Whose branches will not let the summer see
His solemne shadows; but do entertaine.
Eternall winter: so thy sacred traine.
Thrise mightie Cynthia should be frozen dead,
To all the lawlesse flames of Cupids Godhead.
To this end let thy beames divinities,
For euer shine vpon their sparckling eyes,
And be as quench to those pestiferent fires,
That through their eyes, impoison their desires,
Thou never yet wouldst stoope to base assault,
Therefore those Poetes did most highly fault,
That fainde thee fiftie children by Endimion,
And they that write thou hadst but three alone,

Thou never any hadst, but didst affect,
Endimion for his studious intellect.
Thy soule-chast kisses were for vertues sake,
And since his eyes were evermore awake,
To search for knowledge of thy excellence,
And all Astrologie: no negligence,
Or female softnesse fede his learned trance,
Nor was thy vaile once toucht with dalliance,
Wise Poetes faine thy Godhead properlie,
The thresholds of mens doores did fortifie,
And therefore built they thankefull alters there,
Serving thy powre, in most religious feare.
Deare precident for vs to imitate,
Whose dores thou guardst against Imperious fate,
Keeping our peacefull households safe from sack,
And free'st our ships, when others suffer wracke.
Thy virgin chamber then that sacred is,
No more let hold, an idle Salmacis,
Nor let more sleights, Cydippe injurie:
Nor let blacke Jove possest in Scicilie,
Ravish more maids, but maids subdue his might,
With well-steeld lances of thy watchfull sight.
   Then in thy cleare, and Isie Pentacle,
Now execute a Magicke miracle:
Slip everie sort of poisond herbes, and plants,
And bring thy rabid mastiffs to these hants.
Looke with thy fierce aspect, be terror-strong;
Assume thy wondrous shape of halfe a furlong:
Put on thy feete of Serpents, viperous hayres,
And act the fearefulst part of thy affaires:
Convert the violent courses of thy floods,
Remove whole fields of corne, and hugest woods,
Cast hills into the sea, and make the starrs,
Drop out of heaven, and lose thy Mariners.
   So shall the wonders of thy power be seene,
And thou for euer live the Planets Queene.

GEORGE CHAPMAN

Sonet

Fra banc to banc, fra wod to wod, I rin
Ourhailit with my feble fantasie,
Lyc til a leif that fallis from a trie
Or til a reid ourblawin with the wind.
Two gods gyds me: the ane of tham is blind,
Ye, and a bairn brocht up in vanitie;
The nixt a wyf ingenrit of the se,
And lichter nor a dauphin with hir fin.

Unhappie is the man for evirmaire
That teils the sand and sawis in the aire;
Bot twyce unhappier is he, I lairn,
That feidis in his hairt a mad desyre,
And follows on a woman throw the fyre,
Led be a blind and teichit be a bairn.

MARK ALEXANDER BOYD

Decease, release: dum morior orior[1]

The pounded spise both tast & sent doth please
In fadinge smoke the force doth incense showe
The perisht kernell springeth with increase
The lopped tree doth best & soonest growe

Gods spice I was & poundinge was my due
In fadinge breath my incense favoured best
Death was my meane my kernell to renewe
By loppinge shott I upp to heavenly rest

Some thinges more perfit are in their decaye
Like sparke that going out geeves clerest light
Such was my happe whose dolefull dying daye
Begane my joye & termed fortunes spight

Alive a Queene now dead I am a Saint
Once *Mary*[2] cald my name now Martyr is
ffrom earthly raigne debarred by restrainte
In liew whereof I raigne in heavenly blis

My life, my griefe; my death, hath wrought my joye
My freendes, my foyle, my foes, my weale procurd
My speedie death hath scorned longe annoye
And losse of life an endles life assurd.

My scaffolde was the bedd where ease I fownde
The blocke a pillowe of eternall rest.
My headman cast mee in blesfull sownde
His axe cutt of my cares from combred brest

Rue not my death rejoyce at my repose
It was no death to mee but to my woe
The budd was opened to let owt the rose
The cheynes unloosed to let the captive goe

A Prince by birth a prisoner by mishappe
ffrom crowne to crosse from throne to thrall I fell
My right my ruth my tytles wrought my trapp
My weale my woe my worldly heaven my hell

By death from prisoner to a prince enhaunced
ffrom crosse to crowne from thrall to throne againe
My ruth my righte, my trappe my styll advaunced
ffrom woe to weale from hell to heavenly raigne.

ROBERT SOUTHWELL

[1] While I die I pray   [2] Mary Queen of Scots

Where wards are weak

Where wards are weake, & foes encountring strong:
Where mightier doe assault, then doe defend:
The feebler part puts up enforced wrong,
And silent sees, that speech could not amend.

Yet higher powers must thinke, though they repine,
When sunne is set: the little starres will shine.

While Pike doth range, the silly Tench doth flie,
And crouch in privie creekes, with smaller fish:
Yet Pikes are caught when little fish goe bie:
These, fleet a flote; while those, doe fill the dish.
There is a time even for the wormes to creepe:
And sucke the dew while all their foes do sleepe.

The Marlyne cannot ever sore on high,
Nor greedy Grey-hound still pursue the chase:
The tender Larke will finde a time to flie,
And fearefull Hare to runne a quiet race.
He that high growth on Ceders did bestow:
Gave also lowly Mush-rumpts leave to grow.

In Amans pompe poore Mardocheus wept;
Yet God did turne his fate upon his foe.
The Lazar pinde, while Dives feast was kept,
Yet he, to heaven; to hell did Dives goe.
We trample grasse, and prize the flowers of May:
Yet grasse is greene, when flowers doe fade away.

ROBERT SOUTHWELL

A Lover's Complaint

From off a hill whose concave wombe reworded,
A plaintfull story from a sistring vale
My spirrits t'attend this doble voyce accorded,
And downe I laid to list the sad tun'd tale,
Ere long espied a fickle maid full pale
Tearing of papers breaking rings a twaine,
Storming her world with sorrowes, wind and raine.

Upon her head a plattid hive of straw,
Which fortified her visage from the Sunne,

Whereon the thought might thinke sometime it saw
The carkas of a beauty spent and donne,
Time had not sithed all that youth begun,
Nor youth all quit, but spight of heavens fell rage,
Some beauty peept, through lettice of fear'd age.

Oft did she heave her Napkin to her eyne,
Which on it had conceited charecters:
Laundring the silken figures in the brine,
That seasoned woe had pelleted in teares,
And often reading what contents it beares:
As often shriking undistinguisht wo,
In clamours of all size both high and low.

Some-times her leveld eyes their carriage ride,
As they did battry to the spheres intend:
Sometime diverted their poore balls are tide,
To th'orbed earth; sometimes they do extend,
Their view right on, anon their gases lend,
To every place at once and no where fixt,
The mind and sight distractedly commixt.

Her haire nor loose nor ti'd in formall plat,
Proclaimd in her a carelesse hand of pride;
For some untuck'd descended her shev'd hat,
Hanging her pale and pined cheeke beside,
Some in her threeden fillet still did bide,
And trew to bondage would not breake from thence,
Though slackly braided in loose negligence.

A thousand favours from a maund she drew,
Of amber christall and of bedded Jet,
Which one by one she in a river threw,
Upon whose weeping margent she was set,
Like usery applying wet to wet,
Or Monarches hands that lets not bounty fall,
Where want cries some; but where excesse begs all.

Of folded schedulls had she many a one,
Which she perusd, sighd, tore and gave the flud,

Crackt many a ring of Posied gold and bone,
Bidding them find their Sepulchers in mud,
Found yet mo letters sadly pend in blood,
With sleided silke, feate and affectedly
Enswath'd and seald to curious secrecy.

These often bath'd she in her fluxive eies,
And often kist, and often gave to teare,
Cried O false blood thou register of lies,
What unapproved witnes doost thou beare!
Inke would have seem'd more blacke and damned heare.
This said in top of rage the lines she rents,
Big discontent, so breaking their contents.

A reverend man that graz'd his cattell ny,
Sometime a blusterer that the russle knew
Of Court of Cittie, and had let go by
The swiftest houres observed as they flew,
Towards this afflicted fancy fastly drew:
And priviledg'd by age desires to know
In breefe the grounds and motives of her wo.

So slides he downe uppon his greyned bat;
And comely distant sits he by her side,
When hee againe desires her, being satte,
Her greevance with his hearing to devide
If that from him there may be ought applied
Which may her suffering extasie asswage
Tis promist in the charitie of age.

Father she saies, though in mee you behold
The injury of many a blasting houre;
Let it not tell your Judgement I am old,
Not age, but sorrow, over me hath power;
I might as yet have bene a spreading flower
Fresh to my selfe, if I had selfe applyd
Love to my selfe, and to no Love beside.

But wo is mee, too early I attended
A youthfull suit it was to gaine my grace;
C.E.P.—8

O one by natures outwards so commended,
That maidens eyes stucke over all his face,
Love lackt a dwelling and made him her place.
And when in his faire parts shee didde abide,
Shee was new lodg'd and newly Deified.

His browny locks did hang in crooked curles,
And every light occasion of the wind
Upon his lippes their silken parcels hurles,
Whats sweet to do, to do wil aptly find,
Each eye that saw him did inchaunt the minde:
For on his visage was in little drawne,
What largenesse thinkes in parradise was sawne.

Smal shew of man was yet upon his chinne,
His phenix downe began but to appeare
Like unshorne velvet, on that termlesse skin
Whose bare out-brag'd the web it seem'd to were.
Yet shewed his visage by that cost more deare,
And nice affections wavering stood in doubt
If best were as it was, or best without.

His qualities were beautious as his forme,
For maiden tongu'd he was and thereof free;
Yet if men mov'd him, was he such a storme
As oft twixt May and Aprill is to see,
When windes breath sweet, unruly though they bee.
His rudenesse so with his authoriz'd youth,
Did livery falsenesse in a pride of truth.

Wel could hee ride, and often men would say
That horse his mettell from his rider takes
Proud of subjection, noble by the swaie,
What rounds, what bounds, what course what stop he makes
And controversie hence a question takes,
Whether the horse by him became his deed,
Or he his mannad'g, by'th wel doing Steed.

But quickly on this side the verdict went,
His reall habitude gave life and grace

To appertainings and to ornament,
Accomplisht in him-selfe not in his case:
All ayds them-selves made fairer by their place,
Can for addicions, yet their purpos'd trimme
Peec'd not his grace but were al grac'd by him.

So on the tip of his subduing tongue
All kinde of arguments and question deepe,
Al replication prompt, and reason strong
For his advantage still did wake and sleep,
To make the weeper laugh, the laugher weepe:
He had the dialect and different skil,
Catching al passions in his craft of will.

That hee didde in the general bosome raigne
Of young, of old, and sexes both inchanted,
To dwel with him in thoughts, or to remaine
In personal duty, following where he haunted,
Consent's bewitcht, ere he desire have granted,
And dialogu'd for him what he would say,
Askt their own wils and made their wils obey.

Many there were that did his picture gette
To serve their eies, and in it put their mind,
Like fooles that in th' imagination set
The goodly objects which abroad they find
Of lands and mansions, theirs in thought assign'd,
And labouring in moe pleasures to bestow them,
Then the true gouty Land-lord which doth owe them.

So many have that never toucht his hand
Sweetly suppos'd them mistresse of his heart:
My wofull selfe that did in freedome stand,
And was my owne fee simple (not in part)
What with his art in youth and youth in art
Threw my affections in his charmed power,
Reserv'd the stalke and gave him al my flower.

Yet did I not as some my equals did
Demaund of him, nor being desired yeelded,

Finding my selfe in honour so forbidde,
With safest distance I mine honour sheelded,
Experience for me many bulwarkes builded
Of proofs new bleeding which remaind the soile
Of this false Jewell, and his amorous spoile.

But ah who ever shun'd by precedent,
The destin'd ill she must her selfe assay,
Or forc'd examples gainst her owne content
To put the by-past perrils in her way?
Counsaile may stop a while what will not stay:
For when we rage, advise is often seene
By blunting us to make our wits more keene.

Nor gives it satisfaction to our blood,
That wee must curbe it uppon others proofe,
To be forbod the sweets that seemes so good,
For feare of harmes that preach in our behoofe;
O appetite from judgement stand aloofe!
The one a pallate hath that needs will taste,
Though reason weepe and cry it is thy last.

For further I could say this mans untrue,
And knew the patternes of his foule beguiling,
Heard where his plants in others Orchards grew,
Saw how deceits were guilded in his smiling,
Knew vowes, were ever brokers to defiling,
Thought Characters and words meerly but art,
And bastards of his foule adulterat heart,

And long upon these termes I held my Citty,
Till thus hee gan besiege me: Gentle maid
Have of my suffering youth some feeling pitty
And be not of my holy vowes affraid,
Thats to ye sworne to none was ever said,
For feasts of love I have bene call'd unto
Till now did nere invite nor never vow.

All my offences that abroad you see
Are errors of the blood none of the mind:

Love made them not, with acture they may be,
Where neither Party is nor trew nor kind,
They sought their shame that so their shame did find,
And so much lesse of shame in me remaines,
By how much of me their reproch containes,

Among the many that mine eyes have seene,
Not one whose flame my hart so much as warmed,
Of my affection put to th' smallest teene,
Or any of my leisures ever Charmed,
Harme have I done to them but nere was harmed,
Kept hearts in liveries, but mine owne was free,
And raignd commaunding in his monarchy.

Looke heare what tributes wounded fancies sent me,
Of palyd pearles and rubies red as blood:
Figuring that they their passions likewise lent me
Of greefe and blushes, aptly understood
In bloodlesse white, and the encrimson'd mood,
Effects of terror and deare modesty,
Encampt in hearts but fighting outwardly.

And Lo behold these tallents of their heir,
With twisted mettle amorously empleacht
I have receav'd from many a several faire,
Their kind acceptance, wepingly beseecht,
With th'annexions of faire gems inricht,
And deepe brain'd sonnets that did amplifie
Each stones deare Nature, worth and quallity.

The Diamond? why twas beautifull and hard,
Whereto his invis'd properties did tend,
The deepe greene Emrald in whose fresh regard,
Weake sights their sickly radience do amend.
The heaven hewd Saphir and the Opall blend
With objects manyfold; each severall stone,
With wit well blazond smil'd or made some mone.

Lo all these trophies of affections hot,
Of pensiv'd and subdew'd desires the tender,

Nature hath chargd me that I hoord them not,
But yeeld them up where I my selfe must render:
That is to you my origin and ender:
For these of force must your oblations be,
Since I their Aulter, you enpatrone me.

Oh then advance (of yours) that phraseles hand,
Whose white weighes downe the airy scale of praise,
Take all these similies to your owne command,
Hollowed with sighes that burning lunges did raise:
What me your minister for you obaies
Workes under you, and to your audit comes
Their distract parcells, in combined summes.

Lo this device was sent me from a Nun,
Or Sister sanctified of holiest note,
Which late her noble suit in court did shun,
Whose rarest havings made the blossoms dote,
For she was sought by spirits of ritchest cote,
But kept cold distance, and did thence remove,
To spend her living in eternall love.

But oh my sweet what labour ist to leave,
The thing we have not, mastring what not strives,
Playing the Place which did no forme receive,
Playing patient sports in unconstraind gives,
She that her fame so to her selfe contrives,
The scarres of battaile scapeth by the flight,
And makes her absence valiant, not her might.

Oh pardon me in that my boast is true,
The accident which brought me to her eie,
Upon the moment did her force subdewe,
And now she would the caged cloister flie:
Religious love put out religions eye:
Not to be tempted would she be enur'd,
And now to tempt all liberty procure.

How mightie then you are, Oh heare me tell,
The broken bosoms that to me belong,

Have emptied all their fountaines in my well:
And mine I powre your Ocean all amonge:
I strong ore them and you ore me being strong,
Must for your victorie us all congest,
As compound love to phisick your cold brest.

My parts had powre to charme a sacred Sunne,
Who disciplin'd I dieted in grace,
Beleev'd her eies, when they t'assaile begun,
All vowes and consecrations giving place:
O most potentiall love, vowe, bond, nor space
In thee hath neither sting, knot, nor confine
For thou art all and all things els are thine.

When thou impressest what are precepts worth
Of stale example? when thou wilt inflame,
How coldly those impediments stand forth
Of wealth of filliall feare, lawe, kindred fame,
Loves armes are peace, gainst rule, gainst sence, gainst shame
And sweetens in the suffring pangues it beares,
The *Alloes* of all forces, shockes and feares.

Now all these hearts that doe on mine depend,
Feeling it breake, with bleeding groanes they pine,
And supplicant their sighes to you extend
To leave the battrie that you make gainst mine,
Lending soft audience, to my sweet designe,
And credent soule, to that strong bonded oth,
That shall preferre and undertake my troth.

This said, his watrie eies he did dismount,
Whose sightes till then were leaveld on my face,
Each cheeke a river running from a fount,
With brynish currant downe-ward flowed a pace:
Oh how the channell to the streame gave grace!
Who glaz'd with Christall gate the glowing Roses,
That flame through water which their hew incloses.

Oh father, what a hell of witch-craft lies,
In the small orb of one perticular teare?

But with the inundation of the eies:
What rocky heart to water will not weare?
What brest so cold that is not warmed heare,
Or cleft effect, cold modesty hot wrath:
Both fire from hence, and chill extincture hath.

For loe his passion but an art of craft,
Even there resolv'd my reason into teares,
There my white stole of chastity I daft,
Shooke off my sober gardes, and civill feares,
Appeare to him as he to me appeares:
All melting, though our drops this diffrence bore,
His poison'd me, and mine did him restore.

In him a plenitude of subtle matter,
Applied to Cautills, all straing formes receives,
Of burning blushes, or of weeping water,
Or sounding palenesse: and he takes and leaves,
In eithers aptnesse as it best deceives:
To blush at speeches ranck, to weepe at woes
Or to turne white and sound at tragick showes.

That not a heart which in his levell came,
Could scape the haile of his all hurting ayme,
Shewing faire Nature is both kinde and tame:
And vaild in them did winne whom he would maime,
Against the thing he sought, he would exclaime,
When he most burnt in hart-wisht luxurie,
He preacht pure maide, and praisd cold chastitie.

Thus meerely with the garment of grace,
The naked and concealed feind he coverd,
That th' unexperient gave the tempter place,
Which like a Cherubin above them hoverd,
Who young and simple would not be so loverd.
Aye me I fell, and yet do question make,
What I should doe againe for such a sake.

O that infected moysture of his eye,
O that false fire which in his cheeke so glowd:
O that forc'd thunder from his heart did flye,

O that sad breath his spungie lungs bestowed,
O all that borrowed motion seeming owed,
Would yet againe betray the fore-betrayed,
And new pervert a reconciled Maide.

WILLIAM SHAKESPEARE

Ovid's fifth elegy[1]

Corinnae Concubitus

In summers heate and mid-time of the day
To rest my limbes upon a bed I lay,
One window shut, the other open stood,
Which gave such light as twincles in a wood,
Like twilight glimps at setting of the Sunne
Or night being past, and yet not day begunne.
Such light to shamefast maidens must be showne,
Where they may sport, and seeme to bee unknowne.
Then came *Corinna* in a long loose gowne,
Her white neck hid with tresses hanging downe:
Resembling fayre *Semiramis* going to bed
Or *Layis* of a thousand wooers sped.
I snacht her gowne, being thin, the harme was small.
Yet striv'd she to be covered there withall.
And striving thus as one that would be cast,
Betray'd her selfe, and yelded at the last.
Starke naked as she stood before mine eye,
Not one wen in her body could I spie.
What armes and shoulders did I touch and see,
How apt her breasts were to be prest by me?
How smooth a belly under her wast saw I?
How large a legge, and what a lustie thigh?
To leave the rest, al lik'd me passing well,
I cling'd her naked body, downe she fell,
Judge you the rest: being tirde she bad me kisse,
Jove send me more such after-noones as this.

CHRISTOPHER MARLOWE

[1] Marlowe translated all Ovid's *Amores*, describing them as Elegies

You little Stars that Live in Skies

You little starres that live in skies,
   And glorie in Appollos glorie,
In whose aspect conjoyned lyes
   The heavens' will and Nature's storie,
Joye to bee likened to those eyes,
   Which eyes makes all eyes glad or sorry.
For when you force thoughts from above,
Those over-rule your force by love.

And thou, O love, which in those eyes
   Hast married reason with affection,
And made them Saints of beauties skies,
   Where joyes are shadowes of perfection,
Lend me thy wings, that I may rise
   Up, not by worth but thy Election.
For I have vow'd in strangest fashion
To love and never seeke compassion.

                        ANONYMOUS

Gaze not on youth . . .

Gaze not on Youth; let age containe
Thy wandring eye from objects vaine.

No, I must looke about and see
In love what heavenly objects be.
But when the eye is on the face,
   The minde is in another place.

True pleasure is in chastity.
I onely seeke to please mine eye.
I may be chast, yet gaze my fill.

No, learne of me, and sing this still:
   She, onely she, is ever chast,
   That is with every looke outfact.

                        ANONYMOUS

O I do love, then kiss me

O I do love, then kisse me;
And after Ile not misse thee
With bodies lovely meeting
To dally, pretty sweeting.
Though I am somewhat aged,
Yet is not love assuaged;
But with sweet ardent clips,
Ile lay thee on the lips,
And make thee ever sweare:
Farewell, old batcheler.

ANONYMOUS

Lady, the Silly Flea ...

Lady, the silly flea of all disdained
    Because it hath complained,
    I pitty that poore creature,
    Both black and small of stature.
Were I a flea in bed I would not bite you,
But search some other way for to delight you.

ANONYMOUS

A little pretty bonny lass ...

A little prety bony lass was walking
    In midst of May before the Sun 'gan rise.
I tooke her by the hand and fell to talking
    Of this and that, as best I could devise.
I swore I would, yet still she said I should not
Doe what I would, and yet for all I could not.

ANONYMOUS

Why are our Summer Sports so brittle?

Why are our sommer sports so brittle?
  The leaves already fall,
  The meads are drowned all;
Alas, that sommer lasts so little.
  No pleasure could be tasted
If flowery sommer always lasted.

ANONYMOUS

When I was otherwise than now I am

When I was otherwise then now I am,
  I loved more, but skylled not so much;
Fayre words and smyles could have contented than,
  My simple age and ignorance was such.
But at the length experience made me wonder
That harts and tongues did lodge so farre assunder.

As watermen which on the Thames do row
  Looke to the East, but West keepes on the way,
My soveraigne sweet her countenance setled so
  To feede my hope, while she her snares might laye.
And when she saw that I was in her danger,
Good God, how soone she proved then a ranger.

I could not choose but laugh, although to late,
  To see great craft disifered in a toye.
I love her still, but such conditions hate
  Which so prophanes my Paradise of joy.
Love whetts the witts, whose paine is but a pleasure,
A toy by fitts to play withall at leasure.

ANONYMOUS

Whether men do laugh or weep

Whether men doe laugh or weepe,
Whether they doe wake or sleepe,
Whether they die yoong or olde,
Whether they feele heate or cold,
There is underneath the sunne
Nothing in true earnest done.

All our pride is but a jest;
None are worst and none are best.
Griefe and joy and hope and feare
Play their Pageants every where;
Vaine opinion all doth sway,
And the world is but a play.

Powers above in clouds doe sit
Mocking our poore apish wit,
That so lamely with such state
Their high glorie imitate.
No ill can be felt but paine,
And that happie men disdain.

ANONYMOUS

Thus sung Orpheus to his Strings

Thus sung Orphius to his strings,
   When hee was almost slaine,
Whilst the winds, soft murmuring,
   Answerd all his woes againe:
Ah, deare Euridice, he cried;
   And so he died.
'Euridice' the Echoing winds replied.

ANONYMOUS

I sigh, as sure to wear the Fruit

I sigh, as sure to weare the fruit
  Of the willow tree.
I sigh, as sure to lose my sute;
  For it may not bee.
I sigh as one that loves in vaine,
I sigh as one that lives in paine,
    Very sorrie,
    Very weary
  Of my miserie.

I hate my thoughts which, like the flie,
  Flutter in the flame.
I hate my teares which drop and dry,
  Quench and frid the same.
I hate the hart which frozen burnes,
I hate the hart which chosen turnes
    Too and from mee,
    Making of mee
  Nothing but a game.

My thoughts are fuell to desire,
  Which my hart doth move;
My teares are oyle to feed the fire,
  Smart whereof I prove.
She laughes at sighes that come from mee,
I sigh at laughes in her so free,
    Who doth glory
    In the storie
  Of my sorrie love.

Her lovely lookes and loveless mind
  Doe not well agree;
Her quick conceipt and judgement blind
  As ill-suted be.
Her forward wit and froward hart,
That like to knit, this glad to part,
    Makes so prettie
    And so wittie
  Not to pittie mee.

The more I seeke, the lesse I find
   What to trust unto.
The more I hold, the less I bind,
   She doth still undoe.
I weave the web of idle love,
Which endles will and fruitles prove,
   If the pleasure
   For the measure
   Of my treasure goe.

ANONYMOUS

Thanks, Gentle Moon, for thy Obscured Light

Thanks, gentle Moone, for thy obscured light;
   My love and I betraied thou set us free.
   And Zephirus, as many unto thee,
Whose blasts conceald the pleasures of the night;
   Resolve to her thou gave, content to mee.
But be those bowers still fild with serpents' hisses,
That sought by treason to betray our kisses.

And thou, false Arbor, with thy bed of Rose,
   Wherin, wheron, toucht equall with love's fyer,
   We reapt of eyther other love's desire,
Wither the twining plants that thee enclose!
Oh be thy bowers still fild with serpents' hisses,
That sought by treason to betray our kisses.

Torne be the frame, for thou didst thankless hide
   A trayterous spy, her brother and my foe,
   Who sought by death our joyes to undergoe,
And by that death our passions to devide,
   Leaving to our great vows eternall woe.
O be thy bowers still fild with serpents' hisses,
That sought by treason to betray our kisses.

ANONYMOUS

Fly from the World . . .

Flye, flye, flye from the world, O fly, thou poor distrest,
   Where thy diseased sense infectes thy soule,
And wher thy thoghts do multiply unrest,
   Trobling with wishes what they straight controule.
O worlde, O worlde, O worlde betrayers of the mind!
O thoughts, O thoughts, that guide us, being blinde!

Come therefore, Care, Conduct me to my end,
   And steere this shipwracke carcase to the grave.
My sighes a strong and stedfast wind will lende,
   Teares wet the sayles, repentance from rockes save;
Haile death! hayle death! the land I do descry!
Strike sayle! go soule! rest followes them that dye.

                               ANONYMOUS

Every Bush new springing

       Everie bush new springing,
       Every bird now singing,
       Merily sate poore Nico,
       Chanting troli lo loli lo,
       Til her he had espeid
       On whom his hope releid,
       Down a down a down, with a frown,
       O she puld him down.

                        ANONYMOUS

Of all the Birds that I do know

Of all the birds that I doe know,
   Philip my sparrow hath no peer;
For sit she high, or sit she lowe,
   Be she far off or be she near,

There is no bird so fayre, so fine,
Nor yet so fresh as this of mine;
For when she once hath felt a fitte,
Philip will crie still: yet, yet, yet.

Come in a morning merily
    When Philip hath beene latelie fed;
Or in an evening soberlie
    When Philip list to go to bed;
It is a heaven to heare my Phippe,
How she can chirpe with merry lip,
For when she once hath felt a fitte,
Philip will crie still: yet, yet, yet.

She never wanders far abroad,
    But is at home when I do call.
If I command she laies on load
    With lips, with teeth, with tong and all.
She chaunts, she cherpes, she makes such cheare,
That I beleeve she hath no peere.
For when she once hath felt the fitte,
Philip will crie still: yet, yet, yet.

And yet besides all this good sport
    My Philip can both sing and daunce,
With new found toyes of sundrie sort
    My Philip can both pricke and praunce.
And if you say but: fend out, phippe!
Lord, how the peate wil turne and skippe!
For when she once hath felt the fitte,
Philip will crie still: yet, yet, yet.

And to tel truth he were to blame,
    Having so fine a bird as she,
To make him all this goodly game
    Without suspect or jelousie;
He were a churle and knew no good,
Would see her faint for lacke of food,
For when she once hath felt the fitte,
Philip will crie still: yet, yet, yet.

ANONYMOUS

Since Robin Hood . . .

Since Roben Hood, Maid Marian,
  And Little John are gonea,
The hobby horse was quite forgot,
  When Kempe did daunce alonea.
      He did labour
      After the tabor,
      For to dance
      Then into France
      He took paines
To skip it in hope of gaines.
He will trip it trip it trip it on the toe
Diddle diddle diddle doe.

ANONYMOUS

Strike it up, Tabor

    Strike it up, Tabor,
    And pipe us a favour!
Thou shalt be well paid for thy labour.
  I mean to spend my shoe sole
  To dance about the may-pole!
  I will be blithe and brisk,
      Leap and skip,
      Hop and trip
      Turn about
      In the rout,
Until very meary joyntes can scarce friske.

    Lusty Dicke Hopkin,
    Lay on with thy napkin,
The stitching cost me but a dodkin.
  The morris were halfe undone
  Wer't not for Martin of Compton.
  O well said, jiging Alce!

Pritty Gill
Stand you still!
Dapper Jacke
Means to smacke.
How now? fie fie fie! you dance false.

ANONYMOUS

The Ape, the Monkey and Baboon did meet

The Ape, the Monkey and Baboon did meet,
And breaking of their fast in fryday Street,
Two of them sware together solemnly
In their three natures was a simpathie.
Nay, quoth Baboon, I do deny that straine,
I have more knavery in me than you twaine.

Why, quoth the Ape, I have a horse at will
In Parris Garden for to ride on still,
And there show trickes. Tush, quoth the Monkey, I
For better trickes in great men's houses lie.
Tush, quoth Baboone, when men do know I come,
For sport, from City, country, they will runne.

ANONYMOUS

Hawking for the Partridge

Sith Sickles and the shearing scythe
    Hath shorne the Feilds of late,
Now shall our Hawkes and we be blythe.
    Dame Partridge ware your pate!
        Our murdring kites
        In all their flights
        Wil seild or never miss
To trusse you ever and make your bale our blisse.

Whur ret { Duty / Quando / Travell / Jew }   Whur ret { Beauty / Nimble / Trover / Damsell }

Hey dogs hey!

Ware haunt hey { Wanton / Sempster / Callis / Dauncer } ret { Sugar / Faver / Dover / Jerker } ret { Mistress / Minx / Sant / Quoy }

ret { Tricker / Dido / Cherry / Stately } ret { Crafty / Civill / Carver / Ruler } ret { Minion / Lemmon / Courtier / German } Whur! let fly!

O well flowne, eager kyte, marke!
We Faulkners thus make sullen kites
   Yeeld pleasure fit for kings,
And sport with them in those delights,
   And oft in other things.

ANONYMOUS

Tomorrow is the Marriage Day

Tomorrow is the marriage day
Of Mopsus and faire Phillida.
Come, shepherds, bring your garlands gay.

If Love lye in so fowle a nest,
And fowleness on so faire a breast,
What lover may not hope the best?

O do not weepe, fair Bellamoure,
Though he be gone theres many more,
For Love hath many loves in store.

ANONYMOUS

Jockie, thine Hornpipe's dull

Jockie, thine horne pipes dull;
Give wind man, at full.
Fie upon such a sad gull,
Like an hoody doody
   All to moody.
    Pipe it up thicker,
    I'll tread it the quicker.
Why then about it roundly,
And I will foot it soundly,
Ile take my steps the shorter,
As if I trampled mortar.

Darité grows so grave,
I may not her have
In a round, when I crave.
With a hoop, sir, hoy day!
   O you hurt me!
   Set me thy worke by,
   And come to me smurkly.
Then if she chance to glance in,
Give us two roome to dance in.
Though my green jerkin bare is,
Us two to all the parish!

ANONYMOUS

Thule, the Period of Cosmography

Thule, the period of Cosmography,
  Doth vaunt of Hecla, whose sulphurious fire
Doth melt the frozen Clime and thaw the Skie;
  Trinacrian Aetnaes flames ascend not higher.
These things seeme wondrous, yet more wondrous I,
Whose hart with feare doth freeze, with love doth fry.

The Andalusian Merchant, that returnes
  Laden with Cutchinele and China dishes;
Reports in Spain how strangely Fogo burnes
  Amidst an Ocean full of flying fishes.
These things seem wondrous, yet more wondrous I,
Whose hart with feare doth freeze, with love doth frye.

ANONYMOUS

Dainty Sweet Bird . . .

Dainty sweet bird, who art incaged there,
Alas, how like thine and my fortunes are.
Both prisners, both sing, and singing thus
Strive to please her, who hath imprisned us.
Onely in this we differ, thou and I,
Thou livist singing, but I singing die.

ANONYMOUS

Coame, Malkyn, hurle thine oyz at Hodge Trillindle

Coame, Malkyn, hurle thine oyz at Hodge Trillindle,
And zet a zide thy Distave and thy Zpindle.
A little tyny let a ma brast my minde
To theee which I have vownd as ghurst as ghinde.
Yet loave ma, Zweet, a little tyny vit,
And wee a little little Wedelocke wooll gommit.
  Y vaith wooll wee, that wee wooll y vaith lo!

ANONYMOUS

For the Hearne and Duck

Luer, Faulkners! give warning to the Feild!
Let flye! let flye! make mounting hearnes to yeilde.
Dye, fearfull ducks, and climbe no more so high;
The Nyas-Hauke will kisse the Azure Skie.
But when our Soare-Haukes flie and stiffe windes blow,
Then long too late we Faulkners crye hey ho!

ANONYMOUS

Farewell, Sweet Boy, complain not of my truth

Farewell, sweet Boy, complain not of my truth,
   Thy mother lov'd thee not with more devotion;
For to thy boyes play I gave all my youth.
   Young master, I did hope for your promotion.
While some sought honours Princes thoughts observing
   Many woed fame, the child of Pain and Anguish,
Others judged inward good a chief deserving,
   I in thy wanton visions joyd to languish.
I bowed not thy image for succession,
   Nor bound thy bow to shoot reformed kindness;
Thy plays of hope and fear near my confession;
   The spectacles to my life was thy blindness.
But, Cupid, now farewell, I will goe play mee
With thoughts that please mee lesse, and lesse betray me.

FULKE GREVILLE, LORD BROOKE

Come, blessed bird . . .

Come, blessed Bird, and with thy sugred relish
Help our declining quire now to embellish,
For Bonnybootes that so aloft would fetch it,
O he is dead, and none of us can reach it.

Then tune to us, sweet Bird, thy shrill recorder,
For fault of better will serve in the Corus,
Begin and we will follow thee in order.
    Elpin and I and Dorus
Will serve for fault of better in the chorus.
   Then sang the Wood borne minstrel of Diana:
   Long live fair Oriana.

ANONYMOUS

Thus Bonny-boots the Birthday Celebrated

Thus Bonny bootes the birthday celebrated
   Of hir his lady deerest,
Fair Orian, which to his hart was neerest.
   The Nymphs and shepherds feasted
With clowted creame were, and to sing requested.
   Loe heere the faire created,
    (Quoth he), the worlds chiefe goddesse.
Sing then, for she is Bonny-bootes sweet mistres.
   Then sang the shepherds and Nymphs of Diana:
   Long live fair Oriana.

ANONYMOUS

Fly, Love, that art so sprightly

   Fly, Love, that art so sprightly,
   To bonny boots uprightly,
   And when in heaven thou meet him,
   Say that I blindly greete him,
   And that his Oriana,
True widow maid, still followeth Diana.

ANONYMOUS

Our Bonny-boots could toot it, yea and foot it

Our bonny bootes could toote it, yea and foot it.
Say, lusty lads, who now shall bonny boote it?
Who but the jolly shephard, bonny Dorus?
He now must lead the morris daunce before us.

                              ANONYMOUS

Since Bonny-boots was dead . . .

Since Bonny-boots was dead, that so divinely
Could toot and foot it, (O he did it finely!)
    We neare went more a Maying
    Nor had that sweet fa-laing.

                              ANONYMOUS

Live not, poor Bloom, but perish

Live not, poore bloome, but perish,
    Whose Spring frosty Winter blasteth.
Other buds fresh Mayes doe cherish,
    Hyems o're thee his snow casteth,
    And in wither'd armes thee graspeth.

Tyrants, nothing worse you can.
    Now my lively body's yaked
To the dead corps of a man,
    Thus, with loathed burden choked,
    Lingering death with teares invoked.

                              ANONYMOUS

Tan ta ra ran tan tant: cries Mars on bloody rapier

Tan ta ra ran tan tant: cryes Mars on bloudy rapier.
Fa la la fa la, fa la: cries Venus in a Chamber.
    Toodle loodle loo:
    Cryes Pan, that Cuckoo,
    With bels at his shoo,
    And a fiddle too.
Dye me, but I, alas, lye weeping,
For death has slaine my sweeting,
Which hath my heart in keeping.

ANONYMOUS

Come, sirrah Jack, ho!

Come, Sirrah Jacke, hoe!
Fill some tobacco.
    Bring a wire
    And some fire!
    Hast hast away,
    Quicke I say!
    Do not stay!
    Shun delay!
For I drank none good to-day.

I swear that this tobacco
It's perfect Trinidado.
    By the very very mas
    Never never never was
    Better gere
    Than is here.
    By the roode
    For the bloud
It is very very good.

Fill the pipe once more,
My braines daunce trenchmore.
  It is headdy,
  I am geeddy.
  My head and braines,
  Back and reines,
  Jointes and veines
  From all paines
It doth well purge and make it cleane.

For those that do Condemn it,
Or such as not Commend it,
Never were so wise to learne
Good tobacco to discern;
  Let them go
  Plucke a crow,
  And not know,
  As I do,
The sweet of Trinidado.

ANONYMOUS

I am so far from pitying thee

I am so farre from pittying thee,
That wears't a branch of willow-tree,
 That I doe envie thee and all
 That once was high and got a fall:
  O willow, willow, willow-tree,
  I would thou didst belong to me!

Thy wearing willow doth imply
That thou art happier farre then I;
 For once thou wert where thou wouldst be
 Though now thou wear'st the willow-tree:
  O willow, willow, sweet willow,
  Let me once lie upon her pillow!

I doe defie both bough and roote
And all the fiends of Hell to boote,
   One houre of Paradised joye
   Makes Purgatorie seeme a toye:
      O willow, willow, doe thy work,
      Thou canst not make me more accurst!

I have spent all my golden time
In writing many a loving rime,
   I have consumed all my youth
   In vowing of my faith and trueth:
      O willow, willow, willow-tree,
      Yet can I not beleeved bee!

And now alas, it is too late,
Gray hayres, the messenger of fate,
   Bids me to set my heart at rest,
   For beautie loveth yong men best:
      I willow, willow, I must die,
      Thy servant's happier farre then I!

              ANONYMOUS

So quick, so hot . . .[1]

So quicke, so hot, so mad is thy fond sute,
So rude, so tedious growne, in urging mee,
That faine I would with losse make thy tongue mute,
And yeeld some little grace to quiet thee:
   An houre with thee I care not to converse,
   For I would not be counted too perverse,

But roofes too hot would prove for men all fire;
And hils too high for my unused pace,[2]
The grove is charg'd with thornes and the bold bryer;
Gray Snakes the meadowes shrowde in every place:
   A yellow Frog, alas, will fright me so,
   As I should start and tremble as I goe.

Since then I can on earth no fit roome finde,
In heaven I am resolv'd with you to meete,
Till then, for Hopes sweet sake, rest your tir'd minde,
And not so much as see mee in the streete:
  A heavenly meeting one day wee shall have,
  But never, as you dreame, in bed, or grave.

THOMAS CAMPIAN

[1] A girl's dismissal of an over-zealous suitor
[2] These two lines mean: 'to talk with you indoors
(i.e., under "roofs") would only encourage the already
excessive heat of your passion, while I am not used to
outdoor walks'

Sleep, Angry Beauty

Sleepe, angry beauty, sleep, and feare not me.
For who a sleeping Lyon dares provoke?
It shall suffice me here to sit and see
Those lips shut up that never kindely spoke.
  What sight can more content a lovers minde
  Then beauty seeming harmlesse, if not kinde?

My words have charm'd her, for secure shee sleepes;
Though guilty much of wrong done to my love;
And in her slumber, see, shee, close-ey'd, weepes:
Dreames often more then waking passions move.
  Pleade, sleepe, my cause, and make her soft like thee,
  That shee in peace may wake and pitty mee.

THOMAS CAMPIAN

Vain Men, whose Follies . . .

Vaine men, whose follies make a God of Love,
Whose blindnesse beauty doth immortall deeme,
Prayse not what you desire, but what you prove,
Count those things good that are, not those that seeme
I cannot call her true that's false to me,
Nor make of women more then women be.

How faire an entrance breakes the way to love!
How rich of golden hope and gay delight!
What hart cannot a modest beauty move?
Who, seeing cleare day once, will dreame of night?
Shee seem'd a Saint, that brake her faith with mee,
But prov'd a woman as all other be.

So bitter is their sweet, that true content
Unhappy men in them may never finde:
Ah, but without them none; both must consent,
Else uncouth are the joys of eyther kinde.
Let us then prayse their good, forget their ill:
Men must be men, and women women still.

                                    THOMAS CAMPIAN

Dear if I with Guile

Deare if I with guile would guild a true intent
Heaping flattries that in heart were never meant:
            Easely could I then obtaine
                What now in vaine I force;
            Fals-hood much doth gaine,
                Truth yet holds the better course.

Love forbid that through dissembling I should thrive,
Or in praysing you, my selfe of truth deprive:

Let not your high thoughts debase
   A simple truth in me;
Great is beauties grace,
   Truth is yet as fayre as shee.

Prayse is but the winde of pride, if it exceedes;
Wealth, pris'd in it selfe, no outward value needes.
   Fayre you are, and passing fayre;
     You know it, and 'tis true:
   Yet let none despayre
     But to finde as fayre as you.

THOMAS CAMPIAN

Harden now thy Tired Heart . . .

Harden now thy tyred hart, with more then flinty rage;
Ne'er let her false teares henceforth thy constant griefe asswage.
Once true happy dayes thou saw'st when shee stood firme and kinde,
Both as one then liv'd and held one eare, one tongue, one minde:
But now those bright houres be fled, and never may returne;
What then remaines but her untruths to mourne?

Silly Traytresse, who shall now thy carelesse tresses place?
Who thy pretty talke supply, whose eare thy musicke grace?
Who shall thy bright eyes admire? what lips triumph with thine?
Day by day who'll visit thee and say 'th'art onely mine'?
Such a time there was, God wot, but such shall never be:
Too oft, I fear thou wilt remember me.

THOMAS CAMPIAN

An Epistle to Sir Edward Sackville,
now Earl of Dorset

If Sackvile, all that have the power to doe
Great and good turns, as wel could time them too,
And knew their how, and where: we should have, then
Lesse list of proud, hard, or ingratefull Men.
For benefits are ow'd with the same mind
As they are done, and such returnes they find:
You then whose will not only, but desire
To succour my necessities tooke fire,
Not at my prayers, but your sense; which laid
The way to meet, what others would upbraid;
And in the Act did so my blush prevent,
As I did feele it done, as soone as meant:
You cannot doubt, but I who freely know
This Good from you, as freely will it owe;
And though my fortune humble me, to take
The smallest courtesies with thankes, I make
Yet choyce from whom I take them; and would shame
To have such doe me good, I durst not name:
They are the Noblest benefits, and sinke
Deepest in Man, of which when he doth thinke,
The memorie delights him more, from whom
Then what he hath receiv'd. Gifts stinke from some,
They are so long a comming, and so hard;
Where any Deed is forc't, the Grace is mard.
    Can I owe thankes, for Curtesies receiv'd
Against his will that doe's 'hem? that hath weav'd
Excuses, or Delayes? or done 'hem scant,
That they have more opprest me, then my want?
Or if he did it not to succour me,
But by meere Chance? for interest? or to free
Himselfe of farther trouble, or the weight
Of pressure, like one taken in a streight?[1]
All this corrupts the thankes; lesse hath he wonne,
That puts it in his Debt-booke e're't be done;
Or that doth sound a Trumpet, and doth call
His Groomes to witnesse; or else lets it fall

In that proud manner: as a good so gain'd,
Must make me sad for what I have obtain'd.
  No! Gifts and thankes should have one cheerefull face,
So each, that's done, and tane, becomes a Brace.
He neither gives, or do's, that doth delay
A Benefit: or that doth throw't away,
No more then he doth thanke, that will receive
Nought but in corners; and is loath to leave,
Lest Ayre, or Print, but flies it: Such men would
Run from the Conscience of it if they could.
  As I have seene some Infants of the Sword
Well knowne, and practiz'd borrowers on their word,
Give thankes by stealth, and whispering in the eare,
For what they streight would to the world forsweare;
And speaking worst of those, from whom they went
But then, fist fill'd, to put me off the sent.
Now dam'mee, Sir, if you shall not command
My Sword ('tis but a poore Sword understand)
As farre as any poore Sword i' the Land;
Then turning unto him is next at hand,
Dam's whom he damn'd too, is the veriest Gull,
H'as Feathers, and will serve a man to pull.
  Are they not worthy to be answer'd so,
That to such Natures let their full hands flow,
And seeke not wants to succour: but enquire
Like Money-brokers, after Names, and hire
Their bounties forth, to him that last was made,
Or stands to be'n Commission o' the blade?
Still, still, the hunters of false fame apply
Their thoughts and meanes to making loude the cry:
But one is bitten by the Dog he fed,
And hurt seeks Cure; the Surgeon bids take bread,
And spunge-like with it dry up the blood quite:
Then give it to the Hound that did him bite;
Pardon, sayes he, that were a way to see
All the Towne-curs take each their snatch at me.
O, is it so? knowes he so much? and will
Feed those, at whom the Table points at still?
I not deny it, but to helpe the need
Of any, is a Great and generous Deed.

Yea, of th' ingratefull: and he forth must tell
Many a pound, and piece will pace one well;
But these men ever want: their very trade
Is borrowing, that but stopt they doe invade
All as their prize, turne Pyrats here at Land,
Ha' their Bermudas, and their streights i' th' Strand:
Man out their Boates to th' Temple, and not shift
Now, but command; make tribute, what was gift:
And it is paid 'hem with a trembling zeale,
And superstition I dare scarce reveale
If it were cleare, but being so in cloud
Carryed and wrapt, I only am aloud
My wonder! why? the taking a Clownes purse,
Or robbing the poore Market-folkes should nurse
Such a religious horrour in the brests
Of our Towne Gallantry! or why there rests
Such worship due to kicking of a Punck!
Or swaggering with the Watch, or Drawer drunke;
Or feats of darknesse acted in Mid-Sun,
And told of with more Licence then th' were done!
Sure there is Misterie in it, I not know,
That men such reverence to such actions show!
And almost deifie the Authors! make
Lowd sacrifice of drinke, for their health-sake
Reare Suppers in their Names! and spend whole nights
Unto their praise, in certain swearing rites;
Cannot a man be reck'ned in the State
Of Valour, but at this Idolatrous rate?
I thought that Fortitude had beene a meane
'Twixt feare and rashnesse: not a lust obscene,
Or appetite of offending, but a skill,
Or Science of discerning Good and Ill.
And you, Sir, know it well to whom I write,
That with these mixtures we put out her light;
Her ends are honestie, and publike good!
And where they want, she is not understood.
No more are these of us, let them then goe,
I have the lyst of mine owne faults to know,
Looke too and cure; Hee's not a man hath none,
But like to be, that every day mends one,

And feeles it; Else he tarries by the Beast.
Can I discerne how shadowes are decreast,
Or growne, by height or lownesse of the Sunne?
And can I lesse of substance? When I runne,
Ride, saile, am coach'd, know I how farre I have gone,
And my minds motion not? or have I none:
No! he must feele and know, that I will advance:
Men have beene great, but never good by chance,
Or on the sudden. It were strange that he
Who was this Morning such a one, should be
Sydney e're night? or that did go to bed
Coriat, should rise the most sufficient head
Of Christendome? And neither of these know
Were the Rack offer'd them how they came so;
'Tis by degrees that men arrive at glad
Profit in ought: each day some little adde,
In time 'twill be a heape; This is not true
Alone in money, but in manners too.
Yet we must more then move still, or goe on,
We must accomplish; 'Tis the last Key-stone
That makes the Arch. The rest that there were put
Are nothing till that comes to bind and shut.
Then stands it a triumphall marke! then Men
Observe the strength, the height, the why, and when,
It was erected; and still walking under
Meet some new matter to looke up and wonder!
Such Notes are vertuous men! they live as fast
As they are high; are rooted and will last.
They need no stilts, nor rise upon their toes,
As if they would belie their stature; those
Are Dwarfes of Honour, and have neither weight
Nor fashion; if they chance aspire to height,
'Tis like light Canes, that first rise big and brave,
Shoot forth in smooth and comely spaces; have
But few and faire Devisions: but being got
Aloft, grow less and streightned; full of knot;
And last, goe out in nothing: You that see
Their difference, cannot choose which you will be.
You know (without my flatt'ring you) too much
For me to be your Indice. Keep you such,

That I may love your Person (as I doe)
Without your gift, though I can rate that too,
By thanking thus the curtesie to life,
Which you will bury, but therein, the strife
May grow so great to be example, when
(As their true rule or lesson) either men
Donnor's or Donnee's to their practise shall
Find you to reckon nothing, me owe all.

BEN JONSON

¹ caught in a difficult situation

Sonnet

I fear to me such fortune be assign'd
As was to thee, who did so well deserve,
Brave HALKERSTON, even suffer'd here to starve
Amidst base-minded friends, nor true, nor kind.
Why were the Fates and Furies thus combined,
Such worths for such disasters to reserve?
Yet all those evils never made thee swerve
From what became a well-resolved mind;
For swelling greatness never made thee smile,
Despising greatness in extremes of want;
O happy thrice whom no distress could daunt!
Yet thou exclaimed, O time! O age! O isle!
  Where flatterers, fools, bawds, fiddlers, are rewarded
  Whilst virtue starves unpitied, unregarded.

WILLIAM DRUMMOND

To Cynthia on Her Embraces

If thou a reason dost desire to know,
My dearest Cynthia, why I love thee so,
As when I do enjoy all thy love's store,
I am not yet content, but seek for more;
When we do kiss so often as the tale
Of kisses doth outvie the winter's hail:
When I do print them on more close and sweet
Than shells of scollops, cockles when they meet,
Yet am not satisfied: when I do close
Thee nearer to me than the ivy grows
Unto the oak: when those white arms of thine
Clip me more close than doth the elm the vine:
When naked both, thou seemest not to be
Contiguous, but continuous parts of me:
And we in bodies are together brought
So near, our souls may knows each other's thought
Without a whisper: yet I do aspire
To come more close to thee, and to be higher:
No, 'twas well said, that spirits are too high
For bodies, when they meet to satisfy;
Our souls having like forms of light and sense,
Proceeding from the same intelligence,
Desire to mix like to two water drops,
Whose union some little hindrance stops,
Which meeting both together would be one.
For in the steel, and in the adamant stone,
One and the same magnetic soul is cause,
That with such unseen chains each other draws:
So our souls now divided, brook't not well,
That being one, they should asunder dwell.
Then let me die, that so my soul being free,
May join with that her other half in thee,
For when in thy pure self it shall abide,
It shall assume a body glorified,
Being in that high bliss; nor shall we twain
Or wish to meet, or fear to part again.

SIR FRANCIS KYNASTON

To Cynthia on Her Being an Incendiary

Say (sweetest) whether thou didst use me well,
If when in my heart's house I let thee dwell
A welcome inmate, and did not require
More than a kiss a day, for rent or hire:
Thou wert not only pleas'd to stop the rent,
But most ungrateful, burnt the tenement;
Henceforth it will ensue, that thou didst carry
The branded name of an incendiary:
No heart will harbour thee, and thou, like poor
As I, may'st lodging beg from door to door.
If it be so, my ready course will be
To get a licence, and re-edify
My wasted heart. If Cupid should inquire,
By what mishap my heart was set on fire;
I'll say, my happy fortune was to get
Thy beauty's crop, which being green and wet
With show'rs of tears, I did too hasty in,
Before that throughly withered it had bin:
So heating in the mow it soon became
At first a smoke, and afterwards a flame:
At this Love's little King will much admire,
How cold and wet conjoin'd can cause a fire
Having no heat themselves, but I do know
What he will say, for he will bid me go,
And build my heart of stone: so shall I be
Safe from the lightning of thine eyes, and thee,
The cold, and hardness of stone hearts, best serving
For coy green beauties, and them best preserving.
Yet here is danger; for if thou be in't
My heart to stone, and thine harder than flint,
Knocking together may strike fire, and set
Much more on fire, than hath bin burned yet.
If so it hap, then let those flames calcine
My heart to cinders, so it soften thine:
A heart, which until then doth serve the turn
To enflame others, but itself not burn.

SIR FRANCIS KYNASTON

To a Lady in a Garden

Sees not my love how time resumes
The glory which he lent these flowers?
Though none should taste of their perfumes,
Yet must they live but some few hours;
Time what we forbear devours!

Had Helen, or the Egyptian Queen,
Been ne'er so thrifty of their graces,
Those beauties must at length have been
The spoil of age, which finds out faces
In the most retired places.

Should some malignant planet bring
A barren drought, or ceaseless shower,
Upon the autumn or the spring,
And spare us neither fruit nor flower;
Winter would not stay an hour.

Could the resolve of love's neglect
Preserve you from the violation
Of coming years, then more respect
Were due to so divine a fashion,
Nor would I indulge my passion.

EDMUND WALLER

To a Fair Lady, Playing with a Snake

Strange! that such horror and such grace
Should dwell together in one place.
A fury's arm, an angel's face!

'Tis innocence, and youth, which makes
In Chloris' fancy such mistakes,
To start at love, and play with snakes.

By this and by her coldness barred,
Her servants have a task too hard;
The tyrant has a double guard!

Thrice happy snake! that in her sleeve
May boldly creep; we dare not give
Our thoughts so unconfined a leave.

Contented in that nest of snow
He lies, as he his bliss did know,
And to the wood no more would go.

Take heed, fair Eve! you do not make
Another tempter of this snake;
A marble one so warmed would speak.

                    EDMUND WALLER

Upon *Christmas Eve*

Vaile[1] cobwebs from the white-ned floore
And let Arachne spin noe more;
With holly-bushes all adorne
Untill the comeing of the morne
And fancy then the Lord of Light is there
As he did once in Moses-bush appeare.

                    SIR JOHN SUCKLING

[1] lower, remove

Upon Christ *His Birth*

Strange news! a Cittie full? will none give way
To lodge a guest that comes not every day?
Noe inne, nor taverne void? yet I descry
One empty place alone, where wee may ly:

In too much fullnesse is some want: but where?
Mens empty hearts: let's aske for lodgeing there.
But if they not admit us, then wee'le say
Their hearts, as well as inn's, are made of clay.

SIR JOHN SUCKLING

'Love, Reason, Hate'

Love, Reason, Hate, did once bespeak
Three mates to play at barley-break;
Love Folly took; and Reason, Fancy;
And Hate consorts with Pride; so dance they.
Love coupled last, and so it fell,
That Love and Folly were in hell.

They break, and Love would Reason meet,
But Hate was nimbler on her feet;
Fancy looks for Pride, and thither
Hies, and they two hug together:
Yet this new coupling still doth tell,
That Love and Folly were in hell.

The rest do break again, and Pride
Hath now got Reason on her side;
Hate and Fancy meet, and stand
Untouched by Love in Folly's hand;
Folly was dull, but Love ran well:
So Love and Folly were in hell.

SIR JOHN SUCKLING

Proffered Love Rejected

It is not four years ago,
  I offered forty crowns
To lie with her a night or so:
  She answer'd me in frowns.

Not two years since, she meeting me
    Did whisper in my ear,
That she would at my service be,
    If I contented were.

I told her I was cold as snow,
    And had no great desire;
But should be well content to go
    To twenty, but no higher.

Some three months since or thereabout,
    She that so coy had been,
Bethought herself and found me out,
    And was content to sin.

I smil'd at that, and told her I
    Did think it something late,
And that I'd not repentance buy
    At above half the rate.

This present morning early she
    Forsooth came to my bed,
And *gratis* there she offered me
    Her high-priz'd maidenhead.

I told her that I thought it then
    Far dearer than I did,
When I at first the forty crowns
    For one night's lodging bid.

                    SIR JOHN SUCKLING

A Sessions of the Poets

A session was held the other day,
And Apollo himself was at it, they say,
The laurel that had been so long reserved,
Was now to be given to him best deserved.

And

Therefore the wits of the town came thither,
'Twas strange to see how they flocked together,
Each strongly confident of his own sway,
Thought to gain the laurel away that day.

There was Selden, and he sat hard by the chair;
Wenman not far off, which was very fair;
Sands with Townsend, for they kept no order;
Digby and Shillingsworth a little further.

And

There was Lucan's translator, too, and he
That makes God speak so big in's poetry;
Selwin and Waller, and Bartlets both the brothers;
Jack Vaughan and Porter, and divers others.

The first that broke silence was good old Ben,
Prepared before with canary wine,
And he told them plainly he deserved the bays,
For his were called works, where others were but plays.

And

Bid them remember how he had purged the stage
Or errors, that had lasted many an age;
And he hoped they did not think the 'Silent Woman',
The 'Fox', and the 'Alchemist', out-done by no man.

Apollo stopped him there, and bad him not go on,
'Twas merit, he said, and not presumption,
Must carry't; at which Ben turned about,
And in great choler offered to go out.

But

Those that were there thought it not fit
To discontent so ancient a wit;
And therefore Apollo called him back again,
And made him mine host of his own New Inn.

Tom Carew was next, but he had a fault
That would not well stand with a laureat;
His muse was hide-bound, and the issue of's brain
Was seldom brought forth but with trouble and pain.

And

All that were present there did agree,
A laureate muse should be easy and free,
Yet sure 'twas not that, but 'twas thought that, his grace
Considered, he was well he had a cup-bearer's place.

Will. Davenant, ashamed of a foolish mischance,
That he had got lately travelling in France,
Modestly hoped the handsomeness of's muse
Might any deformity about him excuse.

And

Surely the company would have been content,
If they could have found any precedent;
But in all their records either in verse or prose,
There was not one laureate without a nose.

To Will. Bartlet sure all the wits meant well,
But first they would see how his snow would sell:
Will. smiled and swore in their judgments they went less,
That concluded of merit upon success.

Suddenly taking his place again,
He gave way to Selwin, who straight stepped in,
But, alas! he had been so lately a wit,
That Apollo hardly knew him yet.

Toby Matthews (pox on him!) how came he there?
Was whispering nothing in somebody's ear;
When he had the honour to be named in court,
But, sir, you may thank my Lady Carlisle for't:

For had not her care furnished you out
With something of handsome, without all doubt
You and your sorry Lady Muse had been
In the number of those that were not let in.

In haste from the court two or three came in,
And they brought letters, forsooth, from the Queen;
'Twas discreetly done, too, for if th' had come
Without them, th' had scarce been let into the room.

Suckling next was called, but did not appear,
But straight one whispered Apollo i' th' ear,
That of all men living he cared not for 't,
He loved not the Muses so well as his sport.

And prized black eyes, or a lucky hit
At bowls, above all the trophies of wit;
But Apollo was angry, and publicly said,
'Twere fit that a fine were set upon's head.

Wat Montague now stood forth to his trial,
And did not so much as suspect a denial;
But witty Apollo asked him first of all,
If he understood his own pastoral.

For, if he could do it, 'twould plainly appear,
He understood more than any man there,
And did merit the bays above all the rest,
But the Monsieur was modest, and silence confessed.

During all these troubles, in the crowd was hid
One that Apollo soon missed, little Cid;
And having spied him call'd him out of the throng,
And advis'd him in his ear not to write so strong.

Then Murray was summon'd, but 'twas urged that he
Was chief already of another company.

Hales set by himself most gravely did smile
To see them about nothing keep such a coil;
Apollo had spied him, but knowing his mind
Passed by, and call'd Falkland that sat just behind.

But

He was of late so gone with divinity,
That he had almost forgot his poetry;
Though to say the truth (and Apollo did know it)
He might have been both his priest and his poet.

At length who but an Alderman did appear,
At which Will. Davenant began to swear;
But wiser Apollo bad him draw nigher,
And when he was mounted a little higher,

He openly declared that it was the best sign
Of good store of wit to have good store of coin;
And without a syllable more or less said
He put the laurel on the Alderman's head.

At this all the wits were in such amaze
That for a good while they did nothing but gaze
One upon another: not a man in the place
But had discontent writ in great in his face.

Only the small poets cheer'd up again,
Out of hope, as 'twas thought, of borrowing;
But sure they were out, for he forfeits his crown,
When he lends to any poet about the town.

SIR JOHN SUCKLING

Whom do we count a Good Man ...

Whom doe we count a good man, whom but he
Who keepes the lawes and statutes of the Senate,
Who judges in great suits and controversies,
Whose witnesse and opinion winnes the cause;
But his owne house, and the whole neighbourhood
Sees his foule inside through his whited skin.

JOHN MILTON
(from *Tetrachordon*)

Natura naturata

What gives us that fantastic fit,
That all our judgment and our wit
To vulgar custom we submit?

Treason, theft, murder, and all the rest
Of that foul legion we so detest,
Are in their proper names express'd.

Why is it then thought sin or shame
Those necessary parts to name,
From whence we went, and whence we came?

Nature, whate'er she wants, requires;
With love inflaming our desires,
Finds engines fit to quench those fires.

Death she abhors; yet when men die
We are present; but no stander by
Looks on when we that loss supply.

Forbidden wares sell twice as dear;
Even sack, prohibited last year,
A most abominable rate did bear.

'Tis plain our eyes and ears are nice,
Only to raise, by that device,
Of those commodities the price.

Thus reason's shadows us betray,
By tropes and figures led astray,
From Nature, both her guide and way.

SIR JOHN DENHAM

To the Five Members of the Honourable House of Commons

THE HUMBLE PETITION OF THE POETS

After so many concurring petitions
From all ages and sexes, and all conditions,
We come in the rear to present our follies
To Pym, Stroud, Haslerig, Hampden, and Hollis.
Though set form of prayer be an abomination,
Set forms of petitions find great approbation;
Therefore, as others from th' bottom of their souls,
We from the depth and bottom of our bowels,
According unto the bless'd form you have taught us,
We thank you first for the ills you have brought us:

For the good we receive we thank him that gave it,
And you for the confidence only to crave it.
Next in course, we complain of the great violation
Of privilege (like the rest of our nation),
But 'tis none of yours of which we have spoken,
Which never had being until they were broken;
But ours is a privilege ancient and native,
Hangs not on an ord'nance, or power legislative.
And, first, 'tis to speak whatever we please,
Without fear of a prison or pursuivants' fees.
Next, that we only may lie by authority;
But in that also you have got the priority.
Next, an old custom, our fathers did name it
Poetical license, and always did claim it.
By this we have power to change age into youth,
Turn nonsense to sense, and falsehood to truth;
In brief, to make good whatsoever is faulty;
This art some poet, or devil, has taught ye:
And this our property you have invaded,
And a privilege of both Houses have made it.
But that trust above all in poets reposed,
That kings by them only are made and deposed,
This though you cannot do, yet you are willing:
But when we undertake deposing or killing,
They're tyrants and monsters; and yet then the poet
Takes full revenge on the villains that do it:
And when we resume a sceptre or crown,
We are modest, and seek not to make it our own.
But is't not presumption to write verses to you,
Who make better poems by far of the two?
For all those pretty knacks you compose,
Alas! what are they but poems in prose?
And between those and ours there's no difference,
But that yours want the rhyme, the wit, and the sense:
But for lying (the most noble part of a poet)
You have it abundantly, and yourselves know it;
And though you are modest and seem to abhor it,
'T has done you good service, and thank Hell for it:
Although the old maxim remains still in force,
That a sanctified cause must have a sanctified course,

If poverty be a part of our trade,
So far the whole kingdom poets you have made,
Nay, even so far as undoing will do it,
You have made King Charles himself a poet:
But provoke not his Muse, for all the world knows,
Already you have had too much of his prose.

SIR JOHN DENHAM

The Coronet

When for the Thorns with which I long, too long,
   With many a piercing wound,
   My Saviours head have crown'd,
I seek with Garlands to redress that Wrong:
   Through every Garden, every Mead,
I gather flow'rs (my fruits are only flow'rs)
   Dismantling all the fragrant Towers
That once adorned my Shepherdesses head.
   And now when I have summ'd up all my store,
   Thinking (so I my self deceive)
   So rich a Chaplet thence to weave
As never yet the king of Glory wore:
   Alas I find the Serpent old
   That, twining in his speckled breast,
   About the flow'rs disguis'd does fold,
   With wreaths of Fame and Interest.
Ah, foolish Man, that woulds't debase with them
And mortal Glory, Heaven's Diadem!
But thou who only coulds't the Serpent tame,
Either his slipp'ry knots at once untie,
And disintangle all his winding Snare:
Or shatter too with him my curious frame:
And let these wither, so that he may die,
Though set with Skill and chosen out with Care.
That they, while Thou on both their Spoils dost tread,
May crown thy Feet, that could not crown thy Head.

ANDREW MARVELL

Eyes and Tears

How wisely Nature did decree,
With the same Eyes to weep and see!
That, having view'd the object vain,
They might be ready to complain.

And, since the Self-deluding Sight,
In a false Angle takes each hight;
These Tears which better measure all.
Like wat'ry Lines and Plummets fall.

Two Tears, which Sorrow long did weigh
Within the Scales of either Eye,
And then paid out in equal Poise,
Are the true price of all my Joyes.

What in the World most fair appears,
Yea even Laughter, turns to Tears:
And all the Jewels which we prize,
Melt in these pendants of the Eyes.

I have through every Garden been,
Amongst the Red, the White, the Green;
And yet, from all the flow'rs I saw,
No Hony, but these Tears could draw.

So the all-seeing Sun each day
Distills the World with Chymick Ray;
But finds the Essence only Showers,
Which straight in pity back he powers.

Yet happy they whom Grief doth bless,
That weep the more, and see the less:
And, to preserve their Sight more true
Bath still their Eyes in their own Dew.

So *Magdalen*, in Tears more wise
Dissolv'd those captivating Eyes,
Whose liquid Chaines could flowing meet
To fetter her Redeemers feet.

Not full sailes hasting loaden home,
Nor the chast Ladies pregnant Womb,
Nor *Cynthia* Teeming show's so fair,
As two Eyes swoln with weeping are.

The sparkling Glance that shoots Desire,
Drench'd in these Waves, does lose its fire.
Yea oft the Thund'rer pitty takes
And here the hissing Lightning slakes.

The Incense was to Heaven dear,
Not as a Perfume, but a Tear.
And Stars shew lovely in the Night,
But as they seem the Tears of Light.

Ope then mine Eyes your double Sluice,
And practise so your noblest Use.
For others too can see, or sleep;
But only humane Eyes can weep.

Now like two Clouds dissolving, drop,
And at each Tear in distance stop:
Now like two Fountains trickle down:
Now like two floods o'return and drown.

Thus let your Streams o'reflow your Springs,
Till Eyes and Tears be the same things:
And each the other's difference bears;
These weeping Eyes, those seeing Tears.

Magdala, *Lascivos sic quum dimisit Amantes,*
  Fervidaque in castas Lumina solvit aquas;
Haesit in irriguo lachrymarum compede Christus.
  Et tenuit sacros uda Catena pedes.

ANDREW MARVELL

Death

A DIALOGUE

SOULE   'Tis a sad land, that in one day
Hath dull'd thee thus, when death shall freeze
Thy bloud to Ice, and thou must stay
Tenant for Yeares, and Centuries,
How wilt thou brook't?—

BODY   I cannot tell,—
But if all sence wings not with thee,
And something still be left the dead,
I'le wish my Curtaines off to free
Me from so darke, and sad a bed;

A neast of nights, a gloomie sphere,
Where shadowes thicken, and the Cloud
Sits on the Suns brow all the yeare,
And nothing moves without a shrowd;

SOULE   'Tis so: But as thou sawest that night
Wee travell'd in, our first attempts
Were dull, and blind, but Custome straight
Our feares, and falls brought to contempt,

Then, when the gastly *twelve* was past
We breath'd still for a blushing *East*.
And bad the lazie Sunne make hast,
And on sure hopes, though long, did feast;

But when we saw the Clouds to crack
And in those Cranies light appear'd,
We thought the day then was not slack,
And pleas'd our selves with what wee feard;

Just so it is in death. But thou
Shalt in thy mothers bosome sleepe
Whilst I each minute grone to know
How neere Redemption creepes.
Then shall wee meet to mixe again, and met,
'Tis last good-night, our Sunne shall never set.

                                HENRY VAUGHAN

Distraction

O knit me, that am crumbled dust! the heape
    Is all dispers'd, and cheape;
   Give for a handfull, but a thought
    And it is bought;
     Hadst thou
Made me a starre, a pearle, or rain-bow,
    The beames I then had shot
    My light had lessend not,
     But now
I find my selfe the lesse, the more I grow;
    The world
Is full of voices; Man is call'd, and hurl'd
    By each, he answers all,
    Knows ev'ry note and call,
     Hence, still
Fresh dotage tempts, or old usurps his will.
Yet, hadst thou clipt my wings, when Coffin'd in
    This quicken'd masse of sinne,
   And saved that light, which freely thou
    Didst then bestow,
     I feare
I should have spurn'd, and said thou didst forbeare;
    Or that thy store was lesse,
    But now since thou didst blesse
     So much,
I grieve, my God! that thou hast made me such.
     I grieve?
O, yes! thou know'st I doe; Come, and releive
    And tame, and keepe downe with thy light
    Dust that would rise, and dimme my sight,
    Lest left alone too long
    Amidst the noise, and throng,
     Oppressed I
Striving to save the whole, by parcells dye.

        HENRY VAUGHAN

The Evening-watch

A DIALOGUE

BODY   Farewell! I goe to sleep; but when
The day-star springs, I'le wake agen.

SOUL   Goe, sleep in peace; and when thou lyest
Unnumber'd in thy dust, when all this frame
Is but one dramme, and what thou now descriest
     In sev'rall parts shall want a name,
Then may his peace be with thee, and each dust
Writ in his book, who ne'r betray'd mans trust!

BODY   Amen! but hark, e'er we two stray,
How many hours do'st think till day?

SOUL   Ah! go; th'art weak, and sleepie. Heav'n
Is a plain watch, and without figures winds
All ages up; who drew this Circle even
     He fils it; Dayes, and hours are *Blinds*
Yet, this take with thee; The last gasp of time
Is thy first breath, and mans *eternall Prime*.

HENRY VAUGHAN

Sure, there's a Tie of Bodies! . . .

Sure, there's a tye of Bodyes! and as they
     Dissolve (with it,) to Clay,
Love languisheth, and memory doth rust
     O'r-cast with that cold dust;
For things thus *Center'd*, without *Beames*, or *Action*
     Nor give, nor take *Contaction*,
And man is such a Marygold, these fled,
     That shuts, and hangs the head.

2

Absents within the Line Conspire, and *Sense*
    Things distant doth unite,
Herbs sleep unto the *East*, and some fowles thence
    Watch the Returns of light;
But hearts are not so kind: false, short delights
    Tell us the world is brave,
And wrap us in Imaginary flights
    Wide of a faithfull grave;
Thus *Lazarus* was carried out of town;
    For 'tis our foes chief art
By distance all good objects first to drown,
    And then besiege the heart.
But I will be my own *Deaths-head*; and though
    The flatt'rer say, *I live*,
Because Incertainties we cannot know
    Be sure, not to believe.

HENRY VAUGHAN

The Resolve

I have consider'd it; and find
    A longer stay
Is but excus'd neglect. To mind
    One path, and stray
Into another, or to none,
    Cannot be love;
When shal that traveller come home
    That will not move?
If thou wouldst thither, linger not,
    Catch at the place,
Tell youth, and beauty they must rot.
    They'r but a *Case*;
Loose, parcell'd hearts wil freeze: The Sun
    With scatter'd locks
Scarce warms, but by contraction
    Can heat rocks;

Call in thy *Powers*; run, and reach
     Home with the light,
Be there, before the shadows stretch,
     And *Span* up night;
Follow the *Cry* no more: there is
     An ancient way
All strewed with flowers, and happiness
     And fresh as *May*;
These turn, and turn no more; Let wits,
     Smile at fair eies,
Or lips; But who there weeping sits,
     Hath got the *Prize*.

         HENRY VAUGHAN

The Pilgrimage

As travellours when the twilight's come,
And in the sky the stars appear,
The past daies accidents do summe
With, *Thus wee saw there, and thus here.*

Then *Jacob*-like lodge in a place
(A place, and no more, is set down,)
Where till the day restore the race
They rest and dream homes of their own.

So for this night I linger here,
And full of tossings too and fro,
Expect stil when thou wilt appear
That I may get me up, and go.

I long, and grone, and grieve for thee,
For thee my words, my tears do gush,
O that I were but where I see!
Is all the note within my Bush

As Birds rob'd of their native wood,
Although their Diet may be fine,
Yet neither sing, nor like their food,
But with the thought of home do pine;

So do I mourn, and hang my head,
And though thou dost me fullness give,
Yet look I for far better bread
Because by this man cannot live.

O feed me then! and since I may
Have yet more days, more nights to Count,
So strengthen me, Lord, all the way,
That I may travel to thy Mount.

HENRY VAUGHAN

My Mind Keeps out the Host of Sin

My Mind keeps out the Host of Sin;
        Sense lets 'em in:
I'th Phantasie, as i' th' Trojan Horse,
        They Hide their Force.
Till opportunity they find
To Sally, and subdue the Mind.

My Childish Soule oft Cries for what
        It straight doth Hate.
My Lusts, whom Reason should Controle,
        War 'gainst my Soule;
And having got the Victory,
Bring me into Captivity.

My Love against My will is hurl'd
        Upon the World:
I See not in the Darke. I know
        Not what I Doe
When Sin besets me; so befool'd,
I hate to do even what I would.

O, when shall my lost Soule obtaine
Her Selfe againe?
To Act Her owne Hate, and Desire?
O Sacred Fire!
Refine my Heart; and that it be
Kept Pure, O Lord, I give it Thee.

EDMUND ELYS

The Maimed Debauchee

As some, brave *Admiral*, in former War
Depriv'd of Force, but prest with Courage still,
Two Rival Fleets appearing from afar,
Crawls to the top of an adjacent Hill,

From whence (with thoughts full of concern) he views
The Wise, and daring, Conduct of the Fight:
And each bold Action to his mind renews,
His present Glory, and his past Delight.

From his fierce Eyes flashes of Rage he throws,
As from black Clouds when Lightning breaks away,
Transported thinks himself amidst his Foes,
And absent, yet enjoys the bloody Day.

So when my Days of Impotence approach,
And I'me by Love and Wines unlucky chance,
Driv'n from the pleasing Billows of Debauch,
On the dull Shore of lazy Temperance.

My Pains at last some respite shall afford,
While I behold the Battels you maintain:
When Fleets of Glasses sail around the Board,
From whose Broad-Sides Volleys of Wit shall rain.

Nor shall the sight of Honourable Scars,
Which my too forward Valour did procure,
Frighten new-listed Souldiers from the Wars,
Past Joys have more than paid what I endure.

Shou'd some brave Youth (worth being drunk) prove nice,
    And from his fair inviter meanly shrink,
Twould please the Ghost of my departed Vice,
    If, at my Counsel, He repent and drink.

Or shou'd some cold-complexion'd Sot forbid,
    With his dull Morals, our Nights brisk Alarms;
I'le fire his Blood, by telling what I did,
    When I was strong, and able to bear Arms.

I'le tell of Whores attacqu'd their Lords at home,
    Bawds Quarters beaten up, and Fortress won:
Windows demolish'd, Watches overcome,
    And handsom Ills by my contrivance done.

With Tales like these I will such heat inspire,
    As to important mischief shall incline;
I'le make him long some Ancient Church to fire,
    And fear no lewdness they're call'd to by Wine.

Thus Statesman-like I'le saucily impose,
    And, safe from Danger, valiantly advise;
Shelter'd in impotence urge you to blows,
    And, being good for nothing else, be wise.

JOHN WILMOT, 2ND EARL OF ROCHESTER

from *A Hymn to the Pillory*

Hail *Hi'roglyphick*[1] State *Machin*,
Contriv'd to Punish Fancy in:
Men that are Men, in thee can feel no Pain,
And all thy *Insignificants* Disdain.
    Contempt, that false New Word for shame,
    Is without Crime an empty Name.
    A Shadow to Amuse Mankind,
But never frights the Wise or Well-fix'd Mind:
    Vertue despises Humane Scorn,
    And Scandals Innocence adorn.

Exalted on thy *Stool of State*,
What Prospect do I see of Sov'reign Fate;
How th' *Inscrutables* of Providence,
Differ from our contracted Sence;
Here by the Errors of the Town,
The Fools look out and Knaves look on.
Persons or Crimes find here the same respect,
And Vice does Vertue oft Correct,
The undistinguish'd Fury of the Street,
Which Mob and Malice Mankind Greet:
No Byass can the Rabble draw,
But *Dirt* throws *Dirt* without respect to Merit, or to Law

Sometimes the *Air of Scandal* to maintain,
Villains look from thy Lofty Loops in Vain:
But who can judge of Crimes by Punishment,
Where Parties Rule, and Laws Subservient.
Justice with Change of Int'rest Learns to bow,
And what was Merit once, is Murther now:
Actions receive their Tincture from the Times,
And as they change are Vertues made or Crimes.
Thou art the *State-Trap* of the Law,
But neither can keep Knaves, nor Honest Men in Awe;
These are too hard'nd in Offence,
And those upheld by Innocence.

How have thy opening Vacancy receiv'd,
In every Age the Criminals of State?
And how has Mankind been deceiv'd,
When they distinguish Crimes by Fate?
Tell us, *Great Engine*, how to understand,
Or reconcile the Justice of the Land;
How *Bastwick*, *Pryn*, *Hunt*, *Hollingsby* and *Pye*,
Men of unspotted Honesty;
Men that had Learning, Wit and Sence,
And more than most Men have had since,
Could equal Title to thee claim,
With *Oats* and *Fuller*, Men of later Fame:
Even the Learned *Selden* saw,
A Prospect of thee, thro' the Law:

He had thy *Lofty Pinnacles* in view,
But so much Honour never was thy due:
Had the Great *Selden* Triumph'd on thy Stage,
  Selden the Honour of his Age;
  No Man wou'd ever shun thee more,
Or grudge to stand where *Selden* stood before.

  Thou art no shame to Truth and Honesty,
Nor is the Character of such defac'd by thee,
  Who suffer by Oppressive Injury.
  Shame, like the Exhalations of the Sun,
  Falls back where first the motion was begun:
And they who for no Crime shall on thy Brows appear,
Bear less Reproach than they who plac'd 'em there.

DANIEL DEFOE

1 having a hidden meaning, i.e., concealing injustice

The Progress of Beauty

  When first Diana leaves her Bed
Vapors and Steams her Looks disgrace,
A frouzy dirty colour'd red
Sits on her cloudy wrinckled Face.

  But by degrees when mounted high
Her artificiall Face appears
Down from her Window in the Sky,
Her Spots are gone, her Visage clears.

  'Twixt earthly Femals and the Moon
All Parallells exactly run;
If Celia should appear too soon
Alas, the Nymph would be undone.

  To see her from her Pillow rise
All reeking in a cloudy Steam,
Crackt Lips, foul Teeth, and gummy Eyes,
Poor Strephon, how would he blaspheme!

The Soot or Powder which was wont
To make her Hair look black as Jet,
Falls from her Tresses on her Front
A mingled Mass of Dirt and Sweat.

Three Colours, Black, and Red, and White,
So gracefull in their proper Place,
Remove them to a diff'rent Light
They form a frightfull hideous Face,

For instance; when the Lilly slipps
Into the Precincts of the Rose,
And takes Possession of the Lips,
Leaving the Purple to the Nose.

So Celia went entire to bed,
All her Complexions safe and sound,
But when she rose, the black and red
Though still in Sight, had chang'd their Ground.

The Black, which would not be confin'd
A more inferior Station seeks
Leaving the fiery red behind,
And mingles in her muddy Cheeks.

The Paint by Perspiration cracks,
And falls in Rivulets of Sweat,
On either Side you see the Tracks,
While at her Chin the Conflu'ents met.

A Skillfull Houswife thus her Thumb
With Spittle while she spins, anoints,
And thus the brown Meanders come
In trickling Streams betwixt her Joynts.

But Celia can with ease reduce
By help of Pencil, Paint and Brush
Each Colour to it's Place and Use,
And teach her Cheeks again to blush.

She knows her Early self no more,
But fill'd with Admiration, stands,
As Other Painters oft adore
The Workmanship of their own Hands.

Thus after four important Hours
Celia's the Wonder of her Sex;
Say, which among the Heav'nly Pow'rs
Could cause such wonderfull Effects.

Venus, indulgent to her Kind
Gave Women all their Hearts could wish
When first she taught them where to find
White Lead, and Lusitanian Dish.

Love with White lead cements his Wings,
White lead was sent us to repair
Two brightest, brittlest earthly Things
A Lady's Face, and China ware.

She ventures now to lift the Sash,
The Window is her proper Sphear;
Ah Lovely Nymph be not too rash,
Nor let the Beaux approach too near.

Take Pattern by your Sister Star,
Delude at once and Bless our Sight,
When you are seen, be seen from far,
And chiefly chuse to shine by Night.

In the Pell-mell when passing by,
Keep up the Glasses of your Chair,
Then each transported Fop will cry,
G—d d—m me Jack, she's wondrous fair.

But, Art no longer can prevayl
When the Materialls all are gone,
The best Mechanick Hand must fayl
Where Nothing's left to work upon.

Matter, as wise Logicians say,
Cannot without a Form subsist,
And Form, say I, as well as They,
Must fayl if Matter brings no Grist.

And this is fair Diana's Case
For, all Astrologers maintain
Each Night a Bit drops off her Face
When Mortals say she's in her Wain.

While Partridge wisely shews the Cause
Efficient of the Moon's Decay,
That Cancer with his pois'nous Claws
Attacks her in the milky Way:

But Gadbury in Art profound
From her pale Cheeks pretends to show
That Swain Endymion is not sound,
Or else, that Mercury's her Foe.

But, let the Cause be what it will,
In half a Month she looks so thin
That Flamstead can with all his Skill
See but her Forehead and her Chin.

Yet as she wasts, she grows discreet,
Till Midnight never shows her Head;
So rotting Celia stroles the Street
When sober Folks are all a-bed.

For sure if this be Luna's Fate,
Poor Celia, but of mortall Race
In vain expects a longer Date
To the Materialls of Her Face.

When Mercury her Tresses mows
To think of Oyl and Soot, is vain,
No Painting can restore a Nose,
Nor will her Teeth return again.

Two Balls of Glass may serve for Eyes,
White Lead can plaister up a Cleft,
But there alas, are poor Supplyes
If neither Cheeks, nor Lips be left.

Ye Pow'rs who over Love preside,
Since mortal Beautyes drop so soon,
If you would have us well supply'd,
Send us new Nymphs with each new Moon.

JONATHAN SWIFT

The Lady's Dressing Room

Five Hours, (and who can do it less in?)
By haughty *Celia* spent in Dressing;
The Goddess from her Chamber issues,
Array'd in Lace, Brocades and Tissues.

Strephon, who found the Room was void,
And *Betty* otherwise employ'd;
Stole in, and took a strict Survey,
Of all the Litter as it lay;
Whereof, to make the Matter clear,
An Inventory follows here.

And first a dirty Smock appear'd,
Beneath the Arm-pits well besmear'd.
Strephon, the Rogue, display'd it wide,
And turn'd it round on every Side.
On such a Point few Words are best,
And *Strephon* bids us guess the rest;
But swears how damnably the Men lie,
In calling *Celia* sweet and cleanly.
Now listen while he next produces,
The various Combs for various Uses,
Fill'd up with Dirt so closely fixt,
No Brush could force a way betwixt.

A Paste of Composition rare,
Sweat, Dandriff, Powder, Lead and Hair;
A Forehead Cloth with Oyl upon't
To smooth the Wrinkles on her Front;
Here Allum Flower to stop the Steams,
Exhal'd from sour unsavoury Streams,
There Night-gloves made of *Tripsy*'s Hide,
Bequeath'd by *Tripsy* when she dy'd,
With Puppy Water, Beauty's Help
Distill'd from *Tripsy*'s darling Whelp;
Here Gallypots and Vials plac'd,
Some fill'd with Washes, some with Paste,
Some with Pomatum, Paints and Slops,
And Ointments good for scabby Chops.
Hard by a filthy Bason stands,
Fowl'd with the Scouring of her Hands;
The Bason takes whatever comes
The Scrapings of her Teeth and Gums,
A nasty Compound of all Hues,
For here she spits, and here she spues.
But oh! it turn'd poor *Strephon*'s Bowels,
When he beheld and smelt the Towels,
Begumm'd, bematter'd, and beslim'd
With Dirt, and Sweat, and Ear-Wax grim'd.
No Object *Strephon*'s Eye escapes,
Here Pettycoats in frowzy Heaps;
Nor be the Handkerchiefs forgot
All varnish'd o'er with Snuff and Snot.
The Stockings, why shou'd I expose,
Stain'd with the Marks of stinking Toes;
Or greasy Coifs and Pinners reeking,
Which *Celia* slept at least a Week in?
A Pair of Tweezers next he found
To pluck her Brows in Arches round,
Or Hairs that sink the Forehead low,
Or on her Chin like Bristles grow.

The Virtues we must not let pass,
Of *Celia*'s magnifying Glass.
When frighted *Strephon* cast his Eye on't

It shew'd the Visage of a Gyant.
A Glass that can to Sight disclose,
The smallest Worm in *Celia*'s Nose,
And faithfully direct her Nail
To squeeze it out from Head to Tail;
For catch it nicely by the Head,
It must come out alive or dead.

Why *Strephon* will you tell the rest?
And must you needs describe the Chest?
That careless Wench! no Creature warn her
To move it out from yonder Corner;
But leave it standing full in Sight
For you to exercise your Spight.
In vain, the Workmen shew'd his Wit
With Rings and Hinges counterfeit
To make it seem in this Disguise,
A Cabinet to vulgar Eyes;
For *Strephon* ventur'd to look in,
Resolv'd to go thro' thick and thin;
He lifts the Lid, there needs no more,
He smelt it all the Time before.
As from within *Pandora*'s Box,
When *Epimetheus* op'd the Locks,
A sudden universal Crew
Of humane Evils upwards flew;
He still was comforted to find
That *Hope* at last remain'd behind;
So *Strephon* lifting up the Lid,
To view what in the Chest was hid.
The Vapours flew from out the Vent,
But *Strephon* cautious never meant
The Bottom of the Pan to grope,
And fowl his Hands in Search of *Hope*.
O never may such vile Machine
Be once in *Celia*'s Chamber seen!
O may she better learn to keep
'Those Secrets of the hoary deep'!

As Mutton Cutlets, Prime of Meat,
Which tho' with Art you salt and beat,

As Laws of Cookery require,
And toast them at the clearest Fire;
If from adown the hopeful Chops
The Fat upon a Cinder drops,
To stinking Smoak it turns the Flame
Pois'ning the Flesh from whence it came;
And up exhales a greasy Stench,
For which you curse the careless Wench;
So Things, which must not be exprest,
When plumpt into the reeking Chest;
Send up an excremental Smell
To taint the Parts from whence they fell.
The Pettycoats and Gown perfume,
Which waft a Stink round every Room.

Thus finishing his grand Survey,
Disgusted *Strephon* stole away
Repeating in his amorous Fits,
Oh! *Celia, Celia, Celia* shits!

But Vengeance, Goddess never sleeping
Soon punish'd *Strephon* for his Peeping;
His foul Imagination links
Each Dame he sees with all her Stinks:
And, if unsav'ry Odours fly,
Conceives a Lady standing by:
All Women his Description fits,
And both Idea's jump like Wits:
By vicious Fancy coupled fast,
And still appearing in Contrast.
I pity wretched *Strephon* blind
To all the Charms of Female Kind;
Should I the Queen of Love refuse,
Because she rose from stinking Ooze?
To him that looks behind the Scene,
Satira's but some pocky Quean.
When *Celia* in her Glory shows,
If *Strephon* would but stop his Nose;
(Who now so impiously blasphemes
Her Ointments, Daubs, and Paints and Creams,

Her Washes, Slops, and every Clout,
With which he makes so foul a Rout;)
He soon would learn to think like me,
And bless his ravisht Sight to see
Such Order from Confusion sprung,
Such gaudy Tulips rais'd from Dung.

JONATHAN SWIFT

Shall I Repine

If neither brass nor marble can withstand
The mortal force of Time's dystructive hand
If mountains sink to vales, if cityes dye
And lessening rivers mourn their fountains dry
When my old cassock says a Welch divine
Is out at elbows why should I repine?

JONATHAN SWIFT

A Libel on D[octor] D[elaney] and a certain great Lord

Deluded Mortals, whom the *Great*
Chuse for Companions *tete à tete*,
Who at their Dinners, *en famille*
Get Leave to sit whene'er you will;
Then, boasting tell us where you din'd,
And, how his *Lordship* was so kind;
How many pleasant Things he spoke,
And, how you *laugh'd* at every *Joke*:
Swear, he's a most facetious Man,
That you and he are *Cup* and *Cann*.
You Travel with a heavy Load,
And quite mistake *Preferment*'s Road.

Suppose my *Lord* and you alone;
Hint the least Int'rest of your own;
His Visage drops, he knits his Brow,
He cannot talk of Bus'ness now;
Or, mention but a vacant *Post*,
He'll turn it off with; *Name your Toast*.
Nor could the nicest Artist Paint,
A Countenance with more Constraint.

For, as their Appetites to quench,
Lords keep a Pimp to bring a Wench;
So, Men of Wit are but a kind
Of Pandars to a vicious Mind,
Who proper Objects must provide
To gratify their Lust of Pride,
When weary'd with Intrigues of State,
They find an idle Hour to Prate.
Then, shou'd you dare to ask a *Place*,
You Forfeit all your *Patron*'s Grace,
And disappoint the sole Design,
For which he summon'd you to *Dine*.

Thus, *Congreve* spent, in writing Plays,
And one poor Office, half his Days;
While *Montague*, who claim'd the Station
To be *Maecenas* of the Nation,
For *Poets* open Table kept,
But ne'er consider'd where they Slept.
Himself, as rich as fifty *Jews*,
Was easy, though they wanted Shoes;
And, crazy *Congreve* scarce cou'd spare
A Shilling to discharge his Chair,
Till Prudence taught him to appeal
From *Paean*'s Fire to *Party* Zeal;
Not owing to his happy Vein
The Fortunes of his latter Scene,
Took proper *Principles* to thrive;
And so might ev'ry *Dunce* alive.

Thus, *Steel* who own'd what others writ,
And flourish'd by imputed Wit,

From Lodging in a hundred Jayls,
Was left to starve, and dye in *Wales.*

Thus *Gay,* the *Hare* with many Friends,
Twice sev'n long Years the *Court* attends,
Who, under Tales conveying Truth,
To Virtue form'd a *Princely* Youth,
Who pay'd his Courtship with the Croud,
As far as *Modest Pride* allow'd,
Rejects a servile *Usher*'s Place,
And leaves *St. James*'s in Disgrace.

Thus *Addison* by Lords Carest,
Was left in Foreign Lands distrest,
Forgot at Home, became for Hire,
A trav'lling Tutor to a *Squire;*
But, wisely left the *Muses* Hill,
To Bus'ness shap'd the *Poet*'s Quil,
Let all his barren Lawrel's fade
Took up himself the *Courtier*'s Trade,
And grown a *Minister of State,*
Saw Poets at his Levee wait.

Hail! happy *Pope,* whose gen'rous Mind,
Detesting all the Statesmen kind,
Contemning *Courts,* at *Courts* unseen,
Refus'd the Visits of a Queen;
A Soul with ev'ry Virtue fraught
By *Sages, Priests,* or *Poets* taught;
Whose filial Piety excels
Whatever *Grecian* Story tells:
A Genius for all Stations fit,
Whose *meanest Talent* is his *Wit:*
His Heart too Great, though Fortune little,
To lick a *Rascal Statesman*'s Spittle.
Appealing to the Nation's Taste,
Above the Reach of Want is plac't:
By *Homer* dead was taught to thrive,
Which *Homer* never cou'd alive.
And, sits aloft on *Pindus* Head,
Despising *Slaves* that *cringe* for Bread.

True *Politicians* only Pay
For solid Work, but not for Play;
Nor ever chuse to Work with Tools
Forg'd up in *Colleges* and *Schools.*
Consider how much more is due
To all their *Journey-Men*, than you,
At Table you can *Horace* quote;
They at a Pinch can bribe a Vote:
You shew your Skill in *Grecian* Story.
But, they can manage *Whig* and *Tory:*
You, as a *Critick*, are so curious
To find a Verse in *Virgil* Spurious;
But, they can *smoak* the deep Designs,
When *Bolingbroke* with *Pult'ney* Dines.

Besides; your Patron may upbraid ye,
That you have got a Place already,
An Officer for your Talents fit,
To Flatter, Carve, and shew your Wit;
To snuff the Lights, and stir the Fire,
And get a *Dinner* for your Hire,
What Claim have you to *Place*, or *Pension?*
He overpays in Condescension.

But, Rev'rend *Doctor*, you, we know,
Cou'd never Condescend so low;
The *Vice-Roy*, whom you now attend,
Wou'd, if he durst, be more your Friend;
Nor will in you those Gifts despise,
By which himself was taught to rise:
When he has Virtue to retire,
He'll Grieve he did not raise you higher,
And place you in a better Station,
Although it might have pleas'd the Nation.

This may be true—submitting still
To W—'s more than R—l Will.
And what Condition can be worse?
He comes to *drain* a *Beggar's Purse:*
He comes to tye our Chains on faster,
And shew us, *E——* is our Master:

Caressing Knaves and Dunces wooing,
To make them work their own undoing.
What has he else to bait his Traps,
Or bring his *Vermin* in, but *Scraps?*
The Offals of a *Church* distress't,
A hungry *Vicarage* at best;
Or, some remote inferior *Post,*
With forty Pounds a Year at most.

But, here again you interpose;
Your favourite *Lord* is none of those,
Who owe their Virtues to their Stations,
And Characters to Dedications:
For keep him in, or turn him out,
His *Learning* none will call in doubt;
His *Learning*, though a *Poet* said it,
Before a Play, wou'd lose no Credit:
Nor POPE wou'd dare deny him Wit,
Although to Praise it PHILIPS Writ.
I own, he hates an Action base,
His *Virtues* battling with his *Place;*
Nor wants a nice discerning Spirit,
Betwixt a true and spurious Merit;
Can sometimes drop a *Voter*'s Claim,
And give up Party to his Fame.
I do the most that *Friendship* can;
I hate the *Vice-Roy*, love the Man.

But, You, who till your Fortune's made
Must be a Sweet'ner by your Trade,
Shou'd swear he never meant us ill;
We suffer sore against his Will;
That, if we could but see his Heart,
He wou'd have chose a milder part;
We rather should Lament his Case
Who must Obey, or lose his *Place.*

Since this Reflection slipt your Pen,
Insert it when you write agen:
And, to Illustrate it, produce
This *Simile* for his Excuse.

'So, to destroy a guilty Land,
'An *Angel* sent by *Heav'n*'s Command,
'While he obeys *Almighty* Will,
'Perhaps, may feel *Compassion* still,
'And wish the Task had been assign'd
'To *Spirits* of less gentle kind.

But I, in *Politicks* grown old,
Whose Thoughts are of a diff'rent Mold,
Who, from my Soul, sincerely hate
Both —— and *Ministers* of *State*,
Who look on *Courts* with stricter Eyes,
To see the Seeds of *Vice* arise,
Can lend you an Allusion fitter,
Though *flatt'ring Knaves* may call it *bitter*.
Which, if you durst but give it place,
Would shew you many a *Statesman*'s Face.
Fresh from the *Tripod* of Apollo,
I had it in the Words that follow.
(Take Notice, to avoid Offence
I here except *His Excellence*.)

So, to effect his *M—h*'s ends,
From *Hell* a *V—* dev'l ascends,
His *Budget* with *Corruptions* cramm'd,
The Contributions of the *damn'd*;
Which with unsparing Hand, he strows
Through *Courts* and *Senates* as he goes;
And then at *Beelzebub*'s *Black-Hall*,
Complains his *Budget* was too small.

Your *Simile* may better shine
In Verse; but there is *Truth* in mine.
For, no imaginable things
Can differ more than God and ——
And, *Statesmen* by ten thousand odds
Are Angels, just as —— are Gods.

JONATHAN SWIFT

Verses wrote in a lady's ivory table-book

Peruse my Leaves thro' ev'ry Part,
And think thou seest my owners Heart,
Scrawl'd o'er with Trifles thus, and quite
As hard, as sensless, and as light:
Expos'd to every Coxcomb's Eyes,
But hid with Caution from the Wise.
Here you may read (*Dear Charming Saint*)
Beneath (*A new Receit for Paint*)
Here in Beau-spelling (*tru tel deth*)
There in her own (*far an el breth*)
Here (*lovely Nymph pronounce my doom*)
There (*A safe way to use Perfume*)
Here, a Page fill'd with Billet Doux;
On t'other side (*laid out for Shoes*)
(*Madam, I dye without your Grace*)
(Item, *for half a Yard of Lace.*)
Who that had Wit would place it here,
For every peeping Fop to Jear.
To think that your Brains Issue is
Expos'd to th' Excrement of his,
In power of Spittle and a Clout
When e're he please to blot it out;
And then to heighten the Disgrace
Clap his own Nonsense in the place.
Whoe're expects to hold his part
In such a Book and such a Heart,
If he be Wealthy and a Fool
Is in all Points the fittest Tool,
Of whom it may be justly said,
He's a Gold Pencil tipt with Lead.

                    JONATHAN SWIFT

Epigram

Lord *Pam* in the Church (cou'd you think it) kneel'd down,
When told the Lieutenant was just come to Town,
His *Station* despising, unaw'd by the *Place*,
He flies from his *God*, to attend on his *Grace:*
To the *Court* it was fitter to pay his *Devotion*,
Since *God* had no Hand in his Lordship's *Promotion*.

JONATHAN SWIFT

Verses made for Women who cry Apples, &c.

APPLES

Come buy my fine Wares,
Plumbs, Apples and Pears,
A hundred a Penny,
In Conscience too many,
Come, will you have any;
My Children are seven,
I wish them in Heaven,
My Husband's a Sot,
With his Pipe and his Pot,
Not a Farthing will gain 'em,
And I must maintain 'em.

ASPARAGUS

Ripe 'Sparagrass,
Fit for Lad or Lass,
To make their Water pass:
O, 'tis pretty Picking
With a tender Chicken.

ONYONS

Come, follow me by the Smell,
Here's delicate Onyons to sell,
I promise to use you well.
They make the Blood warmer,
You'll feed like a Farmer:
For this is ev'ry Cook's Opinion,
No sav'ry Dish without an Onyon;
But lest your Kissing should be spoyl'd,
Your Onyons must be th'roughly boyl'd;
    Or else you may spare
    Your Mistress a Share,
The Secret will never be known;
    She cannot discover
    The Breath of her Lover,
But think it as sweet as her own.

OYSTERS

Charming Oysters I cry,
My Masters come buy,
So plump and so fresh,
So sweet is their Flesh,
No *Colchester* Oyster,
Is sweeter and moyster,
Your Stomach they settle,
And rouse up your Mettle,
They'll make you a Dad
Of a Lass or a Lad;
And, Madam your Wife
They'll please to the Life;
Be she barren, be she old,
Be she Slut, or be she Scold,
Eat my Oysters, and lye near her,
She'll be fruitful, never fear her.

HERRINGS

Be not sparing,
Leave off swearing
Buy my Herring

Fresh from *Malahide*,
Better ne'er was try'd.
Come eat 'em with pure fresh Butter and Mustard,
Their Bellies are soft, and as white as a Custard.
Come, Six-pence a Dozen to get me some Bread,
Or, like my own Herrings, I soon shall be dead.

ORANGES

Come, buy my fine Oranges, Sauce for your Veal,
And charming when squeez'd in a Pot of brown Ale.
Well roasted, with Sugar and Wine in a Cup,
They'll make a sweet Bishop when Gentlefolks sup.

JONATHAN SWIFT

A Maypole

Depriv'd of Root, and Branch, and Rind,
Yet Flow'rs I bear of ev'ry Kind;
And such is my prolific Pow'r,
They bloom in less than half an Hour:
Yet Standers-by may plainly see
They get no Nourishment from me.
My Head, with Giddiness, goes round;
And yet I firmly stand my Ground:
All over naked I am seen,
And painted like an *Indian* Queen.
No Couple-Beggar in the Land
E'er join'd such Numbers Hand in Hand;
I join them fairly with a *Ring*;
Nor can our Parson blame the Thing:
And tho' no Marriage Words are spoke,
They part not till the *Ring* is broke.
Yet hypocrite Fanaticks cry,
I'm but an Idol rais'd on high;
And once a Weaver in our Town,
A damn'd *Cromwellian*, knock'd me down.

I lay a Prisoner twenty Years;
And then the Jovial Cavaliers
To their old Posts restor'd all Three,
I mean the Church, the King, and Me.

JONATHAN SWIFT

Tophet

Thus Etough looked; so grinned the brawling fiend,
While frighted prelates bowed and called him friend;
I saw them bow, and while they wished him dead,
With servile simper nod the mitred head.
Our mother-church, with half-averted sight,
Blushed as she blessed her grisly proselyte;
Hosannas rung through hell's tremendous borders,
And Satan's self had thoughts of taking orders.

THOMAS GRAY

Impromptu

SUGGESTED BY A VIEW, IN 1766, OF THE SEAT AND
   RUINS OF A DECEASED NOBLEMAN, AT KINGS-
   GATE, KENT.

Old, and abandoned by each venal friend,
   Here Holland formed the pious resolution
To smuggle a few years, and strive to mend
   A broken character and constitution.

On this congenial spot he fixed his choice;
   Earl Goodwin trembled for his neighbouring sand;
Here sea-gulls scream, and cormorants rejoice,
   And mariners, though shipwrecked, dread to land.

Here reign the blustering North and blighting East,
    No tree is heard to whisper, bird to sing;
Yet Nature could not furnish out the feast,
    Art he invokes new horrors still to bring.

Here mouldering fanes and battlements arise,
    Turrets and arches nodding to their fall,
Unpeopled monast'ries delude our eyes,
    And mimic desolation covers all.

'Ah!' said the sighing peer, 'had Bute been true,
    Nor Mungo's, Rigby's, Bradshaw's friendship vain,
Far better scenes than these had blest our view,
    And realised the beauties which we feign;

'Purged by the sword, and purified by fire,
    Then had we seen proud London's hated walls;
Owls would have hooted in St. Peter's choir,
    And foxes stunk and littered in St. Paul's.'

THOMAS GRAY

The Citizen and the Red Lion of Brentford

I love my friend—but love my ease,
And claim a right myself to please
To company however prone.
At times all men wou'd be alone,
Free from each interruption rude
Or what is meant by solitude.
My villa lies within the bills.
So—like a theatre it fills:
To me my kind acquaintance stray,
And Sunday proves no sabbath day:
Yet many a friend and near relation.
Make up a glorious congregation;
They crowd by dozens and by dozens,
And bring me all their country cousins.

Though cringing landlords on the road,
Who find for man and horse abode;
Though gilded grapes to sign-post chain'd,
Invite them to be entertain'd,
And straddling cross his kilderkin,
Though jolly Bacchus calls them in;
Nay—though my landlady wou'd trust 'em,
Pilgarlic's sure of all the custom;
And his whole house is like a fair,
Unless he only treats with air.
What? shall each pert half witted wit,
That calls me Jack, or calls me Kit,
Prey on my time, or on my table?
No—but let's hasten to the fable.
      The eve advanc'd, the Sun declin'd,
Ball to the booby-hutch was join'd,
A wealthy cockney drove away,
To celebrate Saint Saturday;
Wife, daughter, pug, all crouded in,
To meet at country house their kin.
Thro' Brentford, to fair Twickenham's bow'rs,
The ungreas'd grumbling axle scow'rs,
To pass in rural sweets a day,
But there's a lion in the way:
This lion a most furious elf,
Hung up to represent himself,
Redden'd with rage, and shook his mane,
And roar'd, and roar'd, and roar'd again.
Wond'rous, tho' painted on a board,
He roar'd, and roar'd, and roar'd, and roar'd.
'Fool!' (says the majesty of beasts)
'At whose expense a legion feasts,
Foe to yourself, you those pursue,
Who're eating up your cakes and you;
Yes, he shall roost upon my toilet,
Or on my pillow—he can't spoil it,
He'll only make me catch my death.
O Heavens! for a little breath!
Thank God, I never knew resentment,
But am all patience and contentment.

Or else, you paltry knave, I shou'd
(As any other woman wou'd)
Wring off his neck, and down your gullet
Cram it, by way of chick or pullet.—
Well, I must lock up all my rings,
My jewels, and my curious things:
My Chinese toys must go to pot;
My dear, my pinchbecks—and what not?
For all your magpies are, like lawyers,
At once thieves, brawlers, and destroyers.—
You for a wife have search'd the globe.
You've got a very female Job,
Pattern of love, and peace, and unity,
Or how cou'd you expect impunity?
O Lord! this nasty thing will bite,
And scratch and clapper, claw and fight.
O monstrous wretch, thus to devise,
To tear out your poor Sylvia's eyes.
You're a fine Popish plot pursuing,
By presents to affect my ruin;
And thus for good are ill retorting
To ME, who brought you such a fortune;
To ME, you low-liv'd clown, to ME,
Who came of such a family;
ME, who fromage to age p ossess'd
A lion rampant on my crest;
ME, who have fill'd your empty coffers.
ME, who'd so many better offers;
And is my merit thus regarded,
Cuckold, my virtue thus rewarded.
O 'tis past sufferance—Mary—Mary,
I faint—the citron, or the clary.'
    The poor man, who had brought the creature,
Out of pure conjugal good-nature,
Stood at this violent attack.
Like statues made by Roubilliac.
Though form'd beyond all skill antique,
They can't their marble silence break;
They only breathe, and think, and start,
Astonish'd at their maker's art.

Quoth Mag, 'Fair Grizzle, I must grant,
Your spouse a magpye cannot want:
For troth (to give the Dev'l his due)
He keeps a rookery in you.
Don't fear I'll tarry long, sweet lady,
Where there is din enough already,
We never should agree together,
Although we're so much of a feather;
You're fond of peace, no man can doubt it,
Who make such wond'rous noise about it;
And your tongue of immortal mould
Proclaims in thunder you're no scold.
Yes, yes, you're sovereign of the tongue,
And like the king can do no wrong;
Iustly your spouse restrains his voice,
Nor vainly answers words with noise;
This storm, which no soul can endure,
Requires a very different cure;
For such sour verjuice dispositions,
Your crabsticks are the best physicians.'

CHRISTOPHER SMART

from *Jubilate Agno*

III

Let Tobias bless Charity with his Dog, who is faithful, vigilant, and a friend in poverty.

Let Anna bless God with the Cat, who is worthy to be presented before the throne of grace, when he has trampled upon the idol in his prank.

Let Benaiah praise with the Asp—to conquer malice is nobler, than to slay the lion.

Let Barzillai bless with Snail—a friend in need is as the balm of Gilead, or as the slime to the wounded bark.

Let Joab with the Horse worship the Lord God of Hosts

Let Shemaiah bless God with the Caterpillar—the minister of vengeance is the harbinger of mercy.

Let Ahimelech with the Locust bless God from the tyranny of numbers

Let Cornelius with the Swine bless God, which purifyeth all things for the poor.

Let Araunah bless with the Squirrel, which is a gift of homage from the poor man to the wealthy and increaseth goodwill.

Let Bakbakkar bless with the Salamander, which feedeth upon ashes as bread, and whose joy is at the mouth of the furnace.

Let Jabez bless with Tarantula, who maketh his bed in the moss, which he feedeth, that the pilgrim may take heed to his way.

Let Jakim with the Satyr bless God in the dance.

Let Iddo praise the Lord with the Moth—the writings of man perish as the garment, but the Book of God endureth for ever.

Let Nebuchadnezzar bless with the Grasshopper—the pomp and vanities of the World are as the herb of the field, but the glory of the Lord increaseth for ever.

Let Naboth bless with the Canker-worm—envy is cruel and killeth & preyeth upon that which God has given to aspire and bear fruit.

Let Lud bless with the Elk, the strenuous asserter of his liberty, and the maintainer of his ground.

Let Obadiah with the Palmer-worm bless God for the remnant that is left.

Let Agur bless with the Cockatrice—The consolation of the world is deceitful, and temporal honour the crown of him that creepeth.

Let Ithiel bless with the Baboon, whose motions are regular in the wilderness, and who defendeth himself with a staff against the assailant.

Let Ucal bless with the Cameleon, which feedeth on the Flowers and washeth himself in the dew.

Let Lemuel bless with the Wolf, which is a dog without a master, but the Lord hears his cries and feeds him in the desert.

Let Hananiah bless with the Civet, which is pure from benevolence.

Let Azarias bless with the Reindeer, who runneth upon the waters, and wadeth thro' the land in snow.

Let Mishael bless with the Stoat—the praise of the Lord gives propriety to all things.

Let Savaran bless with the Elephant, who gave his life for his country that he might put on immortality.

Let Nehemiah the imitator of God bless with the Monkey, who is workd down from Man.

Let Manasses bless with the Wild-Ass—liberty begetteth insolence, but necessity is the mother of prayer.

Let Jebus bless with the Camelopard, which is good to carry and to parry and to kneel.

Let Huz bless with the Polypus—lively subtlety is acceptable to the Lord.

Let Buz bless with the Jackall—but the Lord is the Lion's provider.

VII

For I am not without authority in my jeopardy, which I derive inevitably from the glory of the name of the Lord.

For I bless God whose name is Jealous—and there is a zeal to deliver us from everlasting burnings.

For in my existimation is good even amongst the slanderers and my memory shall arise for a sweet savour unto the Lord.

For I bless the PRINCE of PEACE and pray that all the guns may be nail'd up, save such are for the rejoicing days.

For I have abstained from the blood of the grape and that even at the Lord's table.

For I have glorified God in GREEK and LATIN, the consecrated languages spoken by the Lord on earth.

For I meditate the peace of Europe amongst family bickerings and domestic jars.

For the HOST is in the WEST—The Lord make us thankful unto salvation.

For I preach the very GOSPEL of CHRIST without comment & with this weapon shall I slay envy.

For I bless God in the rising generation, which is on my side.

For I have translated in the charity, which makes things better & I shall be translated myself at the last.

For he that walked upon the sea, hath prepared the floods with the Gospel of peace.

For the merciful man is merciful to his beast, and to the trees that give them shelter.

For he hath turned the shadow of death into the morning, the Lord
is his name.

For I am come home again, but there is nobody to kill the calf or to
pay the musick.

For the hour of my felicity, like the womb of Sarah, shall come at
the latter end.

For I shou'd have avail'd myself of waggery, had not malice been
multitudinous.

For there are still serpents that can speak—God bless my head, my
heart & my heel.

For I bless God that I am of the same seed with Ehud, Mutius Scaevola
and Colonel Draper.

For the word of God is a sword on my side—no matter what other
weapon a stick or a straw.

For I have adventured myself in the name of the Lord, and he hath
mark'd me for his own.

For I bless God for the Postmaster general & all conveyancers of
letters under his care especially Allen & Shevlock.

For my grounds in New Canaan shall infinitely compensate for the
flats & maynes of Staindrop Moor.

For the praise of God can give to a mute fish the notes of a nightin-
gale.

For I have seen the White Raven & Thomas Hall of Willingham &
am myself a greater curiosity than both.

For I look up to heaven which is my prospect to escape envy by
surmounting it.

For if Pharaoh had known Joseph, he would have blessed God & me
for the illumination of the people.

For I pray God to bless improvements in gardening till London be a
city of palm-trees.

For I pray to give his grace to the poor of England, that Charity be
not offended & that benevolence may increase.

For in my nature I quested for beauty, but God, God hath sent me to
sea for pearls.

For there is a blessing from the STONE of JESUS which is founded upon
hell to the precious jewell on the right hand of God.

For the nightly Visitor is at the window of the impenitent, while I
sing a psalm of my own composing.

For there is a note added to the scale, which the Lord hath made fuller,
stronger & more glorious.

For I offer my goat as he browses the vine, bless the Lord from chambering & drunkeness.

For there is a traveling for the glory of God without going to Italy or France.

For I bless the children of Asher for the evil I did them & the good I might have received at their hands.

For I rejoice like a worm in the rain in him that cherishes and from him that tramples.

For I am ready for the trumpet & alarm to fight to die & to rise again.

For the banish'd of the Lord shall come about again, for so he hath prepared for them.

For sincerity is a jewel which is pure & transparent, eternal & inestimable.

For my hands and my feet are perfect as the sublimity of Naphtali and the felicity of Asher.

For the names and number of animals are as the names and number of the stars.

For I pray the Lord Jesus to translate my MAGNIFICAT into verse and represent it.

For I bless the Lord Jesus from the bottom of Royston Cave to the top of King's Chapel.

For I am a little fellow, which is intitled to the great mess by the benevolence of God my father.

For I this day made over my inheritance to my mother in consideration of her infirmities.

For I this day made over my inheritance to my mother in consideration of her age.

For I this day made over my inheritance to my mother in consideration of her poverty.

For I bless the thirteenth of August, in which I had the grace to obey the voice of Christ in my conscience.

For I bless the thirteenth of August, in which I was willing to run all hazards for the sake of the name of the Lord.

For I bless the thirteenth of August, in which Lord I was willing to be called a fool for the sake of Christ.

For I lent my flocks and my herds and my lands at once unto the Lord.

For nature is more various than observation tho' observers be innumerable.

For Agricola is Γ'εωργος.

For I pray God to bless POLLY in the blessing of Naomi and assign her to the house of DAVID.

For I am in charity with the French who are my foes and Moabites because of the Moabitish woman.

For my Angel is always ready at a pinch to help me out and to keep me up.

For CHRISTOPHER must slay the Dragon with a PAEON's head.

For they have seperated me and my bosom, whereas the right comes by setting us together.

For Silly fellow! Silly fellow! is against me and belongeth neither to me nor my family.

For he that scorneth the scorner hath condescended to my low estate.

For Abiah is the father of Joab and Joab of all Romans and English Men.

For they pass by me in their tour, and the good Samaritan is not yet come.

For I bless God in the behalf of TRINITY COLLEGE in CAMBRIDGE & the society of PURPLES in LONDON.

For I have a nephew CHRISTOPHER to whom I implore the grace of God.

For I pray God bless the CAM—Mr. HIGGS & Mr. & Mrs. WASHBOURNE as the drops of the dew.

For I pray God bless the king of Sardinia and make him an instrument of his peace.

For I am possessed of a cat, surpassing in beauty, from whom I take occasion to bless Almighty God.

For I pray God for the professors of the University of Cambridge to attend & to amend.

For the Fatherless Children and widows are never deserted of the Lord.

XIX

For the Greek & Latin are not dead languages, but taken up & accepted for the sake of him that spake them.

For can is (canis) is cause & effect a dog.

For the English, is concise & strong. Dog & Bull again.

For Newton's notion of colours is αλογος; unphilosophical.

For the colours are spiritual.

For WHITE is the first and the best.

For there are many intermediate colours before you come to
　SILVER.

For the next colour is a lively GREY.

For the next colour is BLUE.

For the next is GREEN of which there are ten thousand distinct
　sorts.

For the next is YELLOW which is more excellent than red, tho Newton
　makes red the prime. God be gracious to John Delap.

For RED is the next working round the Orange.

For Red is of sundry sorts till it deepens to BLACK.

For black blooms and it is PURPLE.

For purple works off to BROWN which is of ten thousand acceptable
　shades.

For the next is PALE. God be gracious to William Whitehead.

For pale works about to White again.

NOW that colour is spiritual appears inasmuch as the blessing of God
　upon all things descends in colour.

For the blessing of health upon the human face is in colour.

For the blessing of God upon purity is in the Virgin's blushes.

For the blessing of God in colour is on him that keeps his virgin.

For I saw a blush in Staindrop Church, which was of God's own
　colouring.

For it was the benevolence of a virgin shewn to me before the whole
　congregation.

For the blessing of God upon the grass is in shades of Green visible to
　a nice observer as they light upon the surface of the earth.

For the blessing of God unto perfection in all bloom & fruit is by
　colouring.

For from hence something in the spirit may be taken off by
　painters.

For Painting is a species of idolatry, tho' not so gross as statuary.

For it is not good to look with earning upon any dead work.

For by so doing something is lost in the spirit & given from life to
　death.

For BULL in the first place is the word of Almighty God.

For he is a creature of infinite magnitude in the height.

For there is the model of every beast of the field in the height.

For they are blessed intelligences & all angels of the living God.

For there are many words under Bull.

For Bull the Month is under it.

For Sea is under Bull.

For Brook is under Bull. God be gracious to Lord Bolinbroke.

For Rock is under Bull.

For Bullfinch is under Bull. God be gracious to the Duke of Cleveland.

For God, which always keeps his work in view has painted a Bullfinch in the heart of a stone. God be gracious to Gosling and Canterbury.

For the Bluecap is under Bull.

For the Humming Bird is under Bull.

For Beetle is under Bull.

For Toad is under Bull.

For Frog is under Bull, which he has a delight to look at.

For the Pheasant-eyed Pink is under Bull. Blessed Jesus RANK EL.

For Bugloss is under Bull.

For Bugle is under Bull.

For Oxeye is under Bull.

For Fire is under Bull.

For I will consider my Cat Jeoffry.

For he is the servant of the Living God, duly and daily serving him.

For at the first glance of the glory of God in the East he worships in his way.

For is this done by wreathing his body seven times round with elegant quickness.

For then he leaps up to catch the musk, which is the blessing of God upon his prayer.

For he rolls upon prank to work it in.

For having done duty and received blessing he begins to consider himself.

For this he performs in ten degrees.

For first he looks upon his fore-paws to see if they are clean.

For secondly he kicks up behind to clear away there.

XX

For thirdly he works it upon stretch with the fore paws extended.

For fourthly he sharpens his claws by wood.

For fifthly he washes himself.

For sixthly he rolls upon wash.

For Seventhly he fleas himself, that he may not be interrupted upon
the beat.

For Eighthly he rubs himself against a post.

For Ninthly he looks up for his instructions.

Tor Tenthly he goes in quest of food.

For having consider'd God and himself he will consider his neighbour.

For if he meets another cat he will kiss her in kindness.

For when he takes his prey he plays with it to give it chance.

For one mouse in seven escapes by his dallying.

For when his day's work is done his business more properly
begins.

For keeps the Lord's watch in the night against the adversary.

For he counteracts the powers of darkness by his electrical skin &
glaring eyes.

For he counteracts the Devil, who is death, by brisking about the
life.

For in his morning orisons he loves the sun and the sun loves him.

For he is of the tribe of Tiger.

For the Cherub Cat is a term of the Angel Tiger.

For he has the subtlety and hissing of a serpent, which in goodness he
suppresses.

For he will not do destruction, if he is well-fed, neither will be spit
without provocation.

For he purrs in thankfulness, when God tells him he's a good Cat.

For he is an instrument for the children to learn benevolence upon.

For every house is incompleat without him & a blessing is lacking in
the spirit.

For the Lord commanded Moses concerning the cats at the departure
of the children of Israel from Egypt.

For every family had one cat at least in the bag.

For the English Cats are the best in Europe.

For he is the cleanest in the use of his fore-paws of any quadrupede.

For the dexterity of his defence is an instance of the love of God to
him exceedingly.

For he is the quickest to his mark of any creature.

For he is tenacious of his point.

For he is a mixture of gravity and waggery.

For he knows that God is his Saviour.

For there is nothing sweeter than his peace when at rest.

For there is nothing brisker than his life when in motion.

For he is of the Lord's poor and so indeed is he called by benevolence
perpetually—Poor Jeoffry! poor Jeoffry! the rat has bit thy throat.

For I bless the name of the Lord Jesus that Jeoffry is better.

For the divine spirit comes about his body to sustain it in compleat
cat.

For his tongue is exceeding pure so that it has in purity what it wants
in musick.

For he is docile and can learn certain things.

For he can set up with gravity which is patience upon approbation.

For he can fetch and carry, which is patience in employment.

For he can jump over a stick which is patience upon proof positive.

For he can spraggle upon waggle at the word of command.

For he can jump from an eminence into his master's bosom.

For he can catch the cork and toss it again.

For he is hated by the hypocrite and miser.

For the former is afraid of detection.

For the latter refuses the charge.

For he camels his back to bear the first notion of business.

For he is good to look on, if a man would express himself neatly.

For he made a great figure in Egypt for his signal service.

For he killed the Icneumon-rat very pernicious by land.

For his ears are so acute that they sting again.

For from this proceeds the passing quickness of his attention.

For by stroaking of him I have found out electricity.

For I perceived God's light about him both wax and fire.

For the Electrical fire is the spiritual substance, which God sends from
heaven to sustain the bodies both of man and beast.

For God has blessed him in the variety of his movements.

For, tho he cannot fly, he is an excellent clamberer.

For his motions upon the face of the earth are more than any other
quadrupede.

For he can tread to all measures upon the musick.

For he can swim for life.

For he can creep.

CHRISTOPHER SMART

Night

When foes insult, and *prudent* friends dispense,
In pity's strains, the worst of insolence,
Oft with thee, LLOYD, I steal an hour from grief,
And in thy social converse find relief.
The mind, of solitude impatient grown,
Loves any sorrows rather than her own.

   Let slaves to business, bodies without soul,
Important blanks in Nature's mighty roll,
Solemnize nonsense in the day's broad glare,
We NIGHT prefer, which heals or hides, our care.

   Rogues justified and by success made bold,
Dull fools and coxcombs sanctified by Gold,
Freely may bask in fortune's partial ray,
And spread their feathers op'ning to the day;
But *thread-bare* Merit dares not shew the head
'Till vain Prosperity retires to bed.
Misfortunes, like the Owl, avoid the light;
The sons of CARE are always sons of NIGHT.

   The Wretch bred up in Method's drowsy school,
Whose only merit is to err by rule,
Who ne'er thro' heat of blood was tripping caught,
 Nor guilty deem'd of one eccentric thought,
Whose soul directed to no use is seen
Unless to move the body's dull Machine;
Which, clock-work like, with the same equal pace,
Still travels on thro' life's insipid space,
Turns up his eyes to think that there should be
Among God's creatures two such things as *we*.
Then for his night-cap calls, and thanks the pow'rs
Which kindly give him grace to keep *good hours*.

   Good hours—Fine words—but was it ever seen
That all men could agree in what they mean?
FLORIO, who many years a course hath run
In downright opposition to the sun,

Expatiates on *good hours*, their cause defends
With as much vigour as our PRUDENT FRIENDS.
Th' uncertain term no settled notion brings,
But still in diff'rent mouths means diff'rent things.
Each takes the phrase in his own private view,
With PRUDENCE it is ten, with FLORIO two.

  Go on, ye fools, who talk for talking sake,
Without distinguishing distinctions make;
Shine forth in native folly, native pride,
Make yourselves rules to all the world beside;
Reason, collected in herself, disdains
The slavish yoke of arbitrary chains,
Steady and true each circumstance she weighs,
Nor to bare *words* inglorious tribute pays.
Men of sense live exempt from vulgar awe,
And Reason to herself alone is law.
That freedom she enjoys with lib'ral mind
Which she as freely grants to all mankind.
No idol titled name her rev'rence stirs,
No hour she blindly to the rest prefers,
All are alike, if they're alike employ'd,
And all are good if *virtuously* enjoy'd.

  Let the sage DOCTOR (think him one we know)
With scraps of antient learning overflow,
In all the dignity of *wig* declare
The fatal consequence of midnight air,
How damps and vapours, as it were by stealth,
Undermine life, and sap the walls of health.
For me let GALEN moulder on the shelf,
I'll live, and be physician to myself.
Whilst soul is join'd to body, whether fate
Allot a longer or a shorter date;
I'll make them live, as brother should with brother,
And keep them in good humour with each other.

  The surest road to health, say what they will,
Is never to suppose we shall be ill.
Most of those evils we poor mortals know
From doctors and imagination flow.

Hence to old women with your boasted rules,
Stale traps, and only sacred now to fools;
As well may sons of physic hope to find
One medicine, as one hour, for all mankind.

   If RUPERT after ten is out of bed
The fool next morning can't hold up his head,
What reason this which *me* to bed must call
Whose head (thank heaven) never aches at all?
In diff'rent courses diff'rent tempers run,
He hates the Moom, I sicken at the sun.
Wound up at twelve at noon, *his* clock goes right,
Mine better goes, wound up at twelve at night.

   Then in Oblivion's grateful cup I drown
The galling sneer, the supercilious frown,
The strange reserve, the proud affected state
Of upstart knaves grown rich and fools grown great.
No more that abject wretch disturbs my rest
Who meanly overlooks a friend distrest.
Purblind to poverty the Worldling goes,
And scarce sees rags an inch beyond his nose,
But from a croud can single out his grace
And cringe and creep to fools who strut in lace.

   Whether those classic regions are survey'd
Where we in earliest youth together stray'd,
Where hand in hand we trod the flow'ry shore,
Tho' now thy happier genius runs before,
When we conspir'd a thankless wretch to raise,
And taught a *stump* to shoot with pilfer'd praise,
Who once for *Rev'rend* merit famous grown
Gratefully strove to kick his MAKER down;
Or if more gen'ral arguments engage,
The court or camp, the pulpit, bar, or stage,
If half-bred surgeons, whom men doctors call,
And lawyers, who were never bred at all,
Those mighty-letter'd monsters of the earth,
Our pity move, or exercise our mirth;
Or if in tittle-tattle tooth-pick way
Our rambling thoughts with easy freedom stray,

A gainer still thy friend himself must find,
His grief suspended, and improv'd his mind.

Whilst peaceful slumbers bless the homely bed,
Where virtue, self-approv'd, reclines her head;
Whilst vice beneath imagin'd horrors mourns,
And conscience plants the villain's couch with thorns,
Impatient of restraint, the active mind,
No more by servile prejudice confin'd,
Leaps from her seat, as wak'ned from a trance,
And darts through Nature at a single glance.
Then we our friends, our foes, ourselves, survey,
And see by Night what fools we are by Day.

Stript of her gaudy plumes and vain disguise
See where Ambition mean and loathsome lies!
Reflexion with relentless hand pulls down
The tyrant's bloody wreath and ravish'd crown.
In vain he tells of battles bravely won,
Of nations conquer'd, and of Worlds undone;
Triumphs like these but ill with Manhood suit,
And sink the conqueror beneath the brute.
But if in searching round the world we find
Some gen'rous youth, the Friend of all mankind,
Whose anger, like the bolt of Jove, is sped
In terrors only at the guilty head,
Whose mercies, like Heav'n's dew, refreshing fall
In gen'ral love and charity to all,
Pleas'd we behold such worth on any throne,
And doubly pleas'd we find it on our own.

Through a false medium things are shewn by day,
Pomp, wealth, and titles judgment lead astray.
How many from appearance borrow state
Whom Night disdains to number with the Great!
Must not we laugh to see yon *lordling* proud
Snuff up vile incense from a fawning croud?
Whilst in his beam surrounding clients play,
Like insects in the sun's enliv'ning ray,
Whilst, Jehu like, he drives at furious rate,
And seems the only charioteer of state,

Talking himself into a little God,
And ruling empires with a single nod,
Who would not think, to hear him law dispense,
That he had Int'rest, and that they had sense?
Injurious thought! beneath NIGHT's honest shade
When pomp is buried and false colours fade,
Plainly we see at that impartial hour
Them dupes to pride, and *him* the tool of pow'r.

God help the man, condemn'd by cruel fate
To court the seeming, or the real great.
Much sorrow shall he feel, and suffer more
Than any slave who labours at the oar.
By slavish-methods must he learn to please,
By smooth-tongu'd flatt'ry, that curst *court-disease*,
Supple to ev'ry wayward mood strike sail,
And shift with shifting humour's peevish gale.
To Nature dead he must adopt vile art,
And wear a smile, with anguish in his heart.
A sense of honour would destroy his schemes,
And conscience ne'er must speak unless in dreams.
When he hath tamely borne for many years
Cold looks, forbidding frowns, contemptuous sneers,
When he at last expects, good easy man,
To reap the profits of his labour'd plan,
Some cringing LACQUEY, or rapacious WHORE,
To favours of the great the surest door,
Some CATAMITE, or PIMP, in credit grown,
Who tempts another's wife, or sells his own,
Steps cross his hopes, the promis'd boon denies,
And for some MINION's MINION claims the prize.

Foe to restraint, unpractis'd in deceit,
Too resolute, from Nature's active heat,
To brook affronts, and tamely pass them by;
Too proud to flatter, too sincere to lie,
Too plain to please, too honest to be great;
Give me, kind Heaven, an humbler, happier state:
Far from the place where men with pride deceive,
Where rascals promise, and where fools believe;

Far from the walk of folly, vice and strife,
Calm, independent, let me steal thro' life,
Nor one vain wish my steady thoughts beguile
To fear his lordship's frown, or court his smile.
Unfit for greatness, I her snares defy,
And look on riches with untainted eye.
To others let the glitt'ring bawbles fall,
Content shall place *us* far above them all.

Spectators only on this bustling stage,
We see what vain designs mankind engage.
Vice after vice with ardour they pursue,
And one old folly brings forth twenty new.
Perplex'd with trifles thro' the vale of life,
Man strives 'gainst man, without a cause for strife;
Armies embattled meet, and thousands bleed,
For some vile spot which cannot fifty feed.
Squirrels for nuts contend, and, wrong or right,
For the world's empire kings ambitious fight.
What odds?—*to us* 'tis all the self-same thing,
A NUT, a WORLD, a SQUIRREL, and a KING.

Britons, like Roman spirits fam'd of old,
Are cast by Nature in a PATRIOT mould;
No private joy, no private grief they know,
Their soul's engross'd by public weal or woe.
Inglorious ease like ours, they greatly scorn:
Let care with nobler wreaths their brows adorn.
Gladly they toil beneath the statesman's pains,
Give them but credit for a statesman's brains.
All would be deem'd e'en from the cradle fit
To rule in politics as well as wit.
The grave, the gay, the fopling, and the dunce,
Start up (God bless us!) statesmen all at once.

His mighty charge of souls the priest forgets,
The court-bred lord his promises and debts,
Soldiers their fame, misers forget their pelf,
The rake his mistress, and the fop himself,
Whilst thoughts of higher moment claim their care,
And their wise heads the weight of kingdoms bear.

Females themselves the glorious ardour feel,
And boast an equal, or a greater zeal.
From nymph to nymph the state infection flies,
Swells in her breast, and sparkles in her eyes.
O'erwhelm'd by politics lye malice, pride,
Envy and twenty other faults beside.
No more their little flutt'ring hearts confess
A passion for applause, or rage for dress;
No more they pant for PUBLIC RAREE-SHOWS,
Or lose one thought on monkeys or on beaux.
Coquettes no more pursue the jilting plan,
And lustful prudes forget to rail at man.
The darling theme CAECILIA's self will chuse,
Nor thinks of scandal whilst she talks of news.

The CIT, a COMMON-COUNCIL-MAN by place,
Ten thousand mighty nothings in his face,
By situation as by nature great,
With nice precision parcels out the state,
Proves and disproves, affirms and then denies,
Objects himself, and to himself replies,
Wielding aloft the Politician rod,
Makes P[ITT] by turns a devil and a god,
Maintains e'en to the very teeth of pow'r
The same thing right and wrong in half an hour,
Now all is well, now he suspects a plot,
And plainly proves, WHATEVER IS, IS NOT.
Fearfully wise, he shakes his empty head,
And deals out empires as he deals out thread.
His useless scales are in a corner flung,
And Europe's balance hangs upon his tongue.

Peace to such triflers, be our happier plan
To pass thro' life as easy as we can.
Who's in or out, who moves this grand machine,
Nor stirs my curiosity nor spleen.
Secrets of state no more I wish to know
Than secret movements of a PUPPET-SHEW;
Let but the puppets move, I've my desire,
Unseen the hand which *guides* the MASTER-WIRE.

What is't to us, if taxes rise or fall,
Thanks to our fortune *we* pay none at all.
Let muckworms, who in dirty acres deal,
Lament those hardships which *we* cannot feel.
His GRACE, who smarts, may bellow if he please,
But must I bellow too, who sit at ease?
By custom safe the poet's numbers flow,
Free as the light and air some years ago.
No statesman e'er will find it worth his pains
To tax our labours, and excise our brains.
Burthens like these vile earthly buildings bear,
No tribute 's laid on *Castles* in the *Air*.

Let then the flames of war destructive reign,
And ENGLAND's terrors awe *imperious* SPAIN;
Let ev'ry *venal clan* and *neutral* tribe
Learn to receive conditions, not prescribe;
Let each new-year call loud for new supplies,
And tax on tax with doubled burthen rise;
Exempt *we* sit, by no rude cares opprest,
And, having little, are with little blest.
All real ills in dark oblivion lye,
And joys, by fancy form'd, their place supply.
NIGHT's laughing hours unheeded slip away,
Nor one dull thought foretells approach of DAY.

Thus have we liv'd, and whilst the fates afford
Plain Plenty to supply the frugal board,
Whilst MIRTH, with DECENCY his lovely bride,
And Wine's gay GOD, with TEMP'RANCE by his side,
Their welcome visit pay; whilst HEALTH attends
The narrow circle of our chosen Friends,
Whilst frank GOOD-HUMOUR consecrates the treat,
And — — makes society complete,
Thus WILL we live, tho' in our teeth are hurl'd
Those *Hackney Strumpets*, PRUDENCE and the WORLD.

PRUDENCE, of old a sacred term, imply'd
Virtue with godlike wisdom for her guide,
But now in gen'ral use is known to mean
The stalking-horse of vice, and folly's screen.

The sense perverted we retain the name,
Hypocrisy and Prudence are the same.

A Tutor once, more read in men than books,
A kind of crafty knowledge in his looks,
Demurely sly, with high preferment blest,
His fav'rite Pupil in these words addrest:

Would'st thou, my son, be wise and virtuous deem'd,
By all mankind a prodigy esteem'd?
Be this thy rule; be what men *prudent* call;
PRUDENCE, almighty PRUDENCE gives thee all.
Keep up appearances; there lies the test,
The world will give thee credit for the rest.
Outward be fair, however foul within;
Sin if thou wilt, but then in secret sin.
This maxim's into common favour grown,
Vice is no longer vice unless 'tis known.
Virtue indeed may barefac'd take the field,
But vice is virtue, when 'tis well conceal'd.
Should raging passions drive thee to a whore,
Let PRUDENCE lead thee to a *postern* door;
Stay out all night, but take especial care
That PRUDENCE bring thee back to early prayer.
As one with watching and with study faint,
Reel in a drunkard, and reel out a saint.

With joy the youth this useful lesson heard,
And in his mem'ry stor'd each precious word,
Successfully pursued the plan, and *now*,
'Room for my LORD—VIRTUE, stand by and bow.'

And is this all—is this the wordling's art,
To mask, but not amend a vicious heart?
Shall lukewarm caution and demeanour grave,
For wise and good stamp ev'ry supple knave?
Shall wretches whom no real virtue warms,
Gild fair their names and states with empty forms,
Whilst VIRTUE seeks in vain the wish'd-for prize,
Because, disdaining ill, she hates disguise;

Because she frankly pours forth all her store,
Seems what she *is*, and scorns to pass for more?
Well—be it so—let vile dissemblers hold
Unenvy'd pow'r, and boast their dear-bought gold,
Me neither pow'r shall tempt, nor thirst of pelf,
To flatter others, or deny myself,
Might the whole world be plac'd within my span,
I would not be *that* THING, *that* PRUDENT MAN.

    What, cries Sir PLIANT, would you then oppose
Yourself, alone, against an host of foes?
Let not conceit, and peevish lust to rail,
Above all sense of interest prevail.
Throw off for shame this petulance of wit,
Be wise, be modest, and for *once* submit:
Too hard the task 'gainst multitudes to fight,
You must be wrong, the WORLD is in the right.

    What is this WORLD? a term which men have got
To signify not one in ten knows what;
A term, which with no more precision passes
To point out herds of *men* than herds of *asses*;
In common use no more it means we find,
Than many fools in same opinions join'd.

    Can numbers then change Nature's stated laws?
Can numbers make the worse the better cause?
Vice must be vice, virtue be virtue still,
Tho' thousands rail at good and practise ill.
Wouldst thou defend the Gaul's destructive rage
Because vast nations on his part engage?
Tho' to support the rebel CAESAR's cause
Tumultuous legions arm against the laws,
Tho' Scandal would OUR PATRIOT's name impeach,
And rails at virtues which she cannot reach,
What honest man but would with joy submit
To bleed with CATO, and retire with PITT?

    Stedfast and true to virtue's sacred laws,
Unmov'd by vulgar censure or applause,

Let the WORLD talk, my Friend; that WORLD, we know,
Which calls us guilty, cannot make us so.
Unaw'd by numbers, follow Nature's plan,
Assert the rights, or quit the name of man.
Consider well, weigh strictly right and wrong;
Resolve not quick, but once resolv'd be strong.
In spite of Dullness, and in spite of Wit,
If to thyself thou canst thyself acquit,
Rather stand up assur'd with conscious pride
Alone, than err with millions on thy side.
                    FINIS

                         CHARLES CHURCHILL

The Shrubbery

Written in a Time of Affliction

Oh happy shades! to me unblest,
    Friendly to peace, but not to me,
How ill the scene that offers rest,
    And heart that cannot rest, agree!

This glassy stream, that spreading pine,
    Those alders quiv'ring to the breeze,
Might soothe a soul less hurt than mine,
    And please, if any thing could please.

But fixt unalterable care
    Foregoes not what she feels within,
Shows the same sadness ev'ry where,
    And slights the season and the scene.

For all that pleas'd in wood or lawn,
    While peace possess'd these silent bow'rs,
Her animating smile withdrawn,
    Has lost its beauties and its pow'rs.

The saint or moralist should tread
   This moss-grown alley, musing slow;
They seek, like me, the secret shade,
   But not, like me, to nourish woe.

Me fruitful scenes and prospects waste
   Alike admonish not to roam;
These tell me of enjoyment past,
   And those of sorrows yet to come.

WILLIAM COWPER

Yardley Oak

Survivor sole, and hardly such, of all
That once liv'd here thy brethren, at my birth
(Since which I number three-score winters past)
A shatter'd veteran, hollow-trunk'd perhaps
As now, and with excoriate forks deform,
Relicts of ages! Could a mind, imbued
With truth from heav'n, created thing adore,
I might with rev'rence kneel and worship thee.

   It seems idolatry with some excuse
When our fore-father Druids in their oaks
Imagin'd sanctity. The conscience yet
Unpurified by an authentic act
Of amnesty, the meed of blood divine,
Lov'd not the light, but gloomy into gloom
Of thickest shades, like Adam after taste
Of fruit prescrib'd, as to a refuge, fled.

   Thou wast a bauble once; a cup and ball,
Which babes might play with; and the thievish jay
Seeking her food, with ease might have purloin'd
The auburn nut that held thee, swallowing down
Thy yet close-folded latitude of boughs
And all thine embryo vastness, at a gulp.
But Fate thy growth decreed: autumnal rains

Beneath thy parent tree mellow'd the soil
Design'd thy cradle, and a skipping deer,
With pointed hoof dibbling the glebe, prapar'd
The soft receptacle in which secure
Thy rudiments should sleep the winter through.

So Fancy dreams—Disprove it, if ye can,
Ye reas'ners broad awake, whose busy search
Of argument, employ'd too oft amiss,
Sifts half the pleasures of short life away.

Thou fell'st mature, and in the loamy clod
Swelling, with vegetative force instinct
Didst burst thine egg, as theirs the fabled Twins
Now stars; two lobes, protruding, pair'd exact;
A leaf succeeded, and another leaf,
And all the elements thy puny growth
Fost'ring propitious, thou becam'st a twig.

Who lived when thou wast such? Oh couldst thou speak,
As in Dodona once thy kindred trees
Oracular, I would not curious ask
The future, best unknown, but at thy mouth
Inquisitive, the less ambiguous past.

By thee I might correct, erroneous oft,
The clock of history, facts and events
Timing more punctual, unrecorded facts
Recov'ring, and misstated setting right—
Desp'rate attempt, till trees shall speak again!

Time made thee what thou wast—King of the woods;
And Time hath made thee what thou art—a cave
For owls to roost in. Once thy spreading boughs
O'erhung the champain; and the numerous flock
That graz'd it stood beneath that ample cope
Uncrowded, yet safe-shelter'd from the storm.
No flock frequents thee now. Thou hast outliv'd
Thy popularity and art become
(Unless verse rescue thee awhile) a thing
Forgotten, as the foliage of thy youth.

While thus through all the stages thou hast push'd
Of treeship, first a seedling hid in grass,

Then twig, then sapling, and, as century roll'd
Slow after century, a giant bulk
Of girth enormous, with moss-cushioned root
Upheav'd above the soil, and sides imboss'd
With prominent wens globose, till at the last
The rottenness, which time is charg'd t'inflinct
On other mighty ones, found also thee—
What exhibitions various hath the world
Witness'd of mutability in all
That we account most durable below!
Change is the diet, on which all subsist
Created changeable, and change at last
Destroys them.—Skies uncertain now the heat
Transmitting cloudless, and the solar beam
Now quenching in a boundless sea of clouds,—
Calm and alternate storm, moisture and drought,
Invigorate by turns the springs of life
In all that live, plant, animal, and man,
And in conclusion mar them. Nature's threads,
Fine passing thought, ev'n in her coarsest works,
Delight in agitation, yet sustain
The force, that agitates not unimpair'd,
But, worn by frequent impulse, to the cause
Of their best tone their dissolution owe.
    Thought cannot spend itself, comparing still
The great and little of thy lot, thy growth
From almost nullity into a state
Of matchless grandeur, and declension thence
Slow into such magnificent decay.
Time was, when, settling on thy leaf, a fly
Could shake thee to the root—and time has been
When tempests could not. At thy firmest age
Thou hadst within thy bole solid contents
That might have ribb'd the sides or plank'd the deck
Of some flagg'd admiral; and tortuous arms,
The ship-wright's darling treasure, didst present
To the four-quarter'd winds, robust and bold,
Warp'd into tough knee-timber, many a load.
But the axe spar'd thee; in those thriftier days
Oaks fell not, hewn by thousands, to supply

The bottomless demands of contest wag'd
For senatorial honours. Thus to Time
The task was left to whittle thee away
With his sly scythe, whose ever-nibbling edge
Noiseless, an atom and an atom more
Disjoining from the rest, has unobserv'd,
Achiev'd a labour, which had, far and wide,
(By man performed) made all the forest ring.

Embowell'd now, and of thy ancient self
Possessing nought but the scoop'd rind, that seems
An huge throat calling to the clouds for drink,
Which it would give in riv'lets to thy root,
Thou temptest none, but rather much forbid'st
The feller's toil, which thou couldst ill requite.
Yet is thy root sincere, sound as the rock,
A quarry of stout spurs and knotted fangs,
Which, crook'd into a thousand whimsies, clasp
The stubborn soil, and hold thee still erect.

So stands a kingdom, whose foundations yet
Fail not, in virtue and in wisdom laid,
Though all the superstructure, by the tooth
Pulveriz'd of venality, a shell
Stands now, and semblance only of itself.

Thine arms have left thee. Winds have rent them off
Long since, and rovers of the forest wild
With bow and shaft have burnt them. Some have left
A splinter'd stump bleach'd to a snowy white;
And some memorial none where once they grew.
Yet life still lingers in thee, and puts forth
Proof not contemptible of what she can,
Even where death predominates. The spring
Thee finds not less alive to her sweet force
Than yonder upstarts of the neighbour wood,
So much thy juniors, who their birth receiv'd
Half a millennium since the date of thine.

But since, although well qualified by age
To teach, no spirit dwells in thee, nor voice
May be expected from thee, seated here

On thy distorted root, with hearers none
Or prompter, save the scene, I will perform
Myself the oracle, and will discourse
In my own ear such matter as I may.
Thou, like myself, hast stage by stage attain'd
Life's wintry bourn; thou, after many years,
I after few; but few or many prove
A span in retrospect; for I can touch
With my least finger's end my own decease
And with extended thumb my natal hour,
And hadst thou also skill in measurement
As I, the past would seem as short to thee.
Evil and few—said Jacob—at an age
Thrice mine, and few and evil, I may think
The Prediluvian race, whose buxom youth
Endured two centuries, accounted theirs.

  'Shortliv'd as foliage is the race of man.
The wind shakes down the leaves, the budding grove
Soon teems with others, and in spring they grow.
So pass mankind. One generation meets
Its destin'd period, and a new succeeds.'
Such was the tender but undue complaint
Of the Maeonian in old time; for who
Would drawl out centuries in tedious strife
Severe with mental and corporeal ill
And would not rather chuse a shorter race
To glory, a few decads here below?

  One man alone, the Father of us all,
Drew not his life from woman; never gaz'd,
With mute unconsciousness of what he saw
On all around him; learn'd not by degrees,
Nor owed articulation to his ear;
But, moulded by his Maker into Man
At once, upstood intelligent, survey'd
All creatures, with precision understood
Their purport, uses, properties, assign'd
To each his name significant, and, fill'd
With love and wisdom, render'd back to heav'n
In praise harmonious the first air he drew.

He was excus'd the penalties of dull
Minority. No tutor charg'd his hand
With the thought-tracing quill, or task'd his mind
With problems; history, not wanted yet,
Lean'd on her elbow, watching Time, whose course,
Eventful, should supply her with a theme;

WILLIAM COWPER

The Caverns of the Grave I've seen

The Caverns of the Grave I've seen,
And these I shew'd to England's Queen.
But now the Caves of Hell I view:
Who shall I dare to shew them to?
What mighty Soul in Beauty's form
Shall dauntless View the Infernal Storm?
Egremont's Countess can controll
The flames of Hell that round me roll.
If she refuse, I still go on
Till the Heavens and Earth are gone,
Still admir'd by Noble minds,
Follow'd by Envy on the winds,
Re-engrav'd Time after Time,
Ever in their youthfull prime,
My designs unchang'd remain.
Time may rage but rage in vain.
For above Time's troubled Fountains
On the Great Atlantic Mountains,
In my Golden House on high,
There they Shine Eternally.

WILLIAM BLAKE

William Bond

I wonder whether the Girls are mad,
And I wonder whether they mean to kill,
And I wonder if William Bond will die,
For assuredly he is very ill.

He went to Church in a May morning
Attended by Fairies, one, two and three;
But the Angels of Providence drove them away,
And he returned home in Misery.

He went not out to the Field nor Fold,
He went not out to the Village nor Town,
But he came home in a black, black cloud,
And took to his Bed and there lay down.

And an Angel of Providence at his Feet,
And an Angel of Providence at his Head,
And in the midst a Black, Black Cloud,
And in the midst the Sick Man on his Bed.

And on his Right hand was Mary Green,
And on his Left hand was his sister Jane,
And their tears fell thro' the black, black Cloud
To drive away the sick man's pain.

'O William, if thou dost another Love,
'Dost another Love better than poor Mary,
'Go and take that other to be thy Wife,
'And Mary Green shall her servant be.'

'Yes, Mary, I do another Love,
'Another I Love far better than thee,
'And Another I will have for my Wife;
'Then what have I to do with thee?

'For thou art Melancholy Pale,
'And on thy Head is the cold Moon's shine,
'But she is ruddy and bright as day,
'And the sun beams dazzle from her eyne.'

Mary trembled and Mary chill'd
And Mary fell down on the right hand floor,
That William Bond and his Sister Jane
Scarce could recover Mary more.

When Mary woke and found her Laid
On the Right hand of her William dear,
On the Right hand of his loved Bed,
And saw her William Bond so near,

The Fairies that fled from William Bond
Danced around her Shining Head;
They danced over the Pillow white,
And the Angels of Providence left the Bed.

I thought Love liv'd in the hot sun shine,
But O, he lives in the Moony light!
I thought to find Love in the heat of day,
But sweet Love is the Comforter of Night.

Seek Love in the Pity of others' Woe,
In the gentle relief of another's care,
In the darkness of night and the winter's snow,
In the naked and outcast, Seek Love there!

WILLIAM BLAKE

The Crystal Cabinet

The Maiden caught me in the Wild,
Where I was dancing merrily;
She put me into her Cabinet
And Lock'd me up with a golden Key.

This Cabinet is form'd of Gold
And Pearl and Crystal shining bright,
And within it opens into a World
And a little lovely Moony Night.

Another England there I saw,
Another London with its Tower,
Another Thames and other Hills,
And another pleasant Surrey Bower.

Another Maiden like herself,
Translucent, lovely, shining clear,
Threefold each in the other clos'd—
O, what a pleasant trembling fear!

O, what a smile! a threefold Smile
Fill'd me, that like a flame I burn'd;
I bent to Kiss the lovely Maid,
And found a Threefold Kiss return'd.

I strove to sieze the inmost Form
With ardor fierce and hands of flame,
But burst the Crystal Cabinet,
And like a Weeping Babe became—

A weeping Babe upon the wild,
And Weeping Woman pale reclin'd,
And in the outward air again
I fill'd with woes the passing Wind.

                              WILLIAM BLAKE

My Spectre around me night and day

I

My Spectre around me night and day
Like a Wild beast guards my way.
My Emanation far within
Weeps incessantly for my Sin.

'Thy weeping thou shall ne'er give o'er:
'I sin against thee more and more,
'And never will from sin be free
'Till she forgives and comes to me.'

'Thou hast parted from my side:
'Once thou wast a virgin bride.
'Never shalt thou a true love find:
'My Spectre follows thee Behind.'

A deep winter dark and cold
(In a dark cold winter night
Within my Heart)
Within my heart thou didst unfold
A fathomless and boundless deep;
There we wander, there we weep.

When my Love did first begin,
Thou didst call that Love a sin:
Secret trembling night and day
Driving all my Loves away.

2

A Fathomless and boundless deep,
There we wander, there we weep;
On the hungry craving wind
My Spectre follows thee behind.

3

He scents thy footsteps in the snow,
Wheresover thou dost go
Thro' the wintry hail and rain.
When wilt thou return again?

4

Dost thou not in Pride and scorn
Fill with tempests all my morn,
And with jealousies and fears
Fill my pleasant nights with tears?

5

Seven of my sweet loves thy knife
Has bereaved of their life.
Their marble tombs I built with tears
And with cold and shuddering fears.

6

Seven more loves weep night and day
Round the tombs where my loves lay,
And seven more loves attend each night
Around my couch with torches bright.

7

And seven more Loves in my bed
Crown with wine my mournful head,
Pitying and forgiving all
Thy transgressions, great and small.

8

When wilt thou return and view
My loves, and them to life renew?
When wilt thou return and live?
When wilt thou pity as I forgive?

9

'Never, Never I return:
'Still for Victory I burn.
'Living, thee alone I'll have
'And when dead I'll be thy grave.

10

'Thro' the Heaven and Earth and Hell
'Thou shall never never quell:
I will fly and thou pursue,
'Night and Morn the flight renew.'

11

Till I turn from Female Love,
And root up the Infernal Grove,
I shall never worthy be
To Step into Eternity.

12

And, to end thy cruel mocks,
Annihilate thee on the rocks,
And another form create
To be subservient to my Fate.

13

Let us agree to give up Love,
And root up the infernal grove;
Then shall we return and see
The worlds of happy Eternity.

14

And throughout all Eternity
I forgive you, you forgive me.
As our dear Redeemer said:
'This the Wine and this the Bread.'

(Additional stanzas)

1

O'er my Sins Thou sit and moan:
Hast thou no sins of thy own?
O'er my Sins thou sit and weep,
And lull thy own sins fast asleep.

2

What Transgressions I commit
Are for thy Transgressions fit.
They thy Harlots, thou their Slave,
And my Bed becomes their grave.

Poor pale pitiable form
That I follow in a Storm,
Iron tears and groans of lead
Bind around my aking head.

And let us go to the [*word illegible*] downs
With many pleasing wiles
The Woman that does not love your Frowns
Will never endure your smiles.

WILLIAM BLAKE

I Murder Hate by Field or Flood

1

I murder hate by field or flood,
  Tho' Glory's name may screen us.
In wars at hame I'll spend my blood—
  Life-giving wars of Venus.
The deities that I adore
  Are Social Peace and Plenty:
I'm better pleas'd to make one more
  Than be the death of twenty.

2

I would not die like Socrates,
  For all the fuss of Plato;
Nor would I with Leonidas,
  Nor yet would I with Cato;
The zealots of the Church and State
  Shall ne'er my mortal foes be;
But let me have bold Zimri's fate
  Within the arms of Cozbi.

ROBERT BURNS

The Pains of Sleep

Ere on my bed my limbs I lay,
It hath not been my use to pray
With moving lips or bended knees;
But silently, by slow degrees,
My spirits I to Love compose,
In humble trust mine eye-lids close,
With reverential resignation,
No wish conceived, no thought expressed,
Only a sense of supplication;
A sense o'er all my soul impressed
That I am weak, yet not unblest,

Since in me, round me, everywhere
Eternal Strength and Wisdom are.

But yesternight I prayed aloud
In anguish and in agony,
Up-starting from the fiendish crowd
Of shapes and thoughts that tortured me:
A lurid light, a trampling throng,
Sense of intolerable wrong,
And whom I scorned, those only strong!
Thirst of revenge, the powerless will
Still baffled, and yet burning still!
Desire with loathing strangely mixed
On wild or hateful objects fixed.
Fantastic passions! maddening brawl!
And shame and terror over all!
Deeds to be hid which were not hid,
Which all confused I could not know
Whether I suffered, or I did:
For all seemed guilt, remorse or woe,
My own or others still the same
Life-stifling fear, soul-stifling shame.

So two nights passed: the night's dismay
Saddened and stunned the coming day.
Sleep, the wide blessing, seemed to me
Distemper's worst calamity.
The third night, when my own loud scream
Had waked me from the fiendish dream,
O'ercome with sufferings strange and wild,
I wept as I had been a child;
And having thus by tears subdued
My anguish to a milder mood,
Such punishments, I said, were due
To natures deepliest stained with sin,—
For aye entempesting anew
The unfathomable hell within,
The horror of their deeds to view,
To know and loathe, yet wish and do!

Such griefs with such men well agree,
But wherefore, wherefore fall on me?
To be beloved is all I need,
And whom I love, I love indeed.

SAMUEL TAYLOR COLERIDGE

A Letter to Sara Hutchinson. [*Dejection*]

APRIL 4, 1802—SUNDAY EVENING

Well! if the Bard was weatherwise, who made
The grand old Ballad of Sir Patrick Spence,
This Night, so tranquil now, will not go hence
Unrous'd by winds, that ply a busier trade
Than that, which moulds yon clouds in lazy flakes,
Or the dull sobbing Draft, that drones and rakes
Upon the Strings of this Eolian Lute,
        Which better far were mute.
For, lo! the New Moon, winter-bright!
And overspread with phantom Light,
(With swimming phantom Light o'erspread
But rimm'd and circled with a silver Thread)
I see the Old Moon in her Lap, foretelling
The coming-on of Rain and squally Blast—
O! Sara! that the Gust ev'n now were swelling,
And the slant Night-shower driving loud and fast!

A Grief without a pang, void, dark, and drear,
A stifling, drowsy, unimpassion'd Grief
That finds no natural Outlet, no Relief
        In word, or sigh, or tear—
This, Sara! well thou know'st,
Is that sore Evil, which I dread the most,
And oft'nest suffer! In this heartless Mood,
To other thoughts by yonder Throstle woo'd,
That pipes within the Larch tree, not unseen,
(The Larch, which pushes out in tassels green
It's bundled Leaflets) woo'd to mild Delights
By all the tender Sounds and gentle Sights

Of this sweet Primrose-month—and *vainly* woo'd
O dearest Sara! in this heartless Mood
All this long Eve, so balmy and serene,
Have I been gazing on the western Sky
And it's peculiar Tint of Yellow Green—
And still I gaze—and with how blank an eye!
And those thin Clouds above, in flakes and bars,
That give away their Motion to the Stars;
Those Stars, that glide behind them, or between,
Now sparkling, now bedimm'd, but always seen;
Yon crescent Moon, as fix'd as if it grew
In it's own cloudless, starless Lake of Blue—
A boat becalm'd! dear William's Sky Canoe!
—I see them all, so excellently fair!
  I see, not feel, how beautiful they are.

      My genial Spirits fail—
      And what can these avail
To lift the smoth'ring Weight from off my Breast?
      It were a vain Endeavor,
      Tho' I should gaze for ever
On that Green Light which lingers in the West!
I may not hope from outward Forms to win
The Passion and the Life whose Fountains are within!
These lifeless Shapes, around, below, Above,
      O what can they impart?
When even the gentle Thought, that thou, my Love!
      Art gazing now, like me,
      And see'st the Heaven, I see—
Sweet Thought it is—yet feebly stirs my Heart!
      Feebly! O feebly!—Yet
      (I well remember it)
In my first Dawn of Youth that Fancy stole
With many secret Yearnings on my Soul.
At eve, sky-gazing in 'ecstatic fit'
(Alas! for cloister'd in a city School
The Sky was all, I knew, of Beautiful)
At the barr'd window often did I sit,
And oft upon the leaded School-roof lay,
      And to myself would say—

There does not live the Man so stripp'd of good affections
As not to love to see a Maiden's quiet Eyes
Uprais'd, and linking on sweet Dreams by dim Connections
To Moon, or Evening Star, or glorious western Skies—
While yet a Boy, this Thought would so pursue me
That often it became a kind of Vision to me!

    Sweet Thought! and dear of old
    To Hearts of finer Mould!
Ten thousand times by Friends and Lovers blest!
    I spake with rash Despair,
    And ere I was aware,
The Weight was somewhat lifted from my Breast!
O Sara! in the weather-fended Wood,
Thy lov'd haunt! where the Stock-doves coo at Noon,
    I guess, that thou hast stood
And watch'd yon Crescent, and it's ghost-like Moon.
And yet, far rather in my present Mood
I would, that thou'dst been sitting all this while
Upon the sod-built Seat of Camomile—
And tho' thy Robin may have ceas'd to sing,
Yet needs for *my* sake must thou love to hear
    The Bee-hive murmuring near,
That ever-busy and most quiet Thing
Which I have heard at Midnight murmuring.

    I feel my spirit moved—
    And wheresoe'er thou be,
    O Sister! O Beloved!
    Those dear mild Eyes, that see
    Even now the Heaven, *I* see—
There is a Prayer in them! It is for *me*—
And I, dear Sara—*I* am blessing *thee*!

It was as calm as this, that happy night
When Mary, thou, and I together were,
The low decaying Fire our only Light,
And listen'd to the Stillness of the Air!
O that affectionate and blameless Maid,
Dear Mary! on her Lap my head she lay'd—

Her Hand was on my Brow,
  Even as my own is now;
And on my Cheek I felt thy eye-lash play.
Such joy I had, that I may truly say,
My Spirit was awe-stricken with the Excess
And trance-like Depth of it's brief Happiness.

Ah fair Remembrances, that so revive
The Heart, and fill it with a living Power,
Where were they, Sara?—or did I not strive
To win them to me?—on the fretting Hour
Then when I wrote thee that complaining Scroll
Which even to bodily Sickness bruis'd thy Soul!
And yet thou blam'st thyself alone! And yet
  Forbidd'st me all Regret!

And must I not regret, that I distress'd
Thee, best belov'd! who lovest me the best?
My better mind had fled, I know not whither,
For O! was this an absent Friend's Employ
To send from far both Pain and Sorrow thither
Where still his Blessings should have call'd down Joy!
I read thy guileless Letter o'er again—
I hear thee of thy blameless Self complain—
And only this I learn—and this, alas! I know—
That thou art weak and pale with Sickness, Grief, and Pain—
  And I—I made thee so!

O for my own sake I regret perforce
Whatever turns thee, Sara! from the Course
Of calm Well-being and a Heart at rest!
When thou, and with thee those, whom thou lov'st best,
Shall dwell together in one happy Home,
One House, the dear *abiding* Home of All,
I too will crown me with a Coronal—
Nor shall this Heart in idle Wishes roam
  Morbidly soft!
No! let me trust, that I shall wear away
In no inglorious Toils the manly Day,
And only now and then, and not too oft,

Some dear and memorable Eve will bless
Dreaming of all your Loves and Quietness.

Be happy, and I need thee not in sight.
Peace in thy Heart, and Quiet in thy Dwelling,
Health in thy Limbs, and in thine Eyes the Light
Of Love, and Hope, and honorable Feeling—
Where e'er I am, I shall be well content!
Not near thee, haply shall be more content!
To all things I prefer the Permanent.
And better seems it for a heart, like mine,
Always to *know*, than sometimes to behold,
    Their Happiness and thine—
For Change doth trouble me with pangs untold!
To see thee, hear thee, feel thee—then to part
    Oh!—it weighs down the Heart!

To *visit* those, I love, as I love thee,
Mary, and William, and dear Dorothy,
It is but a temptation to repine—
The transientness is Poison in the Wine,
Eats out the pith of Joy, makes all Joy hollow,
All Pleasure a dim Dream of Pain to follow!
My own peculiar Lot, my house-hold Life
It is, and will remain, Indifference or Strife.
While *ye* are *well and happy*, 'twould but wrong you
If I should fondly yearn to be among you—
Wherefore, O wherefore! should I wish to be
A wither'd branch upon a blossoming Tree?

But (let me say it! for I vainly strive
To beat away the Thought) but if thou pin'd,
Whate'er the Cause, in body or in mind,
I were the miserablest Man alive
To know it and be absent! Thy Delights
Far off, or near, alike I may partake—
But O! to mourn for thee, and to forsake
All power, all hope of giving comfort to thee—
To know that thou art weak and worn with pain,
And not to hear thee, Sara! not to view thee—
    Not sit beside thy Bed,

Not press thy aching Head,
Not bring thee Health again—
At least to hope, to try—
By this Voice, which thou lov'st, and by this earnest Eye—
Nay, wherefore did I let it haunt my Mind
   The dark distressful Dream!

I turn from it, and listen to the Wind
Which long has rav'd unnotic'd! What a Scream
Of agony by Torture lengthen'd out
That Lute sent forth! O thou wild Storm without!
Jagg'd Rock, or mountain Pond, or blasted Tree,
Or Pine-grove, whither Woodman never clomb,
Or lonely House, long held the Witches' Home,
Methinks were fitter Instruments for Thee,
Mad Lutanist! that in this month of Showers,
Of dark brown Gardens, and of peeping Flowers,
Mak'st Devil's Yule, with worse than wintry Song
The Blossoms, Buds, and timorous Leaves among!
Thou Actor, perfect in all tragic Sounds!
Thou mighty Poet, even to frenzy bold!
   What tell'st thou now about?
'Tis of the Rushing of an Host in Rout—
And many Groans from men with smarting Wounds—
At once they groan with smart, and shudder with the Cold!
'Tis hush'd! there is a Trance of deepest Silence,
Again! but all that Sound, as of a rushing Crowd,
And Groans and tremulous Shudderings, all are over—
And it has other Sounds, and all less deep, less loud!
   A Tale of less Affright,
   And temper'd with Delight,
As William's Self had made the tender Lay—
   'Tis of a little Child
   Upon a heathy Wild,
Not far from home—but it has lost it's way—
And now moans low in utter grief and fear—
And now screams loud, and hopes to make it's Mother hear!

'Tis Midnight! and small Thoughts have I of sleep—
Full seldom may my Friend such Vigils keep—
O breathe She softly in her gentle Sleep!

Cover her, gentle Sleep! with wings of Healing.
And be this Tempest but a Mountain Birth!
May all the Stars hand bright above her Dwelling,
Silent, as tho' they *watch'd* the sleeping Earth!
Healthful and light, my Darling! may'st thou rise
    With clear and cheerful Eyes—
And of the same good Tidings to me send!
    For, oh! beloved Friend!
I am not the buoyant Thing, I was of yore—
When I like an own Child, I to Joy belong'd;
For others mourning oft, myself oft sorely wrong'd,
Yet bearing all things then, as if I nothing bore!

    Yes, dearest Sara! yes!
There *was* a time when tho' my path was rough,
The Joy within me dallied with Distress;
And all Misfortunes were but as the Stuff
Whence Fancy made me Dreams of Happiness:
For Hope grew round me, like the climbing Vine,
And Leaves and Fruitage, not my own, seem'd mine!
But now Ill Tidings bow me down to earth
Nor care I, that they rob me of my Mirth
    But oh! each Visitation
Suspends what Nature gave me at my Birth,
    My shaping Spirit of Imagination!

I speak not now of those habitual Ills
That wear out Life, when two unequal Minds
Meet in one House, and two discordant Wills—
    This leaves me, where it finds,
Past cure, and past Complaint—a fate austere
Too fix'd and hopeless to partake of Fear!

But thou, dear Sara! (dear indeed thou art,
My Comforter! A Heart within my Heart!)
Thou, and the Few, we love, tho' few ye be,
Make up a world of Hopes and Fears for me.
And if Affliction, or distemp'ring Pain,
Or wayward Chance befall you, I complain
Not that I mourn—O Friends, most dear! most true!
    Methinks to weep with you

Were better far than to rejoice alone—
But that my coarse domestic Life has known
No Habits of heart-nursing Sympathy,
No Griefs, but such as dull and deaden me,
No mutual mild Enjoyments of it's own,
No Hopes of it's own Vintage, None, O! none—
Whence when I mourn'd for you, my Heart might borrow
Fair forms and living Motions for it's Sorrow.
For not to think of what I needs must feel,
But to be still and patient all I can;
And haply by abstruse Research to steal
From my own Nature all the Natural Man
This was my sole Resource, my wisest plan!
And that, which suits a part, infects the whole,
And now is almost grown the Temper of my Soul.

My little children are a Joy, a Love,
    A good Gift from above!
But what is Bliss, that still calls up a Woe,
    And makes it doubly keen
Compelling me to *feel*, as well as KNOW,
What a most blessed Lot mine might have been.
Those little Angel Children (woe is me!)
There have been hours, when feeling how they bind
And pluck out the Wing-feathers of my Mind,
Turning my Error to Necessity,
I have half-wish'd, they never had been born!
That seldom! But sad Thoughts they always bring,
And like the Poet's Philomel I sing
My Love-song, with my breast against a Thorn.

With no unthankful Spirit I confess,
This clinging Grief too, in it's turn, awakes
That Love, and Father's Joy; but O! it makes
The Love the greater, and the Joy far less.
These Mountains, too, these Vales, these Woods, these Lakes,
Scenes full of Beauty and of Loftiness
Where all my Life I fondly hop'd to live—
I were sunk low indeed, did they *no* solace give;
But oft I seem to feel, and evermore I fear,
They are not to me the Things, which once they were.

O Sara! we receive but what we give,
And in *our* Life alone does Nature live.
Our's is her Wedding Garment, our's her Shroud—
And would we aught behold of higher Worth
Than that inanimate cold World allow'd
To the poor loveless ever-anxious Crowd,
Ah! from the Soul itself must issue forth
A light, a Glory, and a luminous Cloud
        Enveloping the Earth!
And from the Soul itself must there be se[nt]
A sweet and potent Voice of it's own Bir[th,]
Of all sweet Sounds the Life and Element.

O pure of Heart! thou need'st not ask of me
What this strong music in the Soul may be,
        What, and wherein it doth exist,
This Light, this Glory, this fair luminous Mist,
This beautiful and beauty-making Power!
Joy, innocent Sara! Joy, that ne'er was given
Save to the Pure, and in their purest Hour,
Joy, Sara! is the Spirit and the Power,
That wedding Nature to us gives in Dower
        A new Earth and new Heaven
Undreamt of by the Sensual and the Proud!
Joy is that strong Voice, Joy that Luminous Cloud—
        We, we ourselves rejoice!
And thence flows all that charms or ear or sight.
All melodies the Echoes of that Voice,
All Colors a Suffusion of that Light.

Sister and Friend of my devoutest Choice!
Thou being innocent and full of love
And nested with the Darlings of thy Love,
And feeling in thy Soul, Heart, Lips and Arms
Even what the conjugal and mother Dove
That borrows genial warmth from those, she warms,
Feels in her thrill'd wings, blessedly outspread—
Thou free'd awhile from Cares and human Dread
By the immenseness of the Good and Fair
        Which thou see'st every where—

Thus, thus should'st thou rejoice!
To thee would all Things live from Pole to Pole,
Their Life the Eddying of thy living Soul—
O dear! O Innocent! O full of Love!
A very Friend! A Sister of my Choice—
O dear, as Light and Impulse from above,
Thus may'st thou ever, evermore rejoice!

SAMUEL TAYLOR COLERIDGE

Daniel Defoe

Few will acknowledge all they owe
To persecuted, brave Defoe.
Achilles, in Homeric song,
May, or he may not, live so long
As Crusoe; few their strength had tried
Without so staunch and safe a guide.
What boy is there who never laid
Under his pillow, half afraid,
That precious volume, lest the morrow
For unlearnt lesson might bring sorrow?
But nobler lessons he has taught
Wide-awake scholars who fear'd nought:
A Rodney and a Nelson may
Without him not have won the day.

WALTER SAVAGE LANDOR

The Harper

On the green banks of Shannon, when Sheelah was nigh,
No blithe Irish lad was so happy as I;
No harp like my own could so cheerily play,
And wherever I went was my poor dog Tray.

When at last I was forced from my Sheelah to part,
She said (while the sorrow was big at her heart),
'Oh! remember your Sheelah when far, far away;
And be kind, my dear Pat, to our poor dog Tray.'

Poor dog! he was faithful and kind, to be sure,
And he constantly loved me, although I was poor;
When the sour-looking folk sent me heartless away,
I had always a friend in my poor dog Tray.

When the road was so dark, and the night was so cold,
And Pat and his dog were grown weary and old,
How snugly we slept in my old coat of gray,
And he licked me for kindness—my poor dog Tray.

Though my wallet was scant I remembered his case,
Nor refused my last crust to his pitiful face;
But he died at my feet on a cold winter day,
And I played a sad lament for my poor dog Tray.

Where now shall I go, forsaken and blind?
Can I find one to guide me so faithful and kind?
To my sweet native village, so far, far away,
I can never more return with my poor dog Tray.

THOMAS CAMPBELL

Lines

The cold earth slept below,
    Above the cold sky shone;
And all around, with a chilling sound,
    From caves of ice and fields of snow,
    The breath of night like death did flow
        Beneath the sinking moon.

The wintry hedge was black,
    The green grass was not seen,

The birds did rest on the bare thorn's breast,
    Whose roots, beside the pathway track,
    Had bound their folds o'er mnay a crack
      Which the frost had made between.

    Thine eyes glowed in the glare
      Of the moon's dying light;
As a fen-fire's beam on a sluggish stream
    Gleams dimly, so the moon shone there,
    And it yellowed the strings of thy raven hair,
      That shook in the wind of night.

    The moon made thy lips pale, beloved—
      The wind made thy bosom chill—
The night did shed on thy dear head
    Its frozen dew, and thou didst lie
    Where the bitter breath of the naked sky
      Might visit thee at will.

PERCY BYSSHE SHELLEY

Badger

When midnight comes a host of dogs and men
Go out and track the badger to his den,
And put a sack within the hole, and lie
Till the old grunting badger passes by.
He comes and hears—they let the strongest loose.
The old fox hears the noise and drops the goose.
The poacher shoots and hurries from the cry,
And the old hare half wounded buzzes by.
They get a forkèd stick to bear him down
And clap the dogs and take him to the town,
And bait him all the day with many dogs,
And laugh and shout and fright the scampering hogs.
He runs along and bites at all he meets:
They shout and hollo down the noisy streets.

He turns about to face the loud uproar
And drives the rebels to their very door.
And frequent stone is hurled where'er they go;
When badgers fight, then every one's a foe.
The dogs are clapt and urged to join the fray;
The badger turns and drives them all away.
Though scarcely half as big, demure and small,
He fights with dogs for hours and beats them all.
The heavy mastiff, savage in the fray,
Lies down and licks his feet and turns away.
The bulldog knows his match and waxes cold,
The badger grins and never leaves his hold.
He drives the crowd and follows at their heels
And bites them through—the drunkard swears and reels.

The frighted women take the boys away,
The blackguard laughs and hurries on the fray.
He tries to reach the woods, an awkward race,
But sticks and cudgels quickly stop the chase.
He turns agen and drives the noisy crowd
And beats the many dogs in noises loud.
He drives away and beats them every one,
And then they loose them all and set them on.
He falls as dead and kicked by boys and men,
Then starts and grins and drives the crowd agen;
Till kicked and torn and beaten out he lies
And leaves his hold and cackles, groans, and dies.

JOHN CLARE

Song's Eternity

What is song's eternity?
      Come and see.
Can it noise and bustle be?
      Come and see.
Praises sung or praises said
      Can it be?

Wait awhile and these are dead—
   Sigh, sigh;
Be they high or lowly bred
   They die.

What is song's eternity?
   Come and see.
Melodies of earth and sky,
   Here they be.
Song once sung to Adam's ears
   Can it be?
Ballads of six thousand years
   Thrive, thrive;
Songs awakened with the spheres
   Alive.

Mighty songs that miss decay,
   What are they?
Crowds and cities pass away
   Like a day.
Books are writ and books are read;
   What are they?
Years will lay them with the dead—
   Sigh, sigh;
Trifles unto nothing wed,
   They die.

Dreamers, list the honey-bee;
   Mark the tree
Where the bluecap,[1] 'tootle tee,'
   Sings a glee
Sung to Adam and to Eve—
   Here they be.
When floods covered every bough,
   Noah's ark
Heard that ballad singing now;
   Hark, hark,

'Tootle tootle tootle tee'—
   Can it be
Pride and fame must shadows be?
   Come and see—

Every season owns her own;
    Bird and bee
Sing creation's music on;
    Nature's glee
Is in every mood and tone
    Eternity.

The eternity of song
    Liveth here;
Nature's universal tongue
    Singeth here
Songs I've heard and felt and seen
    Everywhere;
Songs like the grass are evergreen:
    The giver
Said 'Live and be'—and they have been,
    For ever.

JOHN CLARE

blue tit

I Hid my Love

I hid my love when young while I
Couldn't bear the buzzing of a fly;
I hid my love to my despite
Till I could not bear to look at light:
I dare not gaze upon her face
But left her memory in each place;
Where'er I saw a wild flower lie
I kissed and bade my love good-bye.

I met her in the greenest dells,
Where dewdrops pearl the wood bluebells;
The lost breeze kissed her bright blue eye,
The bee kissed and went singing by,
A sunbeam found a passage there,
A gold chain round her neck so fair;

As secret as the wild bee's song
She lay there all the summer long.

I hid my love in field and town
Till e'en the breeze would knock me down;
The Bees seemed singing ballads o'er
The flyes buzz turned a Lion's roar;
And even silence found a tongue,
To haunt me all the summer long;
The riddle nature could not prove
Was nothing else but secret love.

JOHN CLARE

Remembrances

Summer's pleasures they are gone like to visions every one,
And the cloudy days of autumn and of winter cometh on.
I tried to call them back, but unbidden they are gone
Far away from heart and eye and for ever far away.
Dear heart, and can it be that such raptures meet decay?
I thought them all eternal when by Langley Bush I lay,
I thought them joys eternal when I used to shout and play
On its bank at 'clink and bandy,' 'Chock' and 'taw' and 'ducking-
    stone,'
Where silence sitteth now on the wild heath as her own
Like a ruin of the past all alone.

When I used to lie and sing by old Eastwell's boiling spring,
When I used to tie the willow boughs together for a swing,
And fish with crooked pins and thread and never catch a thing,
With heart just like a feather, now as heavy as a stone;
When beneath old Lea Close Oak I the bottom branches broke
To make our harvest cart like so many working folk,
And then to cut a straw at the brook to have a soak.
Oh, I never dreamed of parting or that trouble had a sting,
Or that pleasures like a flock of birds would ever take to wing,
Leaving nothing but a little naked spring.

When jumping time away on old Crossberry Way,
And eating haws like sugar plums ere they had lost the may,
And skipping like a leveret before the peep of day
On the roly-poly up and downs of pleasant Swordy Well,
When in Round Oak's narrow lane as the south got black again
We sought the hollow ash that was shelter from the rain,
With our pockets full of peas we had stolen from the grain;
How delicious was the dinner-time on such a showery day!
Oh, words are poor receipts for what time hath stole away,
The ancient pulpit trees and the play.

When for school o'er Little Field with its brook and wooden brig,
Where I swaggered like a man though I was not half so big,
While I held my little plough though 'twas but a willow twig,
And drove my team along made of nothing but a name,
'Gee hep' and 'hoit' and 'woi'—oh, I never call to mind
These pleasant names of places but I leave a sigh behind,
While I see the little mouldywarps hang sweeing[1] to the wind
On the only aged willow that in all the field remains,
And nature hides her face while they're sweeing in their chains
And in a silent murmuring complains.

Here was commons for their hills, where they seek for freedom still,
Though every common's gone and though traps are set to kill
The little homeless miners—oh, it turns my bosom chill
When I think of old Sneap Green, Puddock's Nook and Hilly Snow,
Where bramble bushes grew and the daisy gemmed in dew
And the hills of silken grass like to cushions to the view,
Where we threw the pismire[2] crumbs when we'd nothing else to do,
All levelled like a desert by the never-weary plough,
All vanished like the sun where that cloud is passing now
And settled here for ever on its brow.

Oh, I never thought that joys would run away from boys,
Or that boys would change their minds and forsake such summer joys;
But alack, I never dreamed that the world had other toys
To petrify first feeling like the fable into stone,
Till I found the pleasure past and the winter come at last,
Then the fields were sudden bare and the sky got overcast,
And boyhood's pleasing haunts, like a blossom in the blast,

Was shrivelled to a withered weed and trampled down and done,
Till vanished was the morning spring and set the summer sun,
And winter fought her battle strife and won.

By Langley Bush I roam, but the bush hath left its hill,
On Cowper Green I stray, 'tis a desert strange and chill,
And the spreading Lea Close Oak, ere decay had penned its will,
To the axe of the spoiler and self-interest fell a prey,
And Crossberry Way and old Round Oak's narrow lane
With its hollow trees like pulpits I shall never see again,
Enclosure like a Buonaparte let not a thing remain,
It levelled every bush and tree and levelled every hill
And hung the moles for traitors—though the brook is running still
It runs a naked stream, cold and chill.

Oh, had I known as then joy had left the paths of men,
I had watched her night and day, be sure, and never slept agen,
And when she turned to go, oh, I'd caught her mantle then,
And wooed her like a lover by my lonely side to stay;
Ay, knelt and worshipped on, as love in beauty's bower,
And clung upon her smiles as a bee upon a flower,
And gave her heart my posies, all cropt in a sunny hour,
As keepsakes and pledges all to never fade away;
But love never heeded to treasure up the may,
So it went the common road to decay.

JOHN CLARE

¹ swinging   ² ant

The Dying Child

He could not die when trees were green,
    For he loved the time too well.
His little hands, when flowers were seen,
    Were held for the bluebell,
      As he was carried o'er the green.

His eye glanced at the white-nosed bee;
  He knew those children of the spring:
When he was well and on the lea
  He held one in his hands to sing,
    Which filled his little heart with glee.

Infants, the children of the spring!
  How can an infant die
When butterflies are on the wing,
  Green grass, and such a sky?
    How can they die at Spring?

He held his hands for daisies white,
  And then for violets blue,
And took them all to bed at night
  That in the green fields grew,
    As childhood's sweet delight.

And then he shut his little eyes,
  And flowers would notice not;
Birds' nests and eggs made no surprise,
  Nor any blossoms got:
    All met with plaintive sighs.

When winter came and blasts did sigh,
  And bare was plain and tree,
As he for ease in bed did lie
  His soul seemed with the free,
    He died so quietly.

JOHN CLARE

A Vision

I lost the love of heaven above,
  I spurned the lust of earth below,
I felt the sweets of fancied love,
  And hell itself my only foe.

I lost earth's joys, but felt the glow
   Of heaven's flame abound in me,
Till loveliness and I did grow
   The bard of immortality.

I loved, but woman fell away;
   I hid me from her faded fame.
I snatched the sun's eternal ray
   And wrote till earth was but a name.

In every language upon earth,
   On every shore, o'er every sea,
I gave my name immortal birth
   And kept my spirit with the free.

JOHN CLARE

Well, honest John

Well, honest John, how fare you now at home?
The spring is come, and birds are building nests;
The old cock-robin to the sty is come,
With olive feathers and its ruddy breast;
And the old cock, with wattles and red comb,
Struts with the hens, and seems to like some best,
Then crows, and looks about for little crumbs,
Swept out by little folks an hour ago;
The pigs sleep in the sty; the bookman[1] comes—
The little boy lets home-close nesting go,
And pockets tops and taws,[2] where daisies blow,
To look at the new number just laid down,
With lots of pictures, and good stories too,
And Jack the Giant-killer's high renown.

JOHN CLARE

[1] travelling vendor of books and pamphlets   [2] marbles

Country Letter

Dear brother Robin, this comes from us all
With our kind love, and could Gip write and all
Though but a dog he'd have his love to spare,
For still he knows, and by your corner chair
The moment he comes in he lies him down
And seems to fancy you are in the town.
This leaves us well in health, thank God for that!
For old acquaintance Sue has kept your hat
Which mother brushes ere she lays it by
And every Sunday goes upstairs to cry.
Iane still is yours till you come back agen
And ne'er so much as dances with the men;
And Ned the woodman every week comes in
And asks about you kindly as our kin;
And he with this and goody Thompson sends
Remembrances with those of all our friends.
Father with us sends love until he hears
And mother she has nothing but her tears,
Yet wishes you like us in health the same
And longs to see a letter with your name,
So, loving brother, don't forget to write.
Old Gip lies on the hearth stone every night;
Mother can't bear to turn him out of doors
And never noises now of dirty floors;
Father will laugh but lets her have her way,
And Gip for kindness get a double pay.
So Robin write and let us quickly see
You don't forget old friends no more than we,
Nor let my mother have so much to blame
To go three journeys ere your letter came.

                                    JOHN CLARE

What is Love?

Say, what is love? To live in vain,
To live, and die, and live again?
Say, what is love? Is it to be
In prison still and still be free—
Or seem as free? Alone, and prove
The hopeless hopes of real love?
Does real love on earth exist?
'Tis like a sunbeam in the mist,
That fades and nowhere will remain,
And nowhere is o'ertook again.
Say, what is love? A blooming name,
A rose-leaf on the page of fame,
That blooms, then fades, to cheat no more,
And is what nothing was before?
Say, what is love? Whate'er it be,
It centres, Mary, still with thee.

JOHN CLARE

The Shepherd's Calendar: February: a Thaw

The snow is gone from cottage tops
The thatch moss glows in brighter green
And eves in quick succession drops
Where grinning icles once hath been
Pit patting wi a pleasant noise
In tubs set by the cottage door
And ducks and geese wi happy joys
Douse in the yard pond brimming oer

The sun peeps thro the window pane
Which children mark wi laughing eye
And in the wet street steal again
To tell each other spring is nigh

And as young hope the past recalls
In playing groups will often draw
Building beside the sunny walls
Their spring-play-huts of sticks or straw

And oft in pleasures dreams they hie
Round homesteads by the village side
Scratting the hedgrow mosses bye
Where painted pooty shells abide
Mistaking oft the ivy spray
For leaves that come wi budding spring
And wondering in their search for play
Why birds delay to build and sing

The milkmaid singing leaves her bed
As glad as happy thoughts can be
While magpies chatter oer her head
As jocund in the change as she
Her cows around the closes stray
Nor lingering wait the foddering boy
Tossing the molehills in their play
And staring round in frolic joy

Ploughman go whistling to their toils
And yoke again the rested plough
And mingling oer the mellow soils
Boys' shouts and whips are noising now
The shepherd now is often seen
By warm banks oer his work to bend
Or oer a gate or stile to lean
Chattering to a passing friend

Odd hive bees fancying winter oer
And dreaming in their combs of spring
Creeps on the slab beside their door
And strokes its leg upon its wing
While wild ones half saleep are humming
Round snowdrop bells a feeble note
And pigions coo of summer coming
Picking their feathers on the cote

The barking dogs by lane and wood
Drive sheep afield from foddering ground
And echo in her summer mood
Briskly mocks the cheery sound
The flocks as from a prison broke
Shake their wet fleeces in the sun
While following fast a misty smoke
Reeks from the moist grass as they run

Nor more behind his masters heels
The dog creeps oer his winter pace
But cocks his tail and oer the fields
Runs many a wild and random chase
Following in spite of chiding calls
The startld cat wi harmless glee
Scaring her up the weed green walls
Or mossy mottld apple tree

As crows from morning perches flye
He barks and follows them in vain
Een larks will catch his nimble eye
And off he starts and barks again
Wi breathless haste and blinded guess
Oft following where the hare hath gone
Forgetting in his joys excess
His frolic puppy days are done

The gossips saunter in the sun
As at the spring from door to door
Of matters in the village done
And secret newsings muttered oer
Young girls when they each other meet
Will stand their tales of love to tell
While going on errands down the street
Or fetching water from the well

A calm of pleasure listens round
And almost whispers winter bye
While fancy dreams of summer sounds
And quiet rapture fills the eye

The sun beams on the hedges lye
The south wind murmurs summer soft
And maids hang out white cloaths to dry
Around the eldern skirted croft

Each barns green thatch reeks in the sun
Its mate the happy sparrow calls
And as nest building spring begun
Peeps in the holes about the walls
The wren a sunny side the stack
Wi short tail ever on the strunt
Cockd gadding up above his back
Again for dancing gnats will hunt

The gladdend swine bolt from the sty
And round the yard in freedom run
Or stretching in their slumbers lye
Beside the cottage in the sun
The young horse whinneys to its mate
And sickens from the threshers door
Rubbing the straw yards banded gate
Longing for freedom on the moor

Hens leave their roosts wi cackling calls
To see the barn door free from snow
And cocks flye up the mossy walls
To clap their spangld wings and crow
About the steeples sunny top
The jackdaw flocks resemble spring
And in the stone archd windows pop
Wi summer noise and wanton wing

The small birds think their wants are oer
To see the snow hills fret again
And from the barns chaff litterd door
Betake them to the greening plain
The woodmans robin startles coy
Nor longer at his elbow comes
To peck wi hungers eager joy
Mong mossy stulps[1] the litterd crumbs

Neath hedge and walls that screen the wind
The gnats for play will flock together
And een poor flyes odd hopes will find
To venture in the mocking weather
From out their hiding holes again
Wi feeble pace they often creep
Along the sun warmd window pane
Like dreaming things that walk in sleep

The mavis thrush wi wild delight
Upon the orchards dripping tree
Mutters to see the day so bright
Spring scraps of young hopes poesy
And oft dame stops her burring wheel
To hear the robins note once more
That tutles² while he pecks his meal
From sweet briar hips beside the door

The hedghog from its hollow root
Sees the wood moss clear of snow
And hunts each hedge for fallen fruit
Crab hip and winter bitten sloe
And oft when checkd by sudden fears
As shepherd dog his haunt espies
He rolls up in a ball of spears
And all his barking rage defies

Thus nature of the spring will dream
While south winds thaw but soon again
Frost breaths upon the stiffening stream
And numbs it into ice—the plain
Soon wears its merry garb of white
And icicles that fret at noon
Will eke their icy tails at night
Beneath the chilly stars and moon

Nature soon sickens of her joys
And all is sad and dumb again
Save merry shouts of sliding boys
About the frozen furrowd plain

The foddering boy forgets his song
And silent goes wi folded arms
And croodling³ shepherds bend along
Crouching to the whizzing storms

JOHN CLARE

¹ tree-stumps   ² tootles
³ to huddle for warmth

Invitation to Eternity

Say, wilt thou go with me, sweet maid,
Say, maiden, wilt thou go with me
Through the valley-depths of shade,
Of night and dark obscurity;
Where the path has lost its way,
Where the sun forgets the day,
Where there's nor light nor life to see,
Sweet maiden, wilt thou go with me?

Where stones will turn to flooding streams,
Where plains will rise like ocean's waves,
Where life will fade like visioned dreams
And mountains darken into caves,
Say, maiden, wilt thou go with me
Through this sad non-identity,
Where parents live and are forgot,
And sisters live and know us not?

Say, maiden, wilt thou go with me
In this strange death-in-life to be,
To live in death and be the same,
Without this life or home or name,
At once to be and not to be—
That was and is not—yet to see
Things pass like shadows, and the sky
Above, below, around us lie?

The land of shadows wilt thou trace,
Nor look nor know each other's face;
The present marred with reason gone,
And past and present all as one?
Say, maiden, can thy life be led
To join the living and the dead?
Then trace thy footsteps on with me;
We are wed to one eternity.

JOHN CLARE

To the Snipe

Lover of swamps
And quagmire overgrown
With hassock-tufts of sedge, where fear encamps
Around thy home alone,

The trembling grass
Quakes from the human foot,
Nor bears the weight of man to let him pass
Where thou, alone and mute,

Sittest at rest
In safety, near the clump
Of huge flag-forest that thy haunts invest
Or some old sallow stump,

Thriving on seams
That tiny islands swell,
Just hilling from the mud and rancid streams,
Suiting thy nature well;

For here thy bill,
Suited by wisdom good,
Of rude unseemly length, doth delve and drill
The jellied mass for food;

And here, mayhap,
When summer suns have drest
The moor's rude, desolate and spongy lap,
May hide thy mystic nest—

Mystic indeed;
For isles that oceans make
Are scarcely more secure for birds to build
Than this flag-hidden lake.

Boys thread the woods
To their remotest shades;
But in these marshy flats, these stagnant floods,
Security pervades.

From year to year
Places untrodden lie,
Where man nor boy nor stock hath ventured near,
Naught gazed on but the sky

And fowl that dread
The very breath of man,
Hiding in spots that never knew his tread,
A wild and timid clan,

Widgeon and teal
And wild duck—restless lot,
That from man's dreaded sight will ever steal
To the most dreary spot.

Here tempests howl
Around each flaggy plot,
Where they who dread man's sight, the water fowl,
Hide and are frightened not.

'Tis power divine
That heartens them to brave
The roughest tempest and at ease recline
On marshes or the wave.

Yet instinct knows
Not safety's bounds: — to shun
The firmer ground where skulking fowler goes
With searching dogs and gun,

By tepid springs
Scarcely one stride across
(Though bramble from its edge a shelter flings
Thy safety is at loss)

— And never choose
The little sinky foss,
Streaking the moors whence spa-red water spews
From pudges fringed with moss;

Freebooters there,
Intent to kill or slay,
Startle with cracking guns the trepid air,
And dogs thy haunts betray.

From danger's reach
Here thou art safe to roam,
Far as these washy flag-sown marshes stretch
A still and quiet home.

In these thy haunts
I've gleaned habitual love;
From the vague world where pride and folly taunts
I muse and look above.

Thy solitudes
The unbounded heaven esteems,
And here my heart warms into higher moods
And dignifying dreams.

I see the sky
Smile on the meanest spot,
Giving to all that creep or walk or fly
A calm and cordial lot.

Thine teaches me
Right feelings to employ—
That in the dreariest places peace will be
A dweller and a joy.

JOHN CLARE

To Homer

Standing aloof in giant ignorance,
    Of thee I hear and of the Cyclades,
As one who sits ashore and longs perchance
    To visit dolphin-coral in deep seas.
So thou wast blind!—but then the veil was rent;
    For Jove uncurtain'd Heaven to let thee live,
And Neptune made for thee a spumy tent,
    And Pan made sing for thee his forest-hive;
Aye, on the shores of darkness there is light,
    And precipices show untrodden green;
There is a budding morrow in midnight;
    There is a triple sight in blindness keen;
Such seeing hadst thou, as it once befel
To Dian, Queen of Earth, and Heaven, and Hell.

(April, 1818)

JOHN KEATS

On Fame

'*You cannot eat your cake and have it too.*'—Proverb.

How fever'd is that man, who cannot look
    Upon his mortal days with temperate blood,
Who vexes all the leaves of his life's book,
    And robs his fair name of its maidenhood;
It is as if the rose should pluck herself,
    Or the ripe plum finger its misty bloom,
As if a clear lake, meddling with itself,
    Should cloud its pureness with a muddy gloom;

But the rose leaves herself upon the briar,
    For winds to kiss and grateful bees to feed,
And the ripe plum still wears its dim attire;
    The undisturbed lake has crystal space;
    Why then should man, teasing the world for grace,
Spoil his salvation by a fierce miscreed?
                (April 30, 1819)

                        JOHN KEATS

Lines supposed to have been Addressed to Fanny Brawne

This living hand, now warm and capable
Of earnest grasping, would, if it were cold
And in the icy silence of the tomb,
So haunt thy days and chill thy dreaming nights
That thou wouldst wish thine own heart dry of blood
So in my veins red life might stream again,
And thou be conscience-calm'd—see here it is—
I hold it towards you.
                (Winter, 1819–1820)

                        JOHN KEATS

What is Young Passion . . .

What is young Passion but a gusty breeze
Ruffling the surface of a shallow flood?
A vernal motion of the vital blood,
That sweetly gushes from a heart at ease,
As sugar'd sap in spicy-budding trees?
And tho' a wish be born with every morrow,
And fondest dreams full oft are types of sorrow,
Eyes that can smile may weep just when they please.
But adult Passion, centred far within,
Hid from the moment's venom and its balm,
Works with the fell inherency of sin,

Nor feels the joy of morn, nor evening calm:
For morn nor eve can change that fiery gloom
That glares within the spirit's living tomb.

HARTLEY COLERIDGE

'Tis strange to Me . . .

'Tis strange to me, who long have seen no face,
That was not like a book, whose every page
I knew by heart, a kindly common-place—
And faithful record of progressive age—
To wander forth, and view an unknown race;
Of all that I have been, to find no trace,
No footstep of my by-gone pilgrimage.
Thousands I pass, and no one stays his pace
To tell me that the day is fair, or rainy—
Each one his object seeks with anxious chase,
And I have not a common hope with any—
Thus like one drop of oil upon a flood,
In uncommunicating solitude—
Single am I amid the countless many.

HARTLEY COLERIDGE

Night

The crackling embers on the hearth are dead;
The indoor note of industry is still;
The latch is fast; upon the window sill
The small birds wait not for their daily bread;
The voiceless flowers—how quietly they shed
Their nightly odours;—and the household rill
Murmurs continuous dulcet sounds that fill

The vacant expectation, and the dread
Of listening night. And haply now she sleeps;
For all the garrulous noises of the air
Are hush'd in peace; the soft dew silent weeps,
Like hopeless lovers for a maid so fair—
Oh! that I were the happy dream that creeps
To her soft heart, to find my image there.

HARTLEY COLERIDGE

How shall a Man fore-doomed . . .

How shall a man fore-doomed to lone estate,
Untimely old, irreverently grey,
Much like a patch of dusty snow in May,
Dead sleeping in a hollow, all too late—
How shall so poor a thing congratulate
The blest completion of a patient wooing,
Or how commend a younger man for doing
What ne'er to do hath been his fault or fate?
There is a fable, that I once did read,
Of a bad angel, that was someway good,
And therefore on the brink of Heaven he stood,
Looking each way, and no way could proceed;
Till at the last he purged away his sin
By loving all the joy he saw within.

HARTLEY COLERIDGE

If I have sinn'd in Act . . .

If I have sinn'd in act, I may repent;
If I have err'd in thought, I may disclaim
My silent error, and yet feel no shame—
But if my soul, big with an ill intent,
Guilty in will, by fate be innocent,

Or being bad, yet murmurs at the curse
And incapacity of being worse
That makes my hungry passion still keep Lent
In keen expectance of a Carnival;
Where, in all worlds, that round the sun revolve
And shed their influence on this passive ball,
Abides a power that can my soul absolve?
Could any sin survive, and be forgiven—
One sinful wish would make a hell of heaven.

HARTLEY COLERIDGE

Full well I know . . .

Full well I know—my Friends—ye look on me
A living spectre of my Father dead—
Had I not borne his name, had I not fed
On him, as one leaf trembling on a tree,
A woeful waste had been my minstrelsy—
Yet have I sung of maidens newly wed
And I have wished that hearts too sharply bled
Should throb with less of pain, and heave more free
By my endeavour. Still alone I sit
Counting each thought as Miser counts a penny,
Wishing to spend my penny-worth of wit
On antic wheel of fortune like a Zany:
You love me for my sire, to you unknown,
Revere me for his sake, and love me for my own.

HARTLEY COLERIDGE

Long time a Child . . .

Long time a child, and still a child, when years
Had painted manhood on my cheek, was I;
For yet I lived like one not born to die;
A thriftless prodigal of smiles and tears,
No hope I needed, and I knew no fears.

But sleep, though sweet, is only sleep, and waking,
I waked to sleep no more, at once o'ertaking
The vanguard of my age, with all arrears
Of duty on my back. Nor child, nor man,
Nor youth, nor sage, I find my head is grey,
For I have lost the race I never ran:
A rathe December blights my lagging May;
And still I am a child, tho' I be old,
Time is my debtor for my years untold.

HARTLEY COLERIDGE

Hawthorne

MAY 23RD, 1864

How beautiful it was, that one bright day
    In the long week of rain!
Though all its splendour could not chase away
    The omnipresent pain.

The lovely town was white with apple-blooms,
    And the great elms o'erhead
Dark shadows wove on their aerial looms
    Shot through with golden thread.

Across the meadows, by the gray old manse,
    The historic river flowed:
I was as one who wanders in a trance,
    Unconscious of his road.

The faces of familiar friends seemed strange;
    Their voices I could hear,
And yet the words they uttered seemed to change
    Their meaning to my ear.

For the one face I looked for was not there,
    The one low voice was mute;
Only an unseen presence filled the air,
    And baffled my pursuit.

Now I look back, and meadow, manse, and stream
    Dimly my thought defines;
I only see—a dream within a dream—
    The hill-top hearsed with pines.

I only hear above his place of rest
    Their tender undertone,
The infinite longings of a troubled breast,
    The voice so like his own.

There in seclusion and remote from men
    The wizard hand lies cold,
Which at its topmost speed let fall the pen,
    And left the tale half told.

Ah! who shall lift that wand of magic power,
    And the lost clew regain?
The unfinished window in Aladdin's tower
    Unfinished must remain!

        HENRY WADSWORTH LONGFELLOW

In the Doorway

The swallow has set her six young on the rail,
    And looks sea-ward:
The water's in stripes like a snake, olive-pale
    To the leeward,—
On the weather-side, black, spotted white with the wind.
'Good fortune departs, and disaster's behind,'—
Hark, the wind with its wants and its infinite wail!

Our fig-tree, that leaned for the saltness, has furled
    Her five fingers,
Each leaf like a hand opened wide to the world
    Where there lingers
No glint of the gold, Summer sent for her sake:
How the vines writhe in rows, each impaled on its stake!
My heart shrivels up and my spirit shrinks curled.

Yet here are we two; we have love, house enough,
    With the field there,
This house of four rooms, that field red and rough,
    Though it yield there,
For the rabbit that robs, scarce a blade or a bent;
If a magpie alight now, it seems an event;
And they both will be gone at November's rebuff.

But why must cold spread? but wherefore bring change
    To the spirit,
God meant should mate his with an infinite range,
    And inherit
His power to put life in the darkness and cold?
Oh, live and love worthily, bear and be bold!
Whom Summer made friends of, let Winter estrange!
               (from *James Lee's Wife*)

ROBERT BROWNING

A Toccata of Galuppi's

Oh, Galuppi, Baldassaro, this is very sad to find!
I can hardly misconceive you; it would prove me deaf and blind;
But although I give you credit, 'tis with such a heavy mind!

Here you come with your old music, and here's all the good it brings.
What, they lived once thus at Venice, where the merchants were the
    kings,
Where St. Mark's is, where the Doges used to wed the sea with rings?

Ay, because the sea's the street there; and 'tis arched by . . . what
    you call
. . . Shylock's bridge with houses on it, where they kept the carnival!
I was never out of England—it's as if I saw it all!

Did young people take their pleasure when the sea was warm in May?
Balls and masks begun at midnight, burning ever to mid-day,
When they made up fresh adventures for the morrow, do you say?

Was a lady such a lady, cheeks so round and lips so red,—
On her neck the small face buoyant, like a bell-flower on its bed,
O'er the breast's superb abundance where a man might base his head?

Well (and it was graceful of them) they'd break talk off and afford
—She, to bite her mask's black velvet, he to finger on his sword,
While you sat and played Toccatas, stately at the clavichord?

What? Those lesser thirds so plaintive, sixths diminished sigh on sigh,
Told them something? Those suspensions, those solutions—'Must we
    die?'
Those commiserating sevenths—'Life might last! we can but try!'

'Were you happy?'—'Yes.'—'And are you still as happy?'—'Yes—
    and you?'
—'Then more kisses'—'Did I stop them, when a million seemed so
    few?'
Hark, the dominant's persistence, till it must be answered to!

So an octave struck the answer. Oh, they praised you, I dare say!
'Brave Galuppi! that was music! good alike at grave and gay!
I can always leave off talking, when I hear a master play.'

Then they left you for their pleasure! till in due time, one by one,
Some with lives that came to nothing, some with deeds as well undone,
Death came tacitly and took them where they never see the sun.

But when I sit down to reason,—think to take my stand nor swerve
Till I triumph o'er a secret wrung from nature's close reserve,
In you come with your cold music, till I creep thro' every nerve.

Yes, you, like a ghostly cricket, creaking where a house was burned—
'Dust and ashes, dead and done with, Venice spent what Venice
    earned!
The soul doubtless, is immortal—where a soul can be discerned.

'Yours for instance, you know physics, something of geology,
Mathematics are your pastime; souls shall rise in their degree;
Butterflies may dread extinction,—you'll not die, it cannot be!

'As for Venice and its people, merely born to bloom and drop,
Here on earth they bore their fruitage, mirth and folly were the crop.
What of soul was left, I wonder, when the kissing had to stop?

'Dust and ashes! So you creak it, and I want the heart to scold.
Dear dead women with such hair, too—what's become of all the gold
Used to hang and brush their bosoms? I feel chilly and grown old.

                                          ROBERT BROWNING

Redbreast, Early in the Morning

Redbreast, early in the morning
Dank and cold and cloudy grey,
Wildly tender is thy music,
Chasing angry thought away.

My heart is not enraptured now,
My eyes are full of tears,
And constant sorrow on my brow
Has done the work of years.

It was not hope that wrecked at once
The spirit's calm in storm,
But a long life of solitude,
Hopes quenched and rising thoughts subdued,
A bleak November's calm.

What woke it then? A little child
Strayed from its father's cottage door,
And in the hour of moonlight wild
Laid lonely on the desert moor.

I heard it then, you heard it too,
And seraph sweet it sang to you;
But like the shriek of misery
That wild, wild music wailed to me.

EMILY BRONTË

I am the Only Being whose Doom

I am the only being whose doom
No tongue would ask, no eye would mourn;
I never caused a thought of gloom,
A smile of joy, since I was born.

In secret pleasure, secret tears,
This changeful life has slipped away,
As friendless after eighteen years,
As lone as on my natal day.

There have been times I cannot hide,
There have been times when this was drear,
When my sad soul forgot its pride
And longed for one to love me here.

But those were in the early glow
Of feelings since subdued by care;
And they have died so long ago,
I hardly now believe they were.

First melted off the hope of youth,
Then fancy's rainbow fast withdrew;
And then experience told me truth
In mortal bosoms never grew.

'Twas grief enough to think mankind
All hollow, servile, insincere;
But worse to trust to my own mind
And find the same corruption there.

EMILY BRONTË

The Night-wind

In summer's mellow midnight,
A cloudless moon shone through
Our open parlour window
And rosetrees wet with dew.

I sat in silent musing,
The soft wind waved my hair:
It told me Heaven was glorious,
And sleeping Earth was fair.

I needed not its breathing
To bring such thoughts to me,
But still it whispered lowly,
'How dark the woods will be!

'The thick leaves in my murmur
Are rustling like a dream,
And all their myriad voices
Instinct with spirit seem.'

I said, 'Go, gentle singer,
Thy wooing voice is kind,
But do not think its music
Has power to reach my mind.

'Play with the scented flower,
The young tree's supple bough,
And leave my human feelings
In their own course to flow.'

The wanderer would not leave me;
Its kiss grew warmer still—
'O come,' it sighed so sweetly,
'I'll win thee 'gainst thy will.

Have we not been from childhood friends?
Have I not loved thee long?
As long as thou hast loved the night
Whose silence wakes my song.

'And when thy heart is laid at rest
Beneath the church-yard stone
I shall have time enough to mourn
And thou to be alone.'

                              EMILY BRONTË

Enough of Thought, Philosopher

'Enough of Thought, Philosopher;
Too long hast thou been dreaming
Unlightened, in this chamber drear
While summer's sun is beaming—
Space-sweeping soul, what sad refrain
Concludes thy musings once again?

'O for the time when I shall sleep
Without identity,
And never care how rain may steep
Or snow may cover me!

'No promised Heaven, these wild Desires
Could all or half fulfil;
No threatened Hell, with quenchless fires,
Subdue this quenchless will!'

—So said I, and still say the same;
—Still to my Death will say—
Three Gods within this little frame
Are warring night and day.

Heaven could not hold them all, and yet
They all are held in me
And must be mine till I forget
My present entity.

O for the time when in my breast
Their struggles will be o'er;
O for the day when I shall rest,
And never suffer more!

'I saw a Spirit standing, Man,
Where thou dost stand—an hour ago;
And round his feet, three rivers ran
Of equal depth and equal flow—

'A Golden stream, and one like blood,
And one like Sapphire, seemed to be,
But where they joined their triple flood
It tumbled in an inky sea.

'The Spirit bent his dazzling gaze
Down on that Ocean's gloomy night,
Then—kindling all with sudden blaze,
The glad deep sparkled wide and bright—
White as the sun; far, far more fair
Than the divided sources were!'

—And even for that Spirit, Seer,
I've watched and sought my lifetime long;
Sought Him in Heaven, Hell, Earth and Air,
An endless search—and always wrong!

Had I but seen his glorious eye
Once light the clouds that 'wilder me,
I ne'er had raised this coward cry
To cease to think and cease to be—

I ne'er had called oblivion blest,
Nor stretching eager hands to Death
Implored to change for lifeless rest
This sentient soul, this living breath.

O let me die, that power and will
Their cruel strife may close,
And vanquished Good, victorious Ill
Be lost in one repose.

EMILY BRONTË

Sic Itur

As, at a railway junction, men
Who came together, taking then
One the train up, one down, again

Meet never! Ah, much more as they
Who take one street's two sides, and say
Hard parting words, but walk away:

Though moving other mates between,
While carts and coaches intervene,
Each to the other goes unseen,

Yet seldom, surely, shall there lack
Knowledge they walk not back to back,
But with an unity of track,

Where common dangers each attend,
And common hopes their guidance lend
To light them to the self-same end.

Whether he then shall cross to thee,
Or thou go thither, or it be
Some midway point, ye yet shall see

Each other yet again shall meet.
Ah, joy! when with the closing street,
Forgivingly at last ye greet!

ARTHUR HUGH CLOUGH

Come Back . . .

Come back again, my olden heart!—
    Ah, fickle spirit and untrue,
I bade the only guide depart
    Whose faithfulness I surely knew:
I said, my heart is all too soft;
He who would climb and soar aloft,
Must needs keep ever at his side
The tonic of a wholesome pride.

Come back again, my olden heart!—
    Alas, I called not then for thee;
I called for Courage, and apart
    From Pride if Courage could not be,

Then welcome, Pride! and I shall find
In thee a power to lift the mind
This low and grovelling joy above—
'Tis but the proud can truly love.

Come back again, my olden heart!—
    With incrustations of the years
Uncased as yet,—as then thou wert,
    Full-filled with shame and coward fears:
Wherewith, amidst a jostling throng
Of deeds, that each and all were wrong,
The doubting soul, from day to day,
Uneasy paralytic lay.

Come back again, my olden heart!—
    I said, Perceptions contradict,
Convictions come, anon depart,
    And but themselves as false convict.
Assumptions hasty, crude, and vain,
Full oft to use will Science deign;
The corks the novice plies to-day
The swimmer soon shall cast away.

Come back again, my olden heart!—
    I said, Behold, I perish quite,
Unless to give me strength to start,
    I make myself my rule of right:
It must be, if I act at all,
To save my shame I have at call
The plea of all men understood,
Because I willed it, it is good.

Come back again, my olden heart!
    I know not if in very deed
This means alone could aid impart
    To serve my sickly spirit's need;
But clear alike of wild self-will,
And fear that faltered, paltered still,
Remorseful thoughts of after days
A way espy betwixt the ways.

Come back again, old heart! Ah me!
        Methinks in those thy coward fears
There might, perchance, a courage be,
        That fails in these the manlier years;
Courage to let the courage sink,
Itself a coward base to think,
Rather than not for heavenly light
Wait on to show the truly right.

ARTHUR HUGH CLOUGH

Shiloh

A Requiem

(April, 1862.)

Skimming lightly, wheeling still,
        The swallows fly low
Over the field in clouded days,
        The forest-field of Shiloh—
Over the field where April rain
Solaced the parched ones stretched in pain
Through the pause of night
That followed the Sunday fight
        Around the church of Shiloh—
The church so lone, the log-built one,
That echoed to many a parting groan
        And natural prayer
        Of dying foemen mingled there—
Foemen at morn, but friends at eve—
        Fame or country least their care:
(What like a bullet can undeceive!)
        But now they lie low,
While over them the swallows skim,
        And all is hushed at Shiloh.

HERMAN MELVILLE

The House-top

A Night Piece

(July, 1863.)

No sleep. The sultriness pervades the air
And binds the brain—a dense oppression, such
As tawny tigers feel in matted shades,
Vexing their blood and making apt for ravage.
Beneath the stars the roofy desert spreads
Vacant as Libya. All is hushed near by.
Yet fitfully from far breaks a mixed surf
Of muffled sound, the Atheist roar of riot.
Yonder, where parching Sirius set in drought,
Balefully glares red Arson—there—and there.
The Town is taken by its rats—ship-rats
And rats of the wharves. All civil charms
And priestly spells which late held hearts in awe—
Fear-bound, subjected to a better sway
Than sway of self; these like a dream dissolve,
And man rebounds whole aeons back in nature.
Hail to the low dull rumble, dull and dead,
And ponderous drag that shakes the wall.
Wise Draco comes, deep in the midnight roll
Of black artillery; he comes, though late;
In code corroborating Calvin's creed
And cynic tyrannies of honest kings;
He comes, nor parlies; and the Town, redeemed,
Gives thanks devout; nor, being thankful, heeds
The grimy slur on the Republic's faith implied,
Which holds that Man is naturally good,
And—more—is Nature's Roman, never to be scourged.

HERMAN MELVILLE

Monody

To have known him, to have loved him
　　After loneness long;
And then to be estranged in life,
　　And neither in the wrong;
And now for death to set his seal—
　　Ease me, a little ease, my song!

By wintry hills his hermit-mound
　　The sheeted snow-drifts drape,
And houseless there the snow-bird flits
　　Beneath the fir-trees' crape:
Glazed now with ice the cloistral vine
　　That hid the shyest grape.

HERMAN MELVILLE

Billy in the Darbies

Good of the Chaplain to enter Lone Bay
And down on his marrow-bones here and pray
For the likes just o' me, Billy Budd.—
But look:
Through the port comes the moonshine astray!
It tips the guard's cutlass and silvers this nook;
But 'twill die in the dawning of Billy's last day.
A jewel-block they'll make of me to-morrow,
Pendant pearl from the yard-arm-end
Like the ear-drop I gave to Bristol-Molly—
Oh, 'tis me, not the sentence, they'll suspend.
Ay, ay, all is up; and I must up too
Early in the morning, aloft from alow.
On an empty stomach, now, never it would do.
They'll give me a nibble—bit of biscuit ere I go.
Sure, a messmate will reach me the last parting cup;
But turning heads away from the hoist and the belay,
Heaven knows who will have the running of me up!

No pipe to those halyards—But aren't it all sham?
A blur's in my eyes; it is dreaming that I am.
A hatchet to my panzer? all adrift to go?
The drum roll to grog, and Billy never know?
But Donald he has promised to stand by the plank;
So I'll shake a friendly hand ere I sink.
But—no! it is dead then I'll be, come to think.
I remember Taff the Welshman when he sank.
And his cheek it was like the budding pink.
But me, they'll lash me in hammock, drop me deep
Fathoms down, fathoms down, how I'll dream fast asleep.
I feel it stealing now. Sentry, are you there?
Just ease these darbies at the wrist,
And roll me over fair.
I am sleepy, and the oozy weeds about me twist.

HERMAN MELVILLE

On the Site of a Mulberry-Tree

Planted by Wm. Shakespeare;
felled by the Rev. F. Gastrell

This tree, here fall'n, no common birth or death
Shared with its kind. The world's enfranchised son,
Who found the trees of Life and Knowledge one,
Here set it, frailer than his laurel-wreath.
Shall not the wretch whose hand it fell beneath
Rank also singly—the supreme unhung?
Lo! Sheppard, Turpin, pleading with black tongue
This viler thief's unsuffocated breath!
We'll search thy glossary, Shakespeare! whence almost,
And whence alone, some name shall be reveal'd
For this deaf drudge, to whom no length of ears
Sufficed to catch the music of the spheres;
Whose soul is carrion now,—too mean to yield
Some Starveling's ninth allotment of a ghost.

DANTE GABRIEL ROSSETTI

The Orchard-Pit

Piled deep below the screening apple-branch
   They lie with bitter apples in their hands:
And some are only ancient bones that blanch,
And some had ships that last year's wind did launch,
   And some were yesterday the lords of lands.

In the soft dell, among the apple-trees,
   High up above the hidden pit she stands,
And there for ever sings, who gave to these,
That lie below, her magic hour of ease,
   And those her apples holden in their hands.

This in my dream is shown me; and her hair
   Crosses my lips and draws my burning breath;
Her song spread golden wings upon the air,
Life's eyes are gleaming from her forehead fair,
   And from her breasts the ravishing eyes of Death.

Men say to me that sleep hath many dreams,
   Yet I knew never but this dream alone:
There, from a dried-up channel, once the stream's,
The glen slopes up; even such in sleep it seems
   As to my waking sight the place well known.

*   *   *   *

My love I call her, and she loves me well:
   But I love her as in the maelstrom's cup
The whirled stone loves the leaf inseparable
That clings to it round all the circling swell,
   And that the same last eddy swallows up.

DANTE GABRIEL ROSSETTI

Dawn on the Night-Journey

Till dawn the wind drove round me. It is past
  And still, and leaves the air to lisp of bird,
  And to the quiet that is almost heard
Of the new-risen day, as yet bound fast
In the first warmth of sunrise. When the last
  Of the sun's hours to-day shall be fulfilled,
  There shall another breath of time be stilled
For me, which now is to my senses cast
As much beyond me as eternity,
  Unknown, kept secret. On the newborn air
The moth quivers in silence. It is vast,
Yes, even beyond the hills upon the sea,
  The day whose end shall give this hour as sheer
As chaos to the irrevocable Past.

DANTE GABRIEL ROSSETTI

A Match with the Moon

Weary already, weary miles to-night
  I walked for bed: and so, to get some ease,
  I dogged the flying moon with similes.
And like a wisp she doubled on my sight
In ponds; and caught in tree-tops like a kite;
  And in a globe of film all vapourish
Swam full-faced like a silly silver fish;—
Last like a bubble shot the welkin's height
Where my road turned, and got behind me, and sent
  My wizened shadow craning round at me,
  And jeered, 'So, step the measure,—one two three!'—
And if I faced on her, looked innocent.
  But just at parting, halfway down a dell,
  She kissed me for good-night. So you'll not tell.

DANTE GABRIEL ROSSETTI

Lost Days

The lost days of my life until to-day,
    What were they, could I see them on the street
    Lie as they fell? Would they be ears of wheat
Sown once for food but trodden into clay?
Or golden coins squandered and still to pay?
    Or drops of blood dabbling the guilty feet?
    Or such spilt water as in dreams must cheat
The throats of men in Hell, who thirst alway?

I do not see them here; but after death
    God knows I know the faces I shall see,
Each one a murdered self, with low last breath.
    'I am thyself,—what hast thou done to me?'
'And I—and I—thyself,' (lo! each one saith),
    'And thou thyself to all eternity!'

            DANTE GABRIEL ROSSETTI

Inclusiveness

The changing guests, each in a different mood,
    Sit at the roadside table and arise:
    And every life among them in likewise
Is a soul's board set daily with new food.
What man has bent o'er his son's sleep, to brood
    How that face shall watch his when cold it lies?—
    Or thought, as his own mother kissed his eyes,
Of what her kiss was when his father wooed?

May not this ancient room thou sit'st in dwell
    In separate living souls for joy or pain?
    Nay, all its corners may be painted plain
Where Heaven shows pictures of some life spent well;
    And may be stamped, a memory all in vain,
Upon the sight of lidless eyes in Hell.

            DANTE GABRIEL ROSSETTI

Without Her

What of her glass without her? the blank grey
  There where the pool is blind of the moon's face.
  Her dress without her? the tossed empty space
Of cloud-rack whence the moon has passed away.
Her paths without her? Day's appointed sway
  Usurped by desolate night. Her pillowed place
  Without her! Tears, Ah me! for love's good grace
And cold forgetfulness of night or day.

What of the heart without her? Nay, poor heart,
  Of thee what word remains ere speech be still?
  A wayfarer by barren ways and chill,
Steep ways and weary, without her thou art,
Where the long cloud, the long wood's counterpart,
  Sheds doubled darkness up the labouring hill.

DANTE GABRIEL ROSSETTI

A Last Confession

(Regno Lombardo-Veneto, 1848)

Our Lombard country-girls along the coast
Wear daggers in their garters; for they know
That they might hate another girl to death
Of meet a German lover. Such a knife
I bought her, with a hilt of horn and pearl.

Father, you cannot know of all my thoughts
That day in going to meet her,—that last day
For the last time, she said;—of all the love
And all the hopeless hope that she might change
And go back with me. Ah! and everywhere,
At places we both knew along the road,

Some fresh shape of herself as once she was
Grew present at my side; until it seemed—
So close they gathered round me—they would all
Be with me when I reached the spot at last,
To plead my cause with her against herself
So changed. O Father, if you knew all this
You cannot know, then you would know too, Father,
And only then, if God can pardon me.
What can be told I'll tell, if you will hear.

I passed a village-fair upon my road,
And thought, being empty-handed, I would take
Some little present: such might prove, I said,
Either a pledge between us, or (God help me!)
A parting gift. And there it was I bought
The knife I spoke of, such as women wear.

That day, some three hours afterwards, I found
For certain, it must be a parting gift.
And, standing silent now at last, I looked
Into her scornful face; and heard the sea
Still trying hard to din into my ears
Some speech it knew which still might change her heart
If only it could make me understand.
One moment thus. Another, and her face
Seemed further off than the last line of sea,
So that I thought, if now she were to speak
I could not hear her. Then again I knew
All, as we stood together on the sand
At Iglio, in the first thin shade o' the hills.

'Take it,' I said, and held it out to her,
While the hilt glanced within my trembling hold;
'Take it and keep it for my sake,' I said.
Her neck unbent not, neither did her eyes
Move, nor her foot left beating of the sand;
Only she put it by from her and laughed.

Father, you hear my speech and not her laugh;
But God heard that. Will God remember all?

It was another laugh than the sweet sound
Which rose from her sweet childish heart, that day
Eleven years before, when first I found her
Alone upon the hill-side; and her curls
Shook down in the warm grass as she looked up
Out of her curls in my eyes bent to hers.
She might have served a painter to pourtray
That heavenly child which in the latter days
Shall walk between the lion and the lamb.
I had been for nights in hiding, worn and sick
And hardly fed; and so her words at first
Seemed fitful like the talking of the trees
And voices in the air that knew my name.
And I remember that I sat me down
Upon the slope with her, and thought the world
Must be all over or had never been,
We seemed there so alone. And soon she told me
Her parents both were gone away from her.

I thought perhaps she meant that they had died;
But when I asked her this, she looked again
Into my face, and said that yestereve
They kissed her long, and wept and made her weep
And gave her all the bread they had with them,
And then had gone together up the hill
Where we were sitting now, and had walked on
Into the great red light: 'and so,' she said,
'I have come up here too; and when this evening
They step out of the light as they stepped in,
I shall be here to kiss them.' And she laughed.

Then I bethought me suddenly of the famine;
And how the church-steps throughout all the town,
When last I had been there a month ago,
Swarmed with starved folk; and how the bread was weighed
By Austrians armed; and women that I knew
For wives and mothers walked the public street,
Saying aloud that if their husbands feared
To snatch the children's food, themselves would stay
Till they had earned it there. So then this child
Was piteous to me; for all told me then

Her parents must have left her to God's chance,
To man's or to the Church's charity,
Because of the great famine, rather than
To watch her growing thin between their knees.
With that, God took my mother's voice and spoke,
And sights and sounds came back and things long since,
And all my childhood found me on the hills;
And so I took her with me.

                      I was young,
Scarce man then, Father; but the cause which gave
The wounds I die of now had brought me then
Some wounds already; and I lived alone,
As any hiding hunted man must live.
It was no easy thing to keep a child
In safety; for herself it was not safe,
And doubled my own danger: but I knew
That God would help me.

                     Yet a little while
Pardon me, Father, if I pause. I think
I have been speaking to you of some matters
There was no need to speak of, have I not?
You do not know how clearly those things stood
Within my mind, which I have spoken of.
Nor how they strove for utterance. Life all past
Is like the sky when the sun sets in it,
Clearest where furthest off.

                   I told you how
She scorned my parting gift and laughed. And yet
A woman's laugh's another thing sometimes:
I think they laugh in Heaven. I know last night
I dreamed I saw into the garden of God,
Where women walked whose painted images
I have seen with candles round them in the church.
They bent this way and that, one to another,
Swaying: and over the long golden hair
Of each there floated like a ring of fire
Which when she stooped stooped with her, and when she rose
Rose with her. Then a breeze flew in among them,
As if a window had been opened in heaven
For God to give his blessing from, before

This world of ours should set; (for in my dream
I thought our world was setting, and the sun
Waned, a spent taper;) and beneath that gust
The rings of light quivered like forest-leaves.
Then all the blessed maidens who were there
Stood up together, as it were a voice
That called them; and they threw their tresses back,
And smote their palms, and all laughed up at once,
For the strong heavenly joy they had in them
To hear God bless the world. Wherewith I woke:
And looking round, I saw as usual
That she was standing there with her long locks
Tressed to her side; and her laugh ended theirs.

For always when I see her now, she laughs.
And yet her childish laughter haunts me too,
The life of this dead terror; as in days
When she a child, dwelt with me. I must tell
Something of those days yet before the end.

I brought her from the city—one such day
When she was still a merry loving child,—
The earliest gift I mind my giving her;
A little image of a flying Love
Made of our coloured glass-ware, in his hands
A dart of gilded metal and a torch.
And him she kissed and me, and fain would know
Why were his poor eyes blindfold, why the wings
And why the arrow. What I knew I told
Of Venus and of Cupid,—strange old tales.
And when she heard that he could rule the loves
Of men and women, still she shook her head
And wondered; and, 'Nay, nay,' she murmured still,
'So strong, and he a younger child than I!'
And then she'd have me fix him on the wall
Fronting her little bed; and then again
She needs must fix him there herself, because
I gave him to her and she loved him so,
And he should make her love me better yet.
If women loved the more, the more they grew

But the fit place upon the wall was high
For her, and so I held her in my arms:
And each time that the heavy pruning-hook
I gave her for a hammer slipped away
As it would often, still she laughed and laughed
And kissed and kissed me. But amid her mirth,
Just as she hung the image on the nail,
It slipped and all its fragments strewed the ground:
And as it fell she screamed, for in her hand
The dart had entered deeply and drawn blood.
And so her laughter turned to tears: and 'Oh!'
I said, the while I bandaged the small hand,—
"That I should be the first to make you bleed,
Who love and love and love you!'—kissing still
The fingers till I got her safe to bed.
And still she sobbed,—'not for the pain at all,'
She said, 'but for the Love, the poor good Love
You gave me.' So she cried herself to sleep.

   Another later thing comes back to me.
'Twas in those hardest foulest days of all,
When still from his shut palace, sitting clean
Above the splash of blood, old Metternich
(May his soul die, and never-dying worms
Feast on its pain for ever!) used to thin
His year's doomed hundreds daintily, each month
Thirties and fifties. This time, as I think,
Was when his thrift forbad the poor to take
That evil brackish salt which the dry rocks
Keep all through winter when the sea draws in.
The first I heard of it was a chance shot
In the street here and there, and on the stones
A stumbling clatter as of horse hemmed round.
Then, when she saw me hurry out of doors,
My gun slung at my shoulder and my knife
Stuck in my girdle, she smoothed down my hair
And laughed to see me look so brave, and leaped
Up to my neck and kissed me. She was still
A child; and yet that kiss was on my lips
So hot all day where the smoke shut us in.

For now, being always with her, the first love
I had—the father's, brother's love—was changed,
I think, in somewise; like a holy thought
Which is a prayer before one knows of it.
The first time I perceived this, I remember,
Was once when after hunting I came home
Weary, and she brought food and fruit for me,
And sat down at my feet upon the floor
Leaning against my side. But when I felt
Her sweet head reach from that low seat of hers
So high as to be laid upon my heart,
I turned and looked upon my darling there
And marked for the first time how tall she was;
And my heart beat with so much violence
Under her cheek. I thought she could not choose
But wonder at it soon and ask me why;
And so I bade her rise and eat with me.
And when, remembering all and counting back
The time, I made out fourteen years for her
And told her so, she gazed at me with eyes
As of the sky and sea on a grey day,
And drew her long hands through her hair, and asked me
If she was not a woman; and then laughed:
And as she stooped in laughing, I could see
Beneath the growing throat the breasts half globed
Like folded lilies deepset in the stream.

Yes, let me think of her as then; for so
Her image, Father, is not like the sights
Which come when you are gone. She had a mouth
Made to bring death to life,—the underlip
Sucked in, as if it strove to kiss itself.
Her face was ever pale, as when one stoops
Over wan water; and the dark crisped hair
And the hair's shadow made it paler still:—
Deep-serried locks, the dimness of the cloud
Where the moon's gaze is set in eddying gloom.
Her body bore her neck as the tree's stem
Bears the top branch; and as the branch sustains
The flower of the year's pride, her high neck bore
C.E.P.—19

That face made wonderful with night and day.
Her voice was swift, yet ever the last words
Fell lingeringly; and rounded finger-tips
She had, that clung a little where they touched
And then were gone o' the instant. Her great eyes,
That sometimes turned half dizzily beneath
The passionate lids, as faint, when she would speak,
Had also in them hidden springs of mirth,
Which under the dark lashes evermore
Shook to her laugh, as when a bird flies low
Between the water and the willow-leaves,
And the shade quivers till he wins the light.

    I was a moody comrade to her then,
For all the love I bore her. Italy,
The weeping desolate mother, long has claimed
Her sons' strong arms to lean on, and their hands
To lop the poisonous thicket from her path,
Cleaving her way to light. And from her need
Had grown the fashion of my whole poor life
Which I was proud to yield her, as my father
Had yielded his. And this had come to be
A game to play, a love to clasp, a hate
To wreak, all things together that a man
Needs for his blood to ripen: till at times
All else seemed shadows, and I wondered still
To see such life pass muster and be deemed
Time's bodily substance. In those hours, no doubt,
To the young girl my eyes were like my soul,
Dark wells of death-in-life that yearned for day.
And though she ruled me always, I remember
That once when I was thus and she still kept
Leaping about the place and laughing, I
Did almost chide her; whereupon she knealt
And putting her two hands into my breast
Sang me a song. Are these tears in my eyes?
'Tis long since I have wept for anything.
I thought that song forgotten out of mind,
And now, just as I spoke it, it came
All back. It is but a rude thing, ill rhymed,

Such as a blind man chaunts and his dog hears
Holding the platter, when the children run
To merrier sport and leave him. Thus it goes:—

> La bella donna[1]
> Piangendo disse:
> 'Come son fisse
> Le stelle in cielo!
> Quel fiato anelo
> Dello stanco sole,
> Quanto m' assonna!
> E la luna, macchiata
> Come uno specchio
> Logoro e vecchio.—
> Faccia affannata,
> Che cosa vuole?
>
> 'Chè stelle, luna, e sole,
> Ciascun m' annoja

[1] She wept, sweet lady,
And said in weeping:
'What spell is keeping
The stars so steady?
Why does the power
Of the sun's noon-hour
To sleep so move me?
And the moon in heaven,
Stained where she passes
As a worn-out glass is,—
Wearily driven,
Why walks she above me?

'Stars, moon, and sun too,
I'm tired of either
And all together!
Whom speak they unto
That I should listen?
For very surely,
Though my arms and shoulders
Dazzle beholders,
And my eyes glisten,
All's nothing purely!
What are words said for
At all about them,
If he they are made for
Can do without them?'

She laughed, sweet lady,
And said in laughing:
'His hand clings half in

My own already!
Oh! do you love me?
Oh! speak of passion
In no new fashion,
No loud inveighings,
But the old sayings
You once said of me.

'You said: "As summer
Through boughs grown brittle,
Comes back a little
Ere frosts benumb her,—
So bring'st thou to me
All leaves and flowers,
Though autumn's gloomy
To-day in the bowers.'

'Oh! does he love me,
When my voice teaches
The very speeches
He then spoke of me?
Alas! what flavour
Still with me lingers?'
(But she laughed as my kisses
Glowed in her fingers
With love's old blisses.)
'Oh! what one favour
Remains to woo him,
Whose whole poor savour
Belongs not to him?'

E m' annojano insieme;
Non me ne preme
Nè ci prendo gioja.
E veramente,
Che le spalle sien franche
E le braccia bianche
E il seno caldo e tondo,
Non mi fa niente.
Chè cosa al mondo
Posso più far di questi
Se non piacciono a te, come dicesti?'

La donna rise
E riprese ridendo:—
'Questa mano che prendo
E dunque mia?
Tu m' ami dunque?
Dimmelo ancora,
Non in modo qualunque,
Ma le parole
Belle e precise
Che dicesti pria.

'*Siccome suole*
La state talora
(*Dicesti*) *un qualche istante*
Tornare innanzi inverno,
Così tu fai ch' io scerno
Le foglie tutte quante,
Ben ch' io certo tenessi
Per passato l' autunno.

'Eccolo il mio alunno!
Io debbo insegnargli
Quei cari detti istessi
Ch' ei mi disse una volta!
Oimè! Che cosa dargli,'
(Ma ridea piano piano
Dei baci in sulla mano,)
'Ch' ei non m' abbia da lungo tempo tolta?'

That I should sing upon this bed!—with you
To listen, and such words still left to say!
Yet was it I that sang? The voice seemed hers,
As on the very day she sang to me;
When, having done, she took out of my hand
Something that I had played with all the while
And laid it down beyond my reach; and so
Turning my face round till it fronted hers,—
'Weeping or laughing, which was best?' she said.

But these are foolish tales. How should I show
The heart that glowed then with love's heat, each day
More and more brightly?—when for long years now
The very flame that flew about the heart,
And gave it fiery wings, has come to be
The lapping blaze of hell's environment
Whose tongues all bid the molten heart despair.

Yet one more thing comes back on me to-night
Which I may tell you: for it bore my soul
Dread firstlings of the brood that rend it now.
It chanced that in our last year's wanderings
We dwelt at Monza, far away from home,
If home we had: and in the Duomo there
I sometimes entered with her when she prayed.
An image of Our Lady stands there, wrought
In marble by some great Italian hand
In the great days when she and Italy
Sat on one throne together: and to her
And to none else my loved one told her heart.
She was a woman then; and as she knelt,—
Her sweet brow in the sweet brow's shadow there,—
They seemed two kindred forms whereby our land
(Whose work still serves the world for miracle)
Made manifest herself in womanhood.
Father, the day I speak of was the first
For weeks that I had borne her company
Into the Duomo; and those weeks had been
Much troubled, for then first the glimpses came
Of some impenetrable restlessness
Growing in her to make her changed and cold.

And as we entered there that day, I bent
My eyes on the fair Image, and I said
Within my heart, 'Oh turn her heart to me!'
And so I left her to her prayers, and went
To gaze upon the pride of Monza's shrine,
Where in the sacristy the light still falls
Upon the Iron Crown of Italy,
On whose crowned heads the day has closed, nor yet
The daybreak gilds another head to crown.
But coming back, I wondered when I saw
That the sweet Lady of her prayers now stood
Alone without her; until further off,
Before some new Madonna gaily decked,
Tinselled and gewgawed, a slight German toy,
I saw her kneel, still praying. At my step
She rose, and side by side we left the church.
I was much moved, and sharply questioned her
Of her transferred devotion; but she seemed
Stubborn and heedless; till she lightly laughed
And said: 'The old Madonna? Aye indeed,
She had my old thoughts,—this one has my new.'
Then silent to the soul I held my way:
And from the fountains of the public place
Unto the pigeon-haunted pinnacles,
Bright wings and water winnowed the bright air;
And stately with her laugh's subsiding smile
She went, with clear-swayed waist and towering neck
And hands held light before her; and the face
Which long had made a day in my life's night
Was night in day to me; as all men's eyes
Turned on her beauty, and she seemed to tread
Beyond my heart to the world made for her.

    Ah there! my wounds will snatch my sense again:
The pain comes billowing on like a full cloud
Of thunder, and the flash that breaks from it
Leaves my brain burning. That's the wound he gave,
The Austrian whose white coat I still made match
With his white face, only the two were red
As suits his trade. The devil makes them wear

White for a livery, that the blood may show
Braver that brings them to him. So he looks
Sheer o'er the field and knows his own at once.

Give me a draught of water in that cup;
My voice feels thick; perhaps you do not hear;
But you *must* hear. If you mistake my words
And so absolve me, I am sure the blessing
Will burn my soul. If you mistake my words
And so absolve me, Father, the great sin
Is yours, not mine: mark this: your soul shall burn
With mine for it. I have seen pictures where
Souls burned with Latin shriekings in their mouths:
Shall my end be as theirs? Nay, but I know
'Tis you shall shriek in Latin. Some bell rings,
Rings through my brain: it strikes the hour in hell.

You see I cannot, Father; I have tried,
But cannot, as you see. These twenty times
Beginning, I have come to the same point
And stopped. Beyond, there are but broken words
Which will not let you understand my tale.
It is that then we have her with us here,
As when she wrung her hair out in my dream
To-night, till all the darkness reeked of it.
Her hair is always wet, for she has kept
Its tresses wrapped about her side for years;
And when she wrung them round over the floor,
I heard the blood between her fingers hiss;
So that I sat up in my bed and screamed
Once and again; and once to once, she laughed.
Look that you turn not now,—she's at your back:
Gather your robe up, Father, and keep close,
Or she'll sit down on it and send you mad.

At Iglio in the first thin shade o' the hills
The sand is black and red. The black was black
When what was spilt that day sank into it,
And the red scarcely darkened. There I stood
This night with her, and saw the sand the same.

.   .   .   .

What would you have me tell you? Father, Father,
How shall I make you know? You have not known
The dreadful soul of woman, who one day
Forgets the old and takes the new to heart,
Forget what man remembers, and therewith
Forgets the man. Nor can I clearly tell
How the change happened between her and me.
Her eyes looked on me from an emptied heart
When most my heart was full of her; and still
In every corner of myself I sought
To find what service failed her; and no less
Than in the good time past, there all was hers.
What do you love? Your Heaven? Conceive it spread
For one first year of all eternity
All round you with all joys and gifts of God;
And then when most your soul is blent with it
And all yields song together,—then it stands
O' the sudden like a pool that once gave back
Your image, but now drowns it and is clear
Again,—or like a sun bewitched, that burns
Your shadow from you, and still shines in sight.
How could you bear it? Would you not cry out,
Among those eyes grown blind to you, those ears
That hear no more your vojce you hear the same,—
'God! what is left but hell for company,
But hell, hell, hell?'—until the name so breathed
Whirled with hot wind and sucked you down in fire?
Even so I stood the day her empty heart
Left her place empty in our home, while yet
I knew not why she went nor where she went
Nor how to reach her: so I stood the day
When to my prayers at last one sight of her
Was granted, and I looked on heaven made pale
With scorn, and heard heaven mock me in that laugh.

    O sweet, long sweet! Was that some ghost of you
Even as your ghost that haunts me now,—twin shapes
Of fear and hatred? May I find you yet
Mine when death wakes? Ah! be it even in flame,
We may have sweetness yet, if you but say

As once in childish sorrow: 'Not my pain,
My pain was nothing: oh your poor poor love,
Your broken love!'

                      My Father, have I not
Yet told you the last things of that last day
On which I went to meet her by the sea?
O God, O God! but I must tell you all.

   Midway upon my journey, when I stopped
To buy the dagger at the village fair,
I saw two cursed rats about the place
I knew for spies—blood-sellers both. That day
Was not yet over; for three hours to come
I prized my life: and so I looked around
For safety. A poor painted mountebank
Was playing tricks and shouting in a crowd.
I knew he must have heard my name, so I
Pushed past and whispered to him who I was,
And of my danger. Straight he hustled me
Into his booth, as it were in the trick,
And brought me out next minute with my face
All smeared in patches, and a zany's gown;
And there I handed him his cups and balls
And swung the sand-bags round to clear the ring
For half an hour. The spies came once and looked:
And while they stopped, and made all sights and sounds
Sharp to my startled senses, I remember
A woman laughed above me. I looked up
And saw where a brown-shouldered harlot leaned
Half through a tavern window thick with vine.
Some man had come behind her in the room
And caught her by her arms, and she had turned
With that coarse empty laugh on him, as now
He munched her neck with kisses, while the vine
Crawled in her back.

                 And three hours afterwards,
When she that I had run all risks to meet
Laughed as I told you, my life burned to death
Within me, for I thought it like the laugh
Heard at the fair. She had not left me long;

But all she might have changed to, or might change to
(I know nought since—she never speaks a word—)
Seemed in that laugh. Have I not told you yet,
Not told you all this time what happened, Father,
When I had offered her the little knife,
And bade her keep it for my sake that loved her,
And she had laughed? Have I not told you yet?

   'Take it,' I said to her the second time,
'Take it and keep it.' And then came a fire
That burnt my hand; and then the fire was blood,
And sea and sky were blood and fire, and all
The day was one red blindness; till it seemed
Within the whirling brain's eclipse, that she
Or I or all things bled or burned to death.
And then I found her laid against my feet
And knew that I had stabbed her, and saw still
Her look in falling. For she took the knife
Deep in her heart, even as I bade her then,
And fell; and her stiff bodice scooped the sand
Into her bosom.   And she keeps it, see,
Do you not see she keeps it?—there, beneath
Wet fingers and wet tresses, in her heart.
For look you, when she stirs her hand, it shows
The little hilt of horn and pearl,—even such
A dagger as our women of the coast
Twist in their garters.   Father, I have done:
And from her side now she unwinds the thick
Dark hair; all round her side it is wet through,
But like the sand at Iglio does not change.
Now you may see the dagger clearly. Father,
I have told all; tell me at once what hope
Can reach me still. For now she draws it out
Slowly, and only smiles as yet: look, Father,
She scarcely smiles: but I shall hear her laugh
Soon, when she shows the crimson blade to God.

DANTE GABRIEL ROSSETTI

Exultation is the Going

Exultation is the going
Of an inland soul to sea,
Past the houses, past the headlands,
Into deep eternity.

Bred as we, among the mountains,
Can the sailor understand
The divine intoxication
Of the first league out from land?

EMILY DICKINSON

I never hear the word 'Escape'

I never hear the word 'escape'
Without a quicker blood,
A sudden expectation,
A flying attitude.

I never hear of prisons broad
By soldiers battered down
But I tug childish at my bars
Only to fail again.

EMILY DICKINSON

I like a Look of Agony

I like a look of agony
Because I know it's true.
Men do not sham convulsion
Nor simulate a throe.

The eyes glaze once, and that is death—
Impossible to feign
The beads upon the forehead
By homely anguish strung.

EMILY DICKINSON

A Clock Stopped

A clock stopped—
Not the mantel's.
Geneva's farthest skill
Can't put the puppet bowing
That just now dangled still.

An awe came on the trinket.
The figures hunched with pain
Then quivered out of decimals
Into degreeless noon.

It will not stir for doctors,
This pendulum of snow.
The shopman importunes it,
While cool concernless No

Nods from the gilded pointers,
Nods from the seconds slim,
Decades of arrogance between
The dial life
And him.

EMILY DICKINSON

I'm Nobody

I'm nobody, who are you?
Are you nobody too?
Then there's a pair of us.
Don't tell—they'd banish us, you know.

How dreary to be somebody,
How public—like a frog—
To tell your name the livelong June
To an admiring bog.

                    EMILY DICKINSON

There's been a Death in the Opposite House

There's been a death in the opposite house
As lately as today.
I know it by the numb look
Such houses have alway.

The neighbours rustle in and out;
The doctor drives away.
A window opens like a pod,
Abrupt, mechanically;

Somebody flings a mattress out.
The children hurry by;
They wonder if it died on that.
I used to as a boy.

The minister goes stiffly in
As if the house were his
And he ownde all the mourners now,
And little boys besides;

And then the milliner, and the man
Of the appalling trade
To take the measure of the house.
There'll be that dark parade

Of tassels and of coaches soon.
It's easy as a sign—
The intuition of the news
In just a country town.

EMILY DICKINSON

I died for Beauty . . .

I died for beauty, but was scarce
Adjusted in the tomb
When one who died for truth was lain
In an adjoining room.

He questioned softly why I failed,
'For beauty' I replied.
'And I for truth. Themselves are one.
We bretheren are' he said.

And so, as kinsmen met a night,
We talked between the rooms,
Until the moss had reached our lips
And covered up our names.

EMILY DICKINSON

I Started Early . . .

I started early, took my dog,
And visited the sea.
The mermaids in the basement
Came out to look at me

And frigates in the upper floor
Extended hempen hands,
Presuming me to be a mouse
Aground upon the sands,

But no man moved me till the tide
Went past my simple shoe
And past my apron and my belt
And past my bodice too,

And made as he would eat me up
As wholly as a dew
Upon a dandelion's sleeve;
And then I started too

And he, he followed close behind;
I felt his silver heel
Upon my ankle, then my shoes
Would overflow with pearl,

Until we met the solid town.
No one he seemed to know
And bowing with a mighty look
At me, the sea withdrew.

EMILY DICKINSON

A Long, Long Sleep . . .

A long, long sleep, a famous sleep
That makes no show for morn
By stretch of limb or stir of lid,
An independent one—

Was ever idleness like this,
Upon a bank of stone
To bask the centuries away
Nor once look up for noon?

EMILY DICKINSON

While We were fearing It . . .

While we were fearing it, it came,
But came with less of fear
Because the fearing it so long
Had almost made it fair.

There is a fitting—a dismay;
A fitting—a despair.
'Tis harder knowing it is due
Than knowing it is here.

The trying on the utmost,
The morning it is new,
Is terribler than wearing it
A whole existence through.

EMILY DICKINSON

The Knight in the Wood

The thing itself was rough and crudely done,
Cut in coarse stone, spitefully placed aside
As merest lumber, where the light was worst,
On a back staircase. Overlooked it lay
In a great Roman palace crammed with art.
It had no number in the list of gems,
Weeded away long since, pushed out and banished,
Before insipid Guidos over-sweet,
And Dolce's rare sensationalities,
And curly chirping angels spruce as birds.
And yet the motive of this thing ill-hewn
And hardly seen *did* touch me. O, indeed,
The skill-less hand that carved it had belonged
To a most yearning and bewildered heart,
There was such desolation in its work;
And through its utter failure the thing spoke

With more of human message, heart to heart,
Than all these faultless, smirking, skin-deep saints;
In artificial troubles picturesque,
And martyred sweetly, not one curl awry.—
Listen; a clumsy knight who rode alone
Upon a stumbling jade in a great wood
Belated. The poor beast with head low-bowed
Snuffing the treacherous ground. The rider leant
Forward to sound the marish with his lance.
You saw the place was deadly; that doomed pair,
The wretched rider and the hide-bound steed
Feared to advance, feared to return—That's all

LORD DE TABLEY

Sonnets

1 THE ARMY SURGEON

Over that breathing waste of friends and foes,
The wounded and the dying, hour by hour,—
In will a thousand, yet but one in power,—
He labours thro' the red and groaning day.
The fearful moorland where the myriads lay
Moved as a moving field of mangled worms.
And as a raw brood, orphaned in the storms,
Thrust up their heads if the wind bend a spray
Above them, but when the bare branch performs
No sweet parental office, sink away
With hopeless chirp of woe, so as he goes
Around his feet in clamorous agony
They rise and fall; and all the seething plain
Bubbles a cauldron vast of many-coloured pain.

2 THE COMMON GRAVE

Last night beneath the foreign stars I stood
And saw the thoughts of those at home go by
To the great grave upon the hill of blood.

Upon the darkness they went visibly,
Each in the vesture of its own distress.
Among them there came One, frail as a sigh,
And like a creature of the wilderness
Dug with her bleeding hands. She neither cried
Nor wept: nor did she see the many stark
And dead that lay unburied at her side.
All night she toiled, and at that time of dawn,
When Day and Night do change their More or Less,
And Day is More, I saw the melting Dark
Stir to the last, and know she laboured on.

SYDNEY DOBELL

Sunken Gold

In dim green depths rot ingot-laden ships,
    While gold doubloons that from the drowned hand fell
    Lie nestled in the ocean's flower bell
With Love's gemmed rings once kissed by now dead lips.
And round some wrought-gold cup the sea-grass whips
    And hides lost pearls, near pearls still in their shell,
    Where seaweed forests fill each ocean dell,
And seek dim sunlight with their countless tips.

So lie the wasted gifts, the long-lost hopes,
    Beneath the now hushed surface of myself,
In lonelier depths than where the diver gropes
    They lie deep, deep; but I at times behold
    In doubtful glimpses, on some reefy shelf,
    The gleam of irrecoverable gold.

EUGENE LEE HAMILTON

The Witch

I have walked a great while over the snow,
And I am not tall nor strong.
My clothes are wet, and my teeth are set,
And the way was hard and long.
I have wandered over the fruitful earth,
But I never came here before.
Oh, lift me over the threshold, and let me in at the door!

The cutting wind is a cruel foe.
I dare not stand in the blast.
My hands are stone, and my voice a groan,
And the worst of death is past.
I am but a little maiden still,
My little white feet are sore.
Oh, lift me over the threshold, and let me in at the door!

Her voice was the voice that women have,
Who plead for their heart's desire.
She came—she came—and the quivering flame
Sank and died in the fire.
It never was lit again on my hearth
Since I hurried across the floor,
To lift her over the threshold, and let her in at the door.

MARY COLERIDGE

Spleen

I was not sorrowful, I could not weep,
And all my memories were put to sleep.

I watched the river grow more white and strange,
All day till evening I watched it change.

All day till evening I watched the rain
Beat wearily upon the window pane.

I was not sorrowful, but only tired
Of everything that ever I desired.

Her lips, her eyes, all day became to me
The shadow of a shadow utterly.

All day mine hunger for her heart became
Oblivion, until the evening came,

And left me sorrowful, inclined to weep,
With all my memories that could not sleep.

ERNEST DOWSON

Dregs

The fire is out, and spent the warmth thereof
(This is the end of every song man sings!)
The golden wine is drunk, the dregs remain,
Bitter as wormwood and as salt as pain;
And health and hope have gone the way of love
Into the drear oblivion of lost things.
Ghosts go along with us until the end;
This was a mistress, this, perhaps, a friend.
With pale, indifferent eyes, we sit and wait
For the dropt curtain and the closing gate:
This is the end of all the songs man sings.

ERNEST DOWSON

A Newspaper is a Collection of Half-injustices

A newspaper is a collection of half-injustices
Which, bawled by boys from mile to mile,
Spreads its curious opinion
To a million merciful and sneering men,
While families cuddle the joys of the fireside

When spurred by tale of dire lone agony.
A newspaper is a court
Where everyone is kindly and unfairly tried
By a squalor of honest men.
A newspaper is a market
Where wisdom sells its freedom
And melons are crowned by the crowd.
A newspaper is a game
Where his error scores the player victory
While another's skill wins death.
A newspaper is a symbol;
It is feckless life's chronicle,
A collection of loud tales
Concentrating eternal stupidities,
That in remote ages lived unhaltered,
Roaming through a fenceless world.

STEPHEN CRANE

A Man said to the Universe

A man said to the universe:
'Sir, I exist!'
'However,' replied the universe,
'The fact has not created in me
A sense of obligation.'

STEPHEN CRANE

Age in Youth

From far she's come, and very old,
And very soiled with wandering.
The dust of seasons she has brought
Unbidden to this field of Spring.

She's halted at the log-barred gate.
The May-day waits, a tangled spill
Of light that weaves and moves along
The daisied margin of the hill,

Where Nature bares her bridal heart,
And on her snowy soul the sun
Languors desirously and dull,
An amorous pale vermilion.

She's halted, propped her rigid arms,
With dead big eyes she drinks the west;
The brown rags hang like clotted dust
About her, save her withered breast.

A very soilure of a dream
Runs in the furrows of her brow,
And with a crazy voice she croons
An ugly catch of long ago.

Its broken rhythm is hard and hoarse,
Its sunken soul of music toils
In precious ashes, dust of youth
And lovely faces sorrow soils.

But look! Along the molten sky
There runs strange havoc of the sun.
'What a strange sight this is,' she says,
'I'll cross the field, I'll follow on.'

The bars are falling from the gate.
The meshes of the meadow yield;
And trudging sunsetward she draws
A journey thro' the daisy field.

The daisies shudder at her hem.
Her dry face laughs with flowery light;
An aureole lifts her soiled gray hair:
'I'll on,' she says, 'to see this sight.'

In the rude math her torn shoe mows
Juices of trod grass and crushed stalk
Mixed with a soiled and earthy dew,
With smear of petals gray as chalk.

The Spring grows sour along her track;
The winy airs of amethyst
Turn acid. 'Just beyond the ledge,'
She says, 'I'll see the sun at rest.'

And to the tremor of her croon,
Her old, old catch of long ago,
The newest daisies of the grass
She shreds and passes on below. . . .

The sun is gone where nothing is
And the black-bladed shadows war.
She came and passed, she passed along
That wet, black curve of scimitar.

In vain the flower-lifting morn
With golden fingers to uprear
The weak Spring here shall pause awhile:
This is a scar upon the year.

TRUMBULL STICKNEY

In Summer

It's growing evening in my soul,
It darkens in.
At the gray window now and then
I hear them toll
The hour-and-day-long chimes of St. Etienne.

Indeed I'd not have lived elsewhere
Nor otherwise,
Nor as the dreary saying is
Been happier,
To wear the love of life within my eyes.

My heart's desolate meadow ways,
All wet and green,
Opened for her to wander in
A little space.
I'd have it even so as it has been.

I've lived the days that fly away,
I have a tale
To tell when age has made me pale
And hair of gray
Excuse the fancy shaking out her sail.

No one shall know what I intend.
Even as I feel
The aching voices make appeal
And swell and blend,
It seems to me I might stoop down to kneel

In memory of that day in June
When, all the land
Lying out in lazy summer fanned
Now and anon
By dying breezes from the Chanel strand,

With nothing in our lives behind,
Nothing before,
In sunlight rich as melting ore
And wide as wind
We clomb the donjon tower of old Gisors

Thro' the portcullis botched in wood
And up, in fear,
A laddered darkness of a stair,
Up to the good
Sun-stricken prospect and the dazzling air.—

Even now I shade my breaking eyes.—
And by her side
Surely she saw my heart divide
Like paradise
For her to walk abroad in at noon-tide.

It swims about my memory.
I feel around
The country steeped in summer swound;
I feel the sigh
That all these years within her breast was bound.

Her fingers in my hand are laid.
I seem to gaze
Into the colours of her face,
And there is made
A quiver in my knees like meadow-grass.

That time I lived the life I have:
A certain flower
Blooms in a hundred years one hour,
And what it gave
Is richer, no, nor more, but all its power.

The chimes have ended for to-day.
After midnight
Solitude blows her candle out;
Dreams go away,
And memory falls from the mast of thought.

                              TRUMBULL STICKNEY

If You should Lightly . . .

If you should lightly, as I've known you, come
And find me of an evening crying here
At open windows of a changing home,
While beyond garden, houses, tree, and dome
Fades out the day and year;

If you should gently touch my shoulder, and
Turning I'd see as with a sweet surprise
You there, above me and about me, stand,
While the warm sunset passed a lucid hand
Over your face and eyes;

C.E.P.—20*

If then you softly, as I've heard you, said
That all was well, I know not what or why,
But just for words' sake told me; while your head
Moved round, you passed away; and in your stead
An autumn night came by:

Still would the happiness of having stood
With one so nearly you tho' gone so soon,
Bring to my solitude a little good,—
As one who's gladdened in a midnight wood
For having seen the moon.

TRUMBULL STICKNEY

Not that, if you had known . . .

Not that, if you had known at all,
You would have done what now you do.
God knows, no blame shall ever fall
Of mine on you.
I only marvel that it all be true.

They say that love's a mustard seed
Upon the acres of the heart;
It spreads from one part like a weed
To another part.
Yet Spring is single and the days depart.

I know not why, but so it is!
That pain is such a simple thing.
Here to your hand I bring my kiss,
And yet nothing
Can tell you nearly what it is I bring.

And why?—It's hard to cipher Fates
And Distances, as yours from me.
Not science even separates
So fixedly;—
And then we tantalise our destiny!

Yes, marvel how the chances cross
And weave these spider-webs of wire.
Men live who say there's gain in loss!
And yet Desire
Revives like ferns on a November fire.

It comes to only a memory.
We have too many memories,
And somehow I believe we die
Of things like these,
Loving what was not, might not be, nor is.

TRUMBULL STICKNEY

Like a Pearl Dropped . . .

Like a pearl dropped in red dark wine,
Your pale face sank within my heart,
Not to be mine, yet always mine.

Your eyes, like flowers from apart
Their frail and shaded gates of dream,
Looked all a meadow's light astart

With sunrise, and your smile did seem
As when below a letting rain
The water-drops with sunset gleam.

I thought my vision was not vain;
I felt my cramped heart stir and move
Which now is pressed with little pain.

I dreamed the dream one wonders of,—
Your face of pearl, so pale and wise.
I saw, and murmured 'Life is Love.'

The dust of folly filled my eyes.
I sang, and opened in your name
Crocuses yellow with moonrise.

I played with shadows at their game;
The meadow thought my song was wind.
I called the sunrise up: it came.

Sweet, sun-warmed grasses did I bind
In fancies of your hair. My song
Was you, and you were all my mind.—

The charm, the splendour, and the wrong
Will drive you thro' the earth, to try
Of you and pleasure which is strong,—

While I remember. Cry on cry
My autumn's gone. A horrid blast
Blows out my sunset from the sky.

Nothing is left and all is past;
Rain settles like a quiet air.
And as a pearl in red wine cast
Glows like a drop of moonlight there,
Your face possesses my despair.

TRUMBULL STICKNEY

If I have wronged You . . .

If I have wronged you in the days
Bygone but unforgotten now,
I make no pleading for your grace.
My tongue is bitter. Leave me, go.

You have no pity, none. You live
Impatient and unreconciled.
Nay, were you a mother, I believe
You never could well love your child.

You've cracked the sense of life and death
With passions in you that despise
The thing you love and choke its breath,
Till unrecriminate it dies,—

It dies to you; and nothing then,
Nor art nor hope nor force nor spell
Can worry back the lost again,—
Lost, lost, and irrecoverable.

And then, God knows, some things there be
Where never pardon yet was known:
What words have leapt from you to me!
Enough, henceforward I'm my own.

Yes, men are selfish—Tell me, you
Who pluck my thoughts for flying fast,
Ask all the years to be, and rue
The unalterably separate past,

What is this that is *generous*?
Can just a word we used to know
In childhood, commonly, to us
Have grown a vulgar riddle so?

Sometimes I think we never met,
Such immense walls of iron and ice
Between us infinitely set
Spring blind into the spirit's skies.

Sometimes I think we never met,—
'T had surely better been, to spare
This nervous wringing of regret,
This hope that tightens to despair.

We have not understood, for all
We deeply lived and clearly said.
And without knowledge love must fall,—
Like this of ours, that lying dead

Clamours for burial. It is time,
It was time in much earlier days,
Before we soiled our lips with crime,
That you and I went our two ways.

TRUMBULL STICKNEY

Now in the Palace Gardens . . .

Now in the palace gardens warm with age,
On lawn and flower-bed this afternoon
The thin November-coloured foliage
Just as last year unfastens lilting down,

And round the terrace in gray attitude
The very statues are becoming sere
With long presentiment of solitude.
Most of the life that I have lived is here,

Here by the path and autumn's earthy grass
And chestnuts standing down the breadths of sky:
Indeed I know not how it came to pass,
The life I lived here so unhappily.

Yet blessing over all! I do not care
What wormwood I have ate to cups of gall;
I care not what despairs are buried there
Under the ground, no, I care not at all.

Nay, if the heart have beaten, let it break!
I have not loved and lived but only this
Betwixt my birth and grave. Dear Spirit, take
The gratitude that pains, so deep it is.

When Spring shall be again, and at your door
You stand to feel the mellower evening wind,
Remember if you will my heart is pure,
Perfectly pure and altogether kind;

That not an aftercry of all our strife
Troubles the love I give you and the faith:
Say to yourself that at the ends of life
My arms are open to you, life and death.—

How much it aches to linger in these things!
I thought the perfect end of love was peace
Over the long-forgiven sufferings.
But something else, I know not what it is,

The words that came so nearly and then not,
The vanity, the error of the whole,
The strong cross-purpose, oh, I know not what
Cries dreadfully in the distracted soul.

The evening fills the garden, hardly red;
And autumn goes away, like one alone.
Would I were with the leaves that thread by thread
Soften to soil, I would that I were one.

TRUMBULL STICKNEY

On some Shells found Inland

These are my murmur-laden shells that keep
A fresh voice tho' the years be very gray.
The wave that washed their lips and tuned their lay
Is gone, gone with the faded ocean sweep,
The royal tide, gray ebb and sunken neap
And purple midday,—gone! To this hot clay
Must sing my shells, where yet the primal day,
Its roar and rhythm and splendour will not sleep.
What hand shall join them to their proper sea

If all be gone? Shall they forever feel
Glories undone and worlds that cannot be?—
'T were mercy to stamp out this agèd wrong,
Dash them to earth and crunch them with the heel
And make a dust of their seraphic song.

TRUMBULL STICKNEY

The Melancholy Year . . .

The melancholy year is dead with rain.
Drop after drop on every branch pursues.
From far away beyond the drizzled flues
A twilight saddens to the window pane.
And dimly thro' the chambers of the brain,
From place to place and gently touching, moves
My one and irrecoverable love's
Dear and lost shape one other time again.
So in the last of autumn for a day
Summer or summer's memory returns.
So in a mountain desolation burns
Some rich belated flower, and with the gray
Sick weather, in the world of rotting ferns
From out the dreadful stones it dies away.

TRUMBULL STICKNEY

With Long Black Wings . . .

With long black wings an angel standing by
Opened his arms, as had he a lover been.
His lips were very cold and lingered thin
Along my lips half-broken with a cry.
From all his body I most dreadfully
Did draw the cruel cold and slowly win
Heart-ache on heart-ache; yet I gathered in
The great black wings that stiffened as to fly.

In that embrace it seemed that years of pain
Passed very slow, and yet my body tight
I held to his till darkness took my brain.
Somehow I woke, and up the dying night
I saw him spread great glittering wings of white.
I knew your brow was cooled, you well again.

TRUMBULL STICKNEY

Leave Him Now Quiet . . .

Leave him now quiet by the way
To rest apart.
I know what draws him to the dust alway
And churns him in the builder's lime:
He has the fright of time.

I heard it knocking in his breast
A minute since;
His human eyes did wince,
He stubborned like the massive slaughter beast
And as a thing o'erwhelmed with sound
Stood bolted to the ground.

Leave him, for rest alone can cure—
If cure there be—
This waif upon the sea.
He is of those who slanted the great door
And listened—wretched little lad—
To what they said.

TRUMBULL STICKNEY

An Athenian Garden

The burned and dusty garden said:
'My leaves are echoes, and thy earth
Is packed with footsteps of the dead.

'The strength of spring-time brought to birth
Some needles on the crooked fir,—
A rose, a laurel—little worth.

'Come here, ye dreaming souls that err
Among the immortals of the grave:
My summer is your sepulchre.

'On earth what darker voices rave
Than now this sea-breeze, driving dust
And whirling radiance wave on wave,

'With lulls so fearful thro' the gust
That on the shapeless flower-bed
Like timber splits the yellow crust.

'O thirsty, thirsty are the dead,
Still thirsty, ever unallayed.
Where is no water, bring no bread.'

I then had almost answer made,
When round the path in pleasure drew
Three golden children to the shade.

They stirred the dust with pail and hoe.
Then did the littlest from his fears
Come up and with his eyes of blue

Give me some berries seriously.
And as he turned to his brother, I
Looked after him thro' happy tears.

TRUMBULL STICKNEY

Near Helikon

By such an all-embalming summer day
As sweetens now among the mountain pines
Down to the cornland yonder and the vines,
To where the sky and sea are mixed in gray,

How do all things together take their way
Harmonious to the harvest, bringing wines
And bread and light and whatsoe'er combines
In the large wreath to make it round and gay.
To me my troubled life doth now appear
Like scarce distinguishable summits hung
Around the blue horizon: places where
Not even a traveller purposeth to steer,—
Whereof a migrant bird in passing sung,
And the girl closed her window not to hear.

TRUMBULL STICKNEY

Six o'clock

Now burst above the city's cold twilight
The piercing whistles and the tower clocks:
For day is done. Along the frozen docks
The workmen set their ragged shirts aright.
Thro' factory doors a stream of dingy light
Follows the scrimmage as it quickly flocks
To hut and home among the snow's gray blocks.—
I love you, human labourers. Good night!
Good-night to all the blackened arms that ache!
Good-night to every sick and sweated brow,
To the poor girl that strength and love forsake,
To the poor boy who can no more! I vow
The victim soon shall shudder at the stake
And fall in blood: we bring him even now.

TRUMBULL STICKNEY

This is the Violin . . .

This is the violin. If you remember—
One afternoon late, in the early days,
One of those inconsolable December
    Twilights of city haze,

You came to teach me how the hardened fingers
Must drop and nail the music down, and how
The sound then drags and nettled cries, then lingers
    After the dying bow.—

For so all that could never be is given
And flutters off these piteously thin
Strings, till the night of a midsummer heaven
    Quivers . . . a violin.

I struggled, and alongside of a duty,
A nagging everyday-long commonplace!
I loved this hopeless exercise of beauty
    Like an allotted grace,—

The changing scales and broken chords, the trying
From sombre notes below to catch the mark,
I have it all thro' my heart, I tell you, crying
    Childishly in the dark.

TRUMBULL STICKNEY

I Hear a River . . .

I hear a river thro' the valley wander
Whose Water runs, the song alone remaining.
A rainbow stands and summer passes under.

TRUMBULL STICKNEY

The Passions that we fought With . . .

The passions that we fought with and subdued
Never quite die. In some maimed serpent's coil
They lurk, ready to spring and vindicate
That power was once our torture and our lord.

TRUMBULL STICKNEY

Mnemosyne

It's autumn in the country I remember.

How warm a wind blew here about the ways!
And shadows on the hillside lay to slumber
During the long sun-sweetened summer-days.

It's cold abroad the country I remember.

The swallows veering skimmed the golden grain
At midday with a wing aslant and limber;
And yellow cattle browsed upon the plain.

It's empty down the country I remember.

I had a sister lovely in my sight:
Her hair was dark, her eyes were very sombre;
We sang together in the woods at night.

It's lonely in the country I remember.

The babble of our children fills my ears,
And on our hearth I stare the perished ember
To flames that show all starry thro' my tears.

It's dark about the country I remember.

There are the mountains where I lived. The path
Is slushed with cattle-tracks and fallen timber,
The stumps are twisted by the tempests' wrath.
But that I knew these places are my own,

I'd ask how come such wretchedness to cumber
The earth, and I to people it alone.

It rains across the country I remember.

TRUMBULL STICKNEY

Be Still. The Hanging Gardens were a Dream

Be still. The Hanging Gardens were a dream
That over Persian roses flew to kiss
The curlèd lashes of Semiramis.
Troy never was, nor green Skamander stream.
Provence and Troubadour are merest lies,
The glorious hair of Venice was a beam
Made with Titian's eye. The sunsets seem,
The world is very old and nothing is.
Be still. Thou foolish thing, thou canst not wake,
Nor thy tears wedge thy soldered lids apart,
But patter in the darkness of thy heart.
Thy brain is plagued. Thou art a frightened owl
Blind with the light of life thou'ldst not forsake,
And error loves and nourishes thy soul.

TRUMBULL STICKNEY

In Ampezzo

Only once more and not again—the larches
Shake to the wind their echo. 'Not again,'—
We see, below the sky that over-arches
Heavy and blue, the plain

Between Tofano lying and Cristallo
In meadowy earths above the ringing stream:
Whence interchangeably desire may follow
Hesitant as in dream,

At sunset, south, by lilac promontories
Under green skies to Italy, or forth
By calms of morning beyond Lavinores
Tyrolward and to north:

As now, this last of latter days, when over
The brownish field by peasants are undone
Some widths of grass, some plots of mountain clover
Under the autumn sun,

With honey-warm perfume that risen lingers
In mazes of low heat, or takes the air,
Passing delicious as a woman's fingers
Passing amid the hair;

When scythes are swishing and the mower's muscle
Spans a repeated crescent to and fro,
Or in dry stalks of corn the sickles rustle,
Tangle, detach and go,

Far thro' the wide blue day and greening meadow
Whose blots of amber beaded are with sheaves,
Whereover pallidly a cloud-shadow
Deadens the earth and leaves:

Whilst high around and near, their heads of iron
Sunken in sky whose azure overlights
Ravine and edges, stand the gray and maron
Desolate Dolomites,—

And older than decay from the small summit
Unfolds a stream of pebbly wreckage down
Under the suns of midday, like some comet
Struck into gravel stone.

Faintly across this gold and amethystine
September, images of summer fade;
And gentle dreams now freshen on the pristine
Viols, awhile unplayed,

Of many a place where lovingly we wander,
More dearly held that quickly we forsake,—
A pine by sullen coasts, an oleander
Reddening on the lake.

And there, each year with more familiar motion,
From many a bird and windy forestries,
Or along shaking fringes of the ocean
Vapors of music rise.

From many easts the morning gives her splendor;
The shadows fill with colors we forget;
Remembered tints at evening grow tender,
Tarnished with violet.

Let us away! soon sheets of winter metal
On this discoloured mountain-land will close,
While elsewhere Spring-time weaves a crimson petal,
Builds and perfumes a rose.

Away! for here the mountain sinks in gravel.
Let us forget the unhappy site with change,
And go, if only happiness be travel
After the new and strange:—

Unless 'twere better to be very single,
To follow some diviner monotone,
And in all beauties, where ourselves commingle,
Love but a love, but one,

Across this shadowy minute of our living,
What time our hearts so magically sing,
To mitigate our fever, simply giving
All in a little thing?

Just as here, past yon dumb and melancholy
Sameness of ruin, while the mountains ail,
Summer and sunset-coloured autumn slowly
Dissipate down the vale;

And all these lines along the sky that measure,
Sorapis and the rocks of Mezzodi
Crumble by foamy miles into the azure
Mediterranean sea:

Whereas to-day at sunrise, under brambles,
A league above the moss and dying pines
I picked this little—in my hand it trembles—
Parcel of columbines.

                              TRUMBULL STICKNEY

At Sainte-Marguérite

The gray tide flows and flounders in the rocks
Along the crannies up the swollen sand.
Far out the reefs lie naked—dunes and blocks
Low in the watery wind. A shaft of land
Going to sea thins out the western strand.

It rains, and all along and always gulls
Career sea-screaming in and weather-glossed.
It blows here, pushing round the cliff; in lulls
Within the humid stone a motion lost
Ekes out the flurried heart-beat of the coast.

It blows and rains a pale and whirling mist
This summer morning. I that hither came—
Was it to pluck this savage from the schist,
This crazy yellowish bloom without a name,
With leathern blade and tortured wiry frame?

Why here alone, away, the forehead pricked
With dripping salt and fingers damp with brine,
Before the offal and the derelict
And where the hungry sea-wolves howl and whine
Like human hours? now that the columbine

Stands somewhere shaded near the fields that fall
Great starry sheaves of the delighted year,
And globing rosy on the garden wall
The peach and apricot and soon the pear
Drip in the teasing hand their sugared tear.

Inland a little way the summer lies.
Inland a little and but yesterday
I saw the weary teams, I heard the cries
Of sicklemen across the fallen hay,
And buried in the sunburned stacks I lay

Tasting the straws and tossing, laughing soft
Into the sky's great eyes of gold and blue
And nodding to the breezy leaves aloft
Over the harvest's mellow residue.
But sudden then—then strangely dark it grew.

How good it is, before the dreary flow
Of cloud and water, here to lie alone
And in this desolation to let go
Down the ravine one with another, down
Across the surf to linger or to drown

The loves that none can give and none receive,
The fearful asking and the small retort,
The life to dream of and the dream to live!
Very much more is nothing than a part,
Nothing at all and darkness in the heart.

I would my manhood now were like the sea.—
Thou at high-tide, when compassing the land
Thou find'st the issue short, questioningly
A moment poised, thy floods then down the strand
Sink without rancor, sink without command,

Sink of themselves in peace without despair,
And turn as still the calm horizon turns,
Till they repose little by little nowhere
And the long light unfathomable burns
Clear from the zenith stars to the sea-ferns.

Thou art thy Priest, thy Victim and thy God.
Thy life is bulwarked with a thread of foam,
And of the sky, the mountains and the sod
Thou askest nothing, evermore at home
In thy own self's perennial masterdom.

TRUMBULL STICKNEY

Notes

page

16. THE CUTTY WREN   Anonymous

M. H. Mason learned this song from her Welsh nurses in Carmarthenshire. In her *Nursery Rhymes and Country Songs* (1878), referring to a slightly different version from Pembrokeshire, she notes that 'It was an ancient custom in South Wales for two or four men to go about on St Stephen's Day carrying a wren fastened on two poles slung on to their shoulders, groaning under its supposed weight, and singing this song'. The wren, smallest of British birds, was considered to be king, and this mock ceremony was evidently a survival connected with the ritual slaughter of the king at the end of the year.

22. NORFOLK SPRANG THEE   Henry Howard, Earl of Surrey

Carved on the tablet near the tomb of Thomas Clere in the Howards' chapel at Lambeth, these lines celebrate the poet's love for his squire, who gave his life for Surrey at the siege of Montreuil in 1544. The genealogical references show Clere's consanguinity with the Howards; the place-names refer to campaigns in which squire and master served together. Clere loved Mary Shelton, a lady-in-waiting at the court of Henry VIII. Surrey has never been given the credit for the Shakespearian sense, here revealed, of the poetic qualities of great names.

22–23. IN THE RUDE AGE ...   Henry Howard, Earl of Surrey
    DIVERS THY DEATH ...
    WYATT RESTETH HERE ...

Three elegies for the poet and diplomat, Sir Thomas Wyatt. Although opposed for family reasons to Wyatt's position in politics and religion, Surrey was a profound admirer and perhaps a close friend. He used his influence at court to get Wyatt freed from the Tower. It is clear from these three elegies that Surrey was deeply incensed at the campaign of vilification of his fellow-poet's character, which did not cease even with his death.

25–33. HOW COLLINGBOURNE WAS CRUELLY EXECUTED ...   William Baldwin

This poem is one of the collection known as *The Mirror for Magistrates* (1559, 1563, 1578, 1587), the first English poetry to deal with historical themes in a really serious manner. Edited by the philosopher and translator William Baldwin, its overt intention was to provide a pattern of examples for statesmen, by which they could escape the errors of past ages. In effect, it was highly subversive; the first edition of 1555 was suppressed. The most famous poem of the collection is Edward Sackville's superb *Induction* to *Henry, Duke of Buckingham*, but the Collingbourne poem—almost certainly by the editor,

Baldwin—does not deserve the total neglect into which it has unaccountably
fallen. Read simply as a vigorous and ironic protest against tyranny, it is highly
effective and easily transcends the crudities of its style; furthermore, it is a
noble and dignified plea for poetic freedom.

35–36.   Richard Stanyhurst

Richard Stanyhurst, a Roman Catholic exile, made many experiments in
quantitative metre, most of them grotesquely bad. But sometimes, as here,
true feeling breaks through to confer upon these experiments an authentic,
if quaint, power.

37. AND IF I DID WHAT THEN?   (?)George Gascoigne

This poem occurs in the prose Adventures of Master F. J. There is some doubt
as to whether Gascoigne wrote it, although it was published under his name. If
it is not his, it is probably by Sir Christopher Hatton.

39–46.   Fulke Greville, Lord Brooke

The Oxgrave representation of Fulke Greville is limited to one poem. Despite
the work of Geoffrey Bullough and Una Ellis-Fermor, Greville is still regarded
merely as the 'friend of Sir Philip Sidney'. He almost certainly wrote most of
his lyrical poems at the same time, and probably in the same house, as Sidney,
when Sidney was writing Astrophel and Stella. Greville's poems are considered,
by contrast, over-cerebral and involute, even though distinguished by a certain
'quaintness'. This judgement does them much less than justice. Leaving aside the
undoubted historical importance of Greville as a precursor of Donne and
the Metaphysicals, his poems—dense, psychologically acute and emotionally
truthful—call for reassessment. While they are perhaps love-poems as intro-
spective as any in the language, and therefore seem to invite the charge of
over-cerebration, they compensate for this by their subtlety and exactness.
Greville may well be called the poet of passive masculine love. And what other
poet voices this state of mind with such intensity and sincerity? His most
famous poem was set to music, and will be found on p. 117.

48–64. THE 11TH: AND LAST BOOK OF THE   Sir Walter Ralegh
            OCEAN TO CYNTHIA

We know nothing of this poem except that it exists in a ms. in Ralegh's own
hand, and that it is addressed to Queen Elizabeth, into whose disfavour he had
fallen. Ralegh refers to himself as the 'Ocean' both because of his naval exploits
and because of the obvious pun on his Christian name. The Ocean is drawn to
Cynthia (the Moon). The text is obscure in places, and we can only guess
what the remainder of the poem was or was intended to be. Some of the
vagaries of spelling have been attributed to the tradition that Ralegh wrote as
he spoke, in the dialect of his native Devon.

   Not even the apparently fragmentary nature of the poem can account for
its neglect. It is one of the most sustained of all confessional poems. It has

perhaps been overlooked because it is so quintessentially of its age. Its consistently high quality throughout its great length is evidence of its passion and sincerity. Ralegh was the last major English poet to be closely associated throughout his active life with national power at its source. In this poem he is able to write both as a lover and as a public man.

65. FEED STILL THYSELF   Sir Walter Ralegh

This poem is only conjecturally by Ralegh, but, as his editor Miss Agnes Latham writes, it has strong temperamental affiliations.

66-90. THE SHADOW OF NIGHT   George Chapman

The Shadow of Night (1594) was Chapman's first published poem. Obscure and convoluted though it is, it contains magnificent passages and repays close reading. Extreme concentration is needed to grasp the thought, but the effort is worthwhile. Chapman's sources in this poem are manifold: Comes's *Mythologiae*, contemporary history, Horace, and much other learned lore. Some critics have relied on evidence from *The Shadow of Night* to suggest the existence of a so-called 'School of Night'—a coterie of poets, including Ralegh, which Shakespeare allegedly caricatured in *Love's Labour's Lost*. However this may be, we believe that the reader can appreciate the poem without knowledge of its lore and its contemporary references, because its basic theme is that of the poet's proper relationship to his environment. Chapman's implied defence of poetry is notable.

91-93.   Robert Southwell

It seems worth while to add these two poems to the canon. At what other period in English poetry could we find, even in the poems of a minor writer, the combination of sincerity and contrivance, wit—even frivolity—and genuine piety as is exemplified in the first of these two poems, a dramatic monologue put into the mouth of the executed Queen of Scots?

93-103. A LOVER'S COMPLAINT   William Shakespeare

This poem was printed with the more famous sonnets by Thomas Thorpe in 1609, and has suffered strange neglect ever since. It bears a close relationship to the sonnets, and would be interesting if only for this reason; but in spite of C. S. Lewis's and others' denigration of it, we think that most major English poets would have been pleased to write it. Far from being a mere *chanson d'aventure*—as Lewis, in one of his too frequent lapses, called it—it is a psychologically cryptic poem that calls for close study. We hope that our reprinting of the 1609 text here will kindle general interest in it.

104-122. WORDS FROM ELIZABETHAN AND JACOBEAN SONG-BOOKS

We give here some lyrics, one of them by Greville, set to music by the Elizabethan and Jacobean madrigalists and lutanists. It is not certainly known who wrote most of these words—evidently not the composers in some cases at least, since the same lyrics turn up in books of songs by different composers. It is surprising, in view of their dazzling poetic quality, that so little attention has been paid to them. Most anthologists have been content to give the words of those madrigals and airs which are best known on account of their music— that is, as songs. It by no means follows, however, that the best of the words attracted the best music. We believe that the lyrics reprinted here can stand by themselves as poetry, without the aid of music. The words of the song-books were reprinted, with enterprise and diligence, by the pioneer, Fellowes, in his collection. But Fellowes modernized, and we have restored the spelling of the music-books.

124. DEAR, IF WITH GUILE . . .   Thomas Campian

The cool realism of Campian's attitude is characteristic: it has neither the anti-romanticism of Donne, nor the gallantry of such Cavaliers as Suckling, nor the cynicism of the Restoration wits, but a commonsense tenderness indicative of an unusually intelligent insight into feminine psychology.

134–140.   Sir John Suckling

The first two poems are not certainly by Suckling, but have been confidently attributed to him in an article published in *Studies in Philology* (LIX, 1962). They have not previously appeared in book form. They show a pious side of Suckling's nature by no means at variance with the gayer moods usually associated with him, as his prose *An Account of Religion by Reason* shows.

146–151.   Henry Vaughan

While everyone knows the handful of poems by which the Breconshire doctor, Henry Vaughan, is usually represented, few seem to have thought it worth while to search *Silex Scintillans* (1650, 1655) for other equally moving poems. Vaughan is often classed as one of the Metaphysicals, but his affinities with this school are less in evidence than his debt to George Herbert, his acknowledged master.

153–155. A HYMN TO THE PILLORY   Daniel Defoe

These lines are the first sixty-one of a much longer poem. Defoe's two satirical poems have been overlooked in favour of satires of less warmth and insight, probably because of his much greater eminence as a prose-writer. Since Defoe himself had stood in the pillory, he knew what he was writing about. Both the whole of this poem and *The True-Born Englishman* are full of humour and humanity in an age better known for wit and callousness.

187–197. NIGHT   Charles Churchill

In an age of satire and *vers de société*, with Pope still uncrowned laureate, truer poetry without hypocrisy and self-inflation is to be found in the writings of minor poets.

206–209. MY SPECTRE AROUND ME NIGHT AND DAY   William Blake

The additional stanzas exist in ms., but cannot confidently be placed in the body of the poem, from which they may have been rejected by Blake. If any single poem contains the whole of Blake's thought, this is it.

212–221. A LETTER TO SARA HUTCHINSON   Samuel Taylor Coleridge

For our reasons for printing this original version of the more famous *Dejection: an Ode*, see Humphry House, *Coleridge*, pp. 133–41, and James Reeves, *Selected Poems of Samuel Taylor Coleridge*, pp. 145–6. Coleridge met Sara Hutchinson, Wordsworth's sister-in-law-to-be, in 1799, and fell in love with her almost at once. Their relationship, intense on his side, cautious and cryptic on hers, lasted until 1810, when Wordsworth and Coleridge became estranged.

221. DANIEL DEFOE   Walter Savage Landor

To search the many volumes of Landor, already exhaustively quarried for his lapidary lyrics, is unrewarding. We confess that we include this one, not only because it has been overlooked, but because we admire Defoe and are grateful for Landor's unpretentious tribute.

223–242.   John Clare

A complete and definitive edition of the works of John Clare is being prepared by Eric Robinson and Geoffrey Summerfield. Meanwhile, most of his poems —those in *The Shepherd's Calendar* are an exception—are not available except in unmodernized, re-punctuated versions. When Professor Tibble published his edition of Clare in 1934 the original versions would doubtless have been unacceptable; the gain to the reader, however, is illustrated by comparing *February* with the other poems in our selection.

243–247.   Hartley Coleridge

Hartley Coleridge may be a minor poet; he may be overshadowed by his titanic father, but he does not deserve the neglect accorded to him by Oxgrave. Saintsbury wrote of him: 'The foiled and marred genius of Hartley Coleridge tried verse as well as prose, and has left its best memorials in the sonnet.' While we are not very happy about 'tried verse' and 'memorials', we are grateful to Saintsbury for his discrimination.

249–250. A TOCCATA OF GALUPPI'S   Robert Browning

It cannot be pretended that Browning's three-thousand columns remain substantially unsearched, and we do not claim that the *Toccata*, surely one of his most attractive poems, is unknown. Yet it is not in Oxgrave, and we feel that many who do not possess the *Poetical Works* might like to have it.

261–280.   Dante Gabriel Rossetti

Rossetti is sometimes called 'soft and styleless' as distinct from his sister, Christina. But whereas her poetry is too often trite in theme—however admirable stylistically—Rossetti's is psychologically dense; despite his occasionally fatal technical fluency, he was always struggling with ideas of a complexity too seldom found in Victorian poetry. *A Last Confession*, an early poem, deserves to be rescued from oblivion both for its dramatic and its psychological virtues. It is by no means merely an imitation of Browning. *The Orchard-Pit* is a fragment—all that survives—of a long poem written towards the end of Rossetti's life.

281–286.   Emily Dickinson

This selection has been made to exclude all the forty-eight poems in F. O. Matthiessen's admirable *Oxford Book of American Verse*.

290. DREGS   Ernest Dowson

It is not easy now to take Dowson's melancholy rhetoric quite seriously, and the decadent's pose is no longer wholly to our taste. But the last five lines of *Dregs* show that Dowson could achieve true poetry.

Index of Titles and First Lines